PATRISTIC MONOGRAPH SERIES NO. 1

CYPRIAN

by

Michael M. Sage

Published by
The Philadelphia Patristic Foundation, Ltd.

1975

Copyright © 1975 The Philadelphia Patristic
Foundation, Ltd.
99 Brattle Street
Cambridge, Massachusetts 02138

Library of Congress Catalogue Number: 75-11008
ISBN: 0-915646-00-5

To Linda

PREFACE

The third century A.D. has long been recognized as a particularly dark and obscure period. The sources available are fragmentary on the whole, and they reveal little beyond imperial biography. It is the purpose of this study to utilize the sources of Christian literature to illuminate this period of Roman history. Secular and ecclesiastical history have been separated far too long. This work attempts to combine the two, in order to better comprehend the context of the Cyprianic corpus through the study of its secular background.

I would like to thank Professor T.D. Barnes for his helpful suggestions and penetrating criticism in the preparation of this work. Thanks are also owed to the encouragement and criticism of Professor J.M. Rist and Father L. Boyle, all of the University of Toronto.

Michael M. Sage
Toronto
June 1974

TABLE OF CONTENTS

ABBREVIATIONS

ACW	J. Quasten, J.C. Plumpe (ed.), *Ancient Christian Writers* (Westminster, Md., 1946 ff.)
AEpigr.	*L'année épigraphique*
Altaner-Stuiber, *Pat.*	B. Altaner, A. Stuiber, *Patrologie. Leben, Schriften und Lehre der Kirchenväter* (Freiburg, 1966)
AP	*Acta Proconsularia*, in *Vita Cypriani*, pp. 190-9
Barnes, *Tert.*	T.D. Barnes, *Tertullian: A Historical and Literary Study* (Oxford, 1971)
BASP	*Bulletin of the American Society of Papyrologists*
Baus, *HCH*	K. Baus, *Handbook of Church History*, I: *From the Apostolic Community to Constantine* (Montreal, 1965), Eng. trans. of 3rd German edition, J. Dolan, H. Jedin (ed.)
Becker (1967)	C. Becker, "Der *Octavius des Minucius Felix*", *SBBayer*, hft. 2 (Munich, 1967)
BMC	*Catalogue of Coins in the British Museum*
BPW	*Berliner Philologische Wochenschrift* (Berlin-Leipzig, 1880-1920)
CAH	*The Cambridge Ancient History*, XII: *The Imperial Crisis and Recovery, A.D. 193-324* (Cambridge, 1939)
CIL	*Corpus Inscriptionum Latinarum*
CPh	*Classical Philology*

ii

CSEL	Corpus Scriptorum Ecclesiasticorum Latinorum (Vienna, 1866 ff.)
FHG	C. Mueller, Fragmenta Historicorum Graecorum (Paris, 1841 ff.)
FGrHist	F. Jacoby, Fragmente der griechischen Historiker (Berlin, 1923 ff.)
Frend, DC	W.H.C. Frend, The Donatist Church. A Movement of Protest in Roman North Africa (Oxford, 1952)
Frend, M&P	W.H.C. Frend, Martyrdom and Persecution in the Early Church. A Study of a Conflict from the Maccabees to Donatus (London, 1965)
Harnack, GAL	A. von Harnack, Geschichte der altchristlichen Literatur bis Eusebius: Die Überlieferung und der Bestand (2 half-volumes Leipzig, 1893-8); Die Chronologie (2 vols. Leipzig, 1904). Refers to Die Chronologie, 2nd vol. (Die Chronologie der Literatur von Irenäus bis Eusebius) unless otherwise noted.
Harnack, HD	A. von Harnack, History of Dogma^3 (7 vols. New York, 1894-9), trans. N. Buchanan
Harnack, M&A	A. von Harnack, Die Mission und Ausbreitung des Christentums in den ersten drei Jahrhunderten^3 (2 vols. Leipzig, 1915). Refers to Volume II.
Hartel	W. Hartel (ed.), Corpus Scriptorum Ecclesiasticorum Latinorum 3, S. Thasci Caecili Cypriani Opera Omnia

	(Vienna, 1868-71), parts 1-3
HJ	*Historisches Jahrbuch*
HThR	*Harvard Theological Review*
ILS	H. Dessau, *Inscriptiones Latinae Selectae* (Berlin, 1892-1916)
JEA	*Journal of Egyptian Archaeology*
JEH	*Journal of Ecclesiastical History*
JRH	*Journal of Religious History*
JRS	*Journal of Roman Studies*
JThS	*Journal of Theological Studies*
Koch, *CU*	H. Koch, *Cyprianische Untersuchungen*, Arbeiten zur Kirchengeschichte, 4 (Bonn, 1926)
Monceaux, *HAC*	P. Monceaux, *Histoire littéraire de l'Afrique chrétienne depuis les origines jusqu'à l'invasion arabe* (7 vols. Paris, 1901-23). Refers to Vol. II unless otherwise noted.
PG	J.P. Migne, *Patrologia Graeca*
PIR	*Prosopographia Imperii Romani*
PL	J.P. Migne, *Patrologia Latina*
PLRE	A.H.M. Jones, J.R. Martindale, and J. Morris, *The Prosopography of the Later Roman Empire*, I: A.D. 260-395 (Cambridge, 1971)
P.Oxy.	*The Oxyrhynchus Papyri* (London, 1898 ff.)
QFIAB	*Quellen und Forschungen aus italienischen Archiven und Bibliotheken*
Quasten, *Pat.*	J. Quasten, *Patrology* (3 vols. Utrecht-Antwerp, 1950-60). Refers to Vol. II unless otherwise noted.

iv

RAC	Reallexikon für Antike und Christentum (Stuttgart, 1941 ff.)
RE	Pauly-Wissowa, Real-Encyclopädie der Klassischen Altertumswissenschaft (1896 ff.)
REL	Revue des études latines
RevBén	Revue bénédictine
RH	Revue historique
RHE	Revue d'histoire ecclésiastique
RIC	H. Mattingly, et al (ed.) The Roman Imperial Coinage (London, 1923 ff.)
Rostovtzeff, SEHRE	M. Rostovtzeff, The Social and Economic History of the Roman Empire² (2 vols. Oxford, 1957)
RP	Revue de philologie
RSR	Recherches de science religieuse
SB	Sitzungsberichte (followed by abbreviated name of academy, e.g., SBBerl)
Schanz-Hosius	M. Schanz, C. Hosius, G. Krüger, Geschichte der römischen Litteratur, III³ (Munich, 1922)
SE	Sententiae episcoporum, in CSEL 3, 1, pp. 435-61
TAPA	Transactions of the American Philological Association
ThQ	Theologische Quartalschrift
ThSt	Theological Studies
TU	Text und Untersuchungen
Vita Cypriani	M. Pellegrino (ed.), Ponzio: Vita e martirio di San Cipriano (Alba, 1955). Also referred to as Pellegrino, Vita

Von Soden,
"Prosop." H. von Soden, "Die Prosopo-
graphie des afrikanischen
Episkopats zur Zeit Cyprians",
QFIAB 12 (1909), pp. 247-70

ZKT Zeitschrift für kirchliche
Theologie

ZNW Zeitschrift für die neutestamentliche Wissenschaft und die
Kunde der älteren Kirche

CYPRIAN

Chapter I: AFRICA AT MID-CENTURY

The extent and expansion of Christianity in Africa in the first half of the third century are problematical. Tertullian provides us with almost all of our information on the question at the opening of the century.[1] He indicates the existence of Christian churches in five towns of Africa: Thysdrus, Hadrumetum, Lambaesis, Uthina and Carthage.[2] He also provides evidence for Christian communities in Mauretania.[3] But as to the distribution of Christians in the African countryside by the year 250, little information is available on which to base any firm conclusions.

Inscriptional evidence is lacking for this period as well. Inscriptions that had previously been identified as Christian are in reality void of any specific Christian indications, and can no longer be used as evidence for the extent of Christianization in Africa.[4] Tertullian remains almost our only guide, but unfortunately most of his

---

1. For earlier developments, see Barnes, Tert., pp. 60-3 on information provided by the Acts of the Scillitan Martyrs.
2. Harnack, M&A, p. 287.
3. Ad Scap. 4.8.
4. For the available information, see Harnack, M&A, pp. 274 ff. Prior to the council of September 256, no geographical distinctions can be drawn, despite Frend, DC, pp. 87 ff.

statements lack geographical exactitude.[1]

The councils held by the African Church prior to Cyprian's episcopate can provide at least some indication of the size of the Christian hierarchy. The council of Agrippinus, on the question of rebaptising heretics, consisted of 70 members according to Augustine.[2] Cyprian supplies the further information that the assembled bishops were from Africa Proconsularis and Numidia.[3] The absence of bishops from Mauretania cannot be used as a basis for inference. The list of bishops who sat in council in Carthage in September 256 contains no certain example of a bishop from Mauretania. Yet Cyprian himself lists his _provincia_ as including Mauretania, and we have other evidence for the existence of African bishoprics in the area.[4] But there was opposition there to Cyprian's point of view, and this may account for the apparent absence of Mauretanian bishops.[5]

Soon after 236, a council which condemned Privatus of Lambaesis was held at Carthage.[6] Cyprian records that 90 bishops attended the meeting. Though this constituted an increase of 20 bishops over the attendance of the council of Agrippinus, we

---

1.   On the absence of Christian epigraphy, see Barnes, _Tert._, pp. 280-2.
2.   _De Unic. Baptism. Contra Petilian._ 13.22. There is no reason to disbelieve this tradition.
3.   Ep. 71.4/774.13.
4.   Ep. 70, 73; also 48.3/607.10.
5.   For the identification, see Von Soden, "Prosop.", p.254, who thinks that some of the five unidentifiable bishoprics may have belonged to Mauretania.
6.   For references, see Appendix I.

2

cannot use this as a basis for estimating the expansion of Christianity. The numbers of bishops attending the councils held during Cyprian's tenure are a warning against the use of such figures in the absence of any control.[1]

Other councils in the period preceding Cyprian's episcopate are mentioned in his correspondence. Writing to the clergy and people of Furni about a priest who had been named tutor of the estate of his relative, Cyprian cites the decision of a council which had taken place iam pridem, forbidding members of the clergy to undertake the function of tutor because it might interfere with the duties of their office.[2] Presumably the priest, Geminius Faustinus, is related to the deceased, Geminius Victor. Whether this decision is the result of one of the councils recorded elsewhere or a separate assembly cannot be ascertained. Cyprian also mentions a council of bishops in which some of the members refused to grant communion to adulterers, but did not on that account withdraw from their fellows who opposed them.[3] But the difficulty of determining whether this is a separate council or merely an action of some otherwise known council makes the information of little worth, though it may be connected with Tertullian's comments in the De Pudicitia, and so would fall circa 210/11.

The first detailed information on the distribution of Christianity in Africa is provided by the Sententiae Episcoporum, the minutes of the council of Carthage beginning

---

1. As Harnack, M&A, pp. 280-1 and especially 284; also Baus, HCH, p. 383.
2. Ep. 1.1/465.4-11.
3. Ep. 55.21/638.23 ff.

on September 1, 256. The names and sees of each of the 87 bishops are supplied. The manuscript tradition is generally good for the names and bishoprics.[1] The bishops are all from Africa Proconsularis or Numidia, and the representatives of Mauretania are conspicuously absent - though there remains the possibility that some may be the representatives of cities that are no longer identifiable.[2] The general absence of bishops from an area is an indication of differences over the theological point in question.[3] The difficulty of travel must also have been a consideration for the majority of council members are from locations reasonably accessible to Carthage.[4]

Both the list and the correspondence allow broad conclusions to be drawn, at least as to the distribution of Christian communities in Africa. But the general paucity of precise information in Cyprian has led to the dangerous use of homonyms as the basis for a percentage of identifi-

---

1. Von Soden, "Prosop."p.249, n.1 and n.2. For the manuscripts, see Hartel's praefatio, and 434.
2. Von Soden, "Prosop.", p. 254.
3. Ep. 71 and 73, addressed to the Mauretanian bishops.
4. For an attempt to identify the locations of the ancient African cities with modern locations, see J. Mesnage, L'Afrique chrétienne: Evêchés et ruines antiques (Paris, 1912); also CIL VIII and supplements. For criticism, see G.C. Picard, La civilisation de l'Afrique romaine (Paris, 1959), p. 22. See also Monceaux, HAC,p.8,n.13, for earlier bibliography. The majority of sites are generally agreed upon.

4

cations of bishops with sees.[1] The real danger here lies in estimating any total number of bishops for the whole of Africa during this period. The severe pressures that Cyprian encountered during his period in office, as well as the mass desertions at the beginning of the Decian Persecution, tell against the expansion of Christianity in the period 200-58, so that the extent of Christianity registered by the Cyprianic corpus should indicate its bounds at mid-century, prior to the troubles of the decade from 250-60.

The total number of identifiable bishops is approximately 135, allowing for mistakes due to homonymy.[2] But the concentration of sees is far from equal. By far the largest number are in Africa Proconsularis, with the greatest concentration along the coast of Proconsularis.[3] Also well-represented was the inland area around

---

1. The basis for this equivalence is Von Soden, "Prosop.", who himself sees the difficulty. For example, Fortunatus from Thuccabor (SE 17) may be the addressee of the Ad Fortunatum, as Schanz-Hosius, p. 352, and others have conjectured; but in the Cyprianic corpus, the name is extremely frequent. At least three and perhaps more individuals of that name can be ascertained: the anti-bishop in Ep. 59 passim; a sub-deacon in letter 36.1; a priest mentioned in 14.4. For the bishop Fortunatus and perhaps other bishops of that name, see Hartel's index, s.v. Fortunatus.
2. Based on Von Soden, "Prosop.", pp. 266-70.
3. A good short summary is given by Monceaux, HAC, pp. 7-9. There is no need to repeat it here.

5

Carthage. Of the 87 listed in the minutes of the council, 54 fall in Proconsularis. Numidia supplies 25 bishops, and 6 are of indeterminate origin.[1] Mauretania is unrepresented, but some of the unknown bishops may have had their sees there.[2]

These results accord well with the distribution of towns in Roman North Africa, with the old province of Africa Proconsularis having the largest concentrations of population in centres of all sizes.[3]

Within Numidia, the populated centre of Cirta provided the impetus towards urbanization.[4] It was only Mauretania in the west that lacked any extensive urbanization and was poorly represented in our list of Christian communities. In spite of Tertullian's boast that conversions had taken place beyond the imperial frontiers in Mauretania, among the Gaetuli and Mauri, Christian expansion in the area is unattested.

The majority of Christians are found in settled urban areas, particularly in the sphere of influence of Carthage; ecclesiastical organization would have been difficult to apply to unsettled and nomadic populations. It was the bishop of Carthage who controlled the entire Christian population

---

1. It accords with Cyprian, who mentions a council composed of 25 Numidian bishops as a possibility, Ep. 59.11.
2. Von Soden, "Prosop.", p. 254.
3. Picard, Civilisation, 60, who divides the majority of land between the territories of cities and imperial saltus of about 1500 sq. km. See also Rostovtzeff, SEHRE, pp. 318 ff.
4. Rostovtzeff, SEHRE, p.323.

of Africa. His predominance was ensured by the importance of Carthage as well as, in the case of Cyprian, by the strength of his own personality. Cyprian claims Mauretania and Numidia as part of his provincia in his correspondence with the bishop of Rome.[1] Carthage was one of the foremost cities of the Empire.[2] Herodian mentions its great size and large population in the course of describing the revolt of the Gordians. In its size and wealth, Carthage was second only to Rome in the West, and disputed with Alexandria for the second spot among the great cities of the Empire.[3] A century later, the author of a geographical compilation of the provinces of the Empire was driven to superlatives in his description of Carthage:

"Ipsa autem regio Africae est valde maxima et bona et dives".[4]

Estimates of population in antiquity are always difficult, but the Augustan city of Carthage may have had 200,000 inhabitants, with a further 300,000 resident in the environs.[5] Far over-shadowing the other

---

1. Ep. 48.3/607.10-11 to Cornelius.
2. For the archeological remains of Roman Carthage, see A. Audollent, Carthage romaine, 146 avant Jésus-Christ - 698 après Jésus-Christ, Bibliothèque des écoles françaises d'Athènes et de Rome, fasc. 84 (Paris, 1901); see also the excellent summary in RE X2 (1930) 2150-2224.
3. Herodian 7.6.1 ff.
4. Expositio Totius Mundi, 61.17 ff. in Sources Chrétiennes, no. 124. His comments about the inhabitants are less than laudatory: "Good men are particularly hard to find."
5. This was about 12% of the total

7

cities of North Africa, it formed a natural centre for both Christian and pagan life. All the councils for which we have information were apparently held under the auspices of the bishop of Carthage. But no record of a graduated hierarchy is preserved, and the most reasonable hypothesis is that the predominance of the bishop of Carthage was a result of the size and the importance of the city, and not the result of an ecclesiastical hierarchy. Of the latter there is no trace.

Any attempt to establish a ratio between bishoprics and population is impossible. Carthage had the resources to supply funds to other churches. During his episcopate, Cyprian sent 100,000 sesterces to help redeem Christians who had been carried off into captivity by raiding barbarian tribes.[1] The poverty and small size of another community is made evident in an offer by Cyprian to support an actor who had turned Christian, if he would give up his profession.[2]

Other means of estimating the total Christian population in Africa during this period are equally uncertain. Tertullian's comments on the number of Christians seem to mirror his penchant for hyperbole rather than reflect accurate estimates. In the Apologeticum, he claims that Christians are

---

5. (cont'd) population of the Roman provinces of North Africa in the Roman period. The estimates are those of Picard, Civilisation, 47;157. See his comments on the figures arrived at by Courtois, pp.47 ff.
1. Ep. 62.4/700.16-9. For the date of this letter, long thought to be 253, see Appendix I.
2. Ep. 2/467-9.

8

everywhere: they are of every age, sex and condition.[1] In a similar vein, he later returns to the theme of Christian numbers: Christians are only of yesterday, yet they fill all the world; only the temples of the gods are left to the pagans.[2] In the same class are Tertullian's remarks in the De Praescriptione Haereticorum, where he mentions the thousands converted to Christianity.[3] His remarks on the numbers in Carthage are likewise suspect, offering little basis for calculation.[4]

Eusebius dates the universal attraction to Christianity from the reign of Commodus when, by the grace of God, peace came to the churches throughout the world, and the souls of the pious of every race began to tread the road of salvation towards the true God.[5] But the statement seems at best an exaggeration. It appears that the work was designed as an introduction to the trial of Apollonius, in which context Eusebius seems more interested in exalting his educational and philosophic attainments. In addition, Eusebius' knowledge is extremely slight on the developments in Christianity in the West.[6]

The Octavius of Minucius Felix offers little beyond certain indefinite hints. Caecilius mentions that Christianity must be totally extirpated. Together with the decay of morals, the Christian conspiracy

---

1. Apol. 1.7.
2. Apol. 37.4.
3. De Praescr. Haeret. 20.
4. Ad Scap. 2, 5.
5. HE 5.21.1.
6. See text p. 52, n.2, on Apollonius, and reference there.

9

grows throughout the entire world.[1] The Christian creed encourages strangers to join, and converts to persevere.[2] Neither statement is very revealing.

Cyprian's evidence on the growth of Christianity follows the same pattern. In citing the decision of the council of Agrippinus, he states that tot milia haereticorum in his provinces, having turned towards the Church, have not hesitated or delayed to undergo rebaptism.[3] So the comments of Cyprian on the activities of bishops before the persecution point to a widespread community. Many neglected their pastoral duties; they were interested only in obtaining money by fraud, if necessary; they resorted to perjury and adultery. At times they left their own congregations in order to wander through foreign provinces in pursuit of gain while their own communities disintegrated.[4] Though the charges may be exaggerated for effect, Cyprian was not describing a small and élite group.

The widespread network of bishops and various other indications would point to a Christian community of some size scattered throughout the cities of Africa Proconsularis and Numidia. Other Christians, though

---

1. Oct. 9.1. In his reply, Octavius cites the daily increase in the numbers of Christians as evidence for the merit of their creed; for Caecilius this points to man's gullibility.

2. Oct. 31.7. For the inapplicability of 33.1 as evidence for Christian numbers, see G.W. Clarke, "The Historical Setting of the Octavius of Minucius Felix", JRH 4 (1966/7) 271, n.30.

3. Ep. 73.3/780.16.

4. De Lapsis 6/240 and 13/241.5.

far fewer in number, are indicated as living in Mauretania. But the question of growth in the first half of the third century remains a problem. The increase in the number of bishops between the council which excommunicated Privatus of Lambaesis and the councils held under Cyprian was nil. The numbers of bishops have led to opposite conclusions as to the expansion of Christianity.[1] The differences in estimates spring from the essential impossibility of arriving at a satisfactory answer; but after the initial councils held at an indeterminate period from the year 190 on, no real growth is discernible. The numbers taking part in the councils under Cyprian fluctuate so widely that it is impossible to use them as a basis for calculating increase or stagnation. The striking figure is the growth shown after the conversion of Constantine.[2]

Even at Carthage the episcopal _fasti_ are almost non-existent. Tertullian, writing _circa_ 210/11 in anger over what he considered the usurpation by a bishop of the right to forgive adultery and fornication, mentions the _edictum peremptorium_ which this _episcopus episcoporum_ had pro-

---

1. Von Soden, "Prosop.", points to the lack of growth, and he assigns the period of expansion in Africa to the years following the persecutions of the mid-third century (265). Baus, _HCH_, p. 311 points to the synods of the first half of the century as particularly significant for the growth of Christianity. Monceaux, _HAC_, p. 6 is also struck by Christian growth; so also Harnack, _M&A_, p. 280 who posits a large growth.
2. Von Soden, "Prosop.", p. 265, is essentially correct.

11

mulgated.[1] Much dispute has been raised as to the see of this bishop. Some claim that he was the bishop of Rome. Attempts were made to identify the specific bishop intended, and the obvious candidate was Callistus.[2] But the situation in Rome during the pontificate of Callistus, as reported by Hippolytus, does not fit the De Pudicitia.[3] More decisive is Tertullian in his reference to omnem ecclesiam Petri propinquam (21.10). Thus a bishop is attested for Carthage in 210/11.[4] No information is preserved, however, as to his name or the duration of his tenure.

The Passion of Perpetua (martyred with her companions at Carthage on March 7, probably in 203) contains visions experienced by Perpetua and Saturus in the period between their apprehension by the Roman authorities and their deaths in the amphitheatre.[5] In one of the visions of Saturus,

---

1. De Pud. 1.6. For dates, see Barnes, Tert., p. 55.
2. Harnack, GAL, pp.260, 286. Also Monceaux, HAC, pp.200, 207; Quasten, Pat.,p. 313; and Schanz-Hosius,p. 304.
3. Philos. 9.12.
4. See Altaner-Stuiber, Pat., p. 159; Barnes, Tert., pp. 247-50.
5. The standard text is C. van Beek, Passio Sanctarum Perpetuae et Felicitatis, I (Neumagen, 1936). More accessible is the text in R. Knopf, G. Krüger, G. Ruhbach, Ausgewählte Märtyrerakten[4], Sammlung ausgewählter kirchen- und dogmengeschichtlicher Quellenschriften, N.F. 3 (Tübingen, 1965),pp. 35-44. For authenticity, see Barnes, Tert., pp.79-80, 263-6. For a valuable introduction, see J.A. Robinson (ed.), "The Passion of S. Perpetua", Texts and Studies,

12

who had first converted Perpetua, both he and Perpetua visit the Lord.[1] After this joyous experience, the future martyrs, on leaving, notice the bishop Optatus outside the entrance on the right, and on the left the presbyter Aspasius. These two stand apart in deep dejection, but upon seeing Perpetua and Saturus fling themselves at their feet and beg to be reconciled.[2]

Thus we have evidence for an Optatus as bishop of Carthage circa 203, and an indication of the existence of a hierarchy which finds confirmation in Tertullian. Both Optatus and Aspasius are portrayed as alive at the time of Perpetua's imprisonment. Pontius confirms that Cyprian was the first bishop in Africa to suffer martyrdom for the faith. There is no evidence, however, for the duration or history of Optatus' pontificate.[3] Some have thought that he was not a Carthaginian, basing themselves on the martyrology included in Bede and elsewhere.[4] Perpetua and her contemporaries have been identified wrongly with the Thuburbitan Martyrs mentioned by Augustine in his sermon, De Contemptu

---

5. (cont'd) Contributions to Biblical and Patristic Literature, vol. 1, n. 2 (Cambridge, 1891), 61-95. Robinson attempts to establish, unsuccessfully, the authorship of Tertullian, but too little is known of African Latin literature for such an attempt to prove fruitful. On this, see Barnes, Tert., 79-80.
  1. Pass. Perpet. 11 ff.
  2. Pass. Perpet. 13 ff.
  3. Audollent, Carthage romaine, 342.
  4. For a refutation and the establishment of the trial at Carthage, see Robinson, "Perpetua", 22-6.

13

Mundi.[1]
An even more elusive figure than
Optatus is Agrippinus, the next bishop about
whom any information has survived. Cyprian
is the single source which preserves his
memory. While involved in the rebaptism
controversy with Stephen, Cyprian answers
the request of Quintus, a Mauretanian bishop,
about his stand.[2] After stating his position
Cyprian adds an historical precedent, citing
Agrippinus:

"...bonae memoriae uir cum ceteris
coepiscopis suis qui illo tempore
in prouincia Africa et Numidia
ecclesiam Domini gubernabant"[3]

In a letter to Jubaianus, also on the question of heretical baptism, Cyprian again
cites Agrippinus as a precedent for his
behaviour.[4] He claims his action is not a
new or sudden innovation: Agrippinus,
holding a large council, had decided that
heretics must be rebaptised. The thousands
of heretics who had come into the Church
from that time until now had all accepted
this.[5] Cyprian only specifies that the
council took place

"...quando anni sint iam multi
et longa aetas"

_____

1. Aug., De Contemptu Mundi, ed. Ben.
V 1338, n. b.
2. On Quintus and his location in
Mauretania, see Von Soden, "Prosop.", 269,
and infra p. 310, n. 3.
3. Ep. 71.4/774.12-14.
4. Ep. 73.3/780.12-15.
5. Ep. 73.3/780.16-19.

14

Augustine tells us that the council consisted of 70 bishops of Proconsularis and Numidia. Though the information he had at hand is unknown, the reference to Numidia and Proconsularis fits Cyprian's statement and may be based upon an accurate tradition.[1] The absence of precise information has given rise to conflicting estimates of Agrippinus' chronological position in the episcopal _fasti_ of Carthage.[2]

Heavy reliance for the date of the council of Agrippinus has been placed on a passage in Tertullian's _De Jejunio_ (13).[3] But Tertullian seems to refer only to councils comprised of persons from several provinces. He specified that they convened universal councils, and that the group was a _representatio totius nominis Christiani_. One can only conjecture how he would have regarded the council of Agrippinus. Did Tertullian consider that an assemblage of

---

1. _De Unico Bapt. Contra Petilian._ 13.22. Of course, the geographical specification may be based on his knowledge of Cyprian.

2. Monceaux, _HAC_ I, 19, places Agrippinus before Optatus, at the end of the second century. C.J. von Hefele, _Histoire des conciles d'après les documents originaux_[2] (Paris, 1907 ff.), ed. and trans. by H. Leclercq, I.1, p. 155, has Agrippinus after 203, based on Tertullian's _De Jejunio_ 13; so also J. Ludwig, _Der heilige Märtyrerbischof Cyprian von Karthago_ (Munich, 1951), p. 15; G. Mongelli, "La chiesa di Cartagine contro Roma durante l'episcopato di S. Cipriano (249-258)", _Miscellanea Francescana_ 59 (1959), p. 131; Harnack, _GAL_, p. 286.

3. _De Jejunio_ 13.

15

bishops from Numidia and Africa fell under this heading? No certain answer is possible. Cyprian's statement that the council took place long ago may be thought to provide some indication, but his terminology is inexact.[1]

The only other bishop of Carthage who can definitely be assigned to the period before Cyprian's episcopate is his probable immediate predecessor, Donatus. Discussing the crisis that had grown up around the question of those Christians who had lapsed in their faith during the persecution Cyprian informs Cornelius that Privatus, the deposed bishop of Lambaesis, had tried to obtain reinstatement from the council being held at Carthage but without success. He mentions that Privatus had been condemned by Fabianus and Donatus, the predecessors of Cornelius and himself.[2] Presumably also the condemnation of Privatus took place in a council at Carthage, and Fabianus sent letters supporting the decision. But this is the full extent of the information available on this shadowy incident - aside from the fact that the council had 90 members.[3]

One more name exists as a possibility for a bishop prior to Cyprian. A certain Cyrus is mentioned by Augustine as bishop of Carthage, but unfortunately no indication is given as to his date. He may as easily have

1. E.g., Ep. 59.10/677.14-9.
2. Ep. 59.10/677.14-9.
3. "90 members", Ep. 59.10/677.14-9. Harnack, M&A, pp. 280-1, thinks the council took place at Lambaesis. Monceaux, HAC, p.5 is right - the council probably occurred at Carthage, but even this cannot be proved.

16

followed Cyprian as preceded him.[1]

The development of the Church hierarchy first meets us in the work of Cyprian; there is no evidence, however, that any of it is his doing. Its size in Carthage is not stated, but some idea of its upper limit is provided by Cyprian's admission that the Church in Rome precedes that of Carthage in size.[2] Under Cornelius, who is contemporaneous with this letter, the Roman clergy was composed of 46 presbyters, 7 deacons, 7 sub-deacons, 42 acolytes, 52 exorcists, readers and door-keepers. In addition, there were more than 1,500 widows and persons in distress receiving support from the Church.[3] The same grades of clergy were represented in the Carthaginian Church.

The most important division was that between the laity in general and the clergy. Terminologically it reproduced the language of municipal government. The clergy, analogous to the governing class of a city, were known as the ordo.[4] The laity were

---

1. Possidius, Vita Sancti Augustini, 8, in PL, 32.33. Augustine, De Depositione Cyri Episcopi Carthaginis, in PL, 46.16. So rightly Monceaux, HAC, p. 5.
2. Ep. 52.2/617.18-619.7
3. HE 6.43.11. See note ad loc. of H.J. Lawlor and J.E.L. Oulton (ed. and trans.) Eusebius: The Ecclesiastical History and the Martyrs of Palestine (London, 1928), II, listing various estimates for the Christian population of Rome inferred from Eusebius' information.
4. For the African clergy, see P. Batiffol, L'église naissante et le catholicisme[6] (Paris, 1913). Also Monceaux, HAC, pp. 113-4.

17

the plebs of the res publica Christiana.[1] Among the clergy, seven degrees of distinction existed; the eighth degree, that of door-keepers present at Rome, is not recorded at Carthage.[2] Represented in the Carthaginian clergy are bishop, presbyter, deacons and readers, all of which were grades of the major clergy.[3] To these grades must be added the acolytes, exorcists and sub-deacons.[4] The last is not mentioned by Tertullian and may be an innovation of the first half of the third century to handle the increasing number of the faithful.[5]

The plebs were also organized into various grades: fideles, or fully baptised Christians, catechumens, penitents, widows,

---

1. Already in Tertullian, De Exhort. Cast. 7; De Idol. 7; De Monog. 11; De Praescr. Haeret. 14. The term is not in Hartel's index. Batiffol, L'église naissante, cites 59.19 as an example of the use of ordo, but this is an error; it cannot be found in Cyprian, who prefers the term clerus; see Hartel's index, s.v.. On the other hand, plebs is very common. See for example, Ep. 14.4/512.19;67.3/737.20; and Hartel's index. Cyprian also uses the variant populus, Ep. 49.2/611.12.
2. At Rome, HE 6.43.11-2.
3. Episcopi: see especially Ep. 3.3/471.16; De Cath. Eccl. Un. 4/213.2, and Hartel's index. Diaconi: Ep. 3.3/471.16; 67.4/738.20. Presbyteri: Ep. 40/585.8 and especially 38/579.14 ff.
4. Acolytes: Ep. 7.34.4/570.14, etc. Exorcists: Ep. 69.15/764.14, etc.
5. So Monceaux, HAC, p. 13.

18

and virgins.[1] The contact between the _plebs_ and the _ordo_ was close and important in the life of the community. The single most important function which was shared by both was the election of various members of the laity to the _clerus_, or the promotion of men within the ecclesiastical hierarchy.

The election of Cyprian himself seems to have been decided by the intervention of the excited populace against the opposition of presbyters.[2] Writing to his clergy from exile, he stresses that he had resolved to decide nothing without their counsel and the consensus of the _plebs_.[3] At a council in 254, in a letter to Spanish bishops who had asked African help in a dispute against Rome, Cyprian and his fellow bishops re-affirmed that, for a valid episcopal election, bishops of the same province must elect the candidate with the approval of the assembled laity.[4] But the most informative piece of evidence is the letter written by Cyprian to his clergy at the end of the

---

1. _Fideles_: _De Op. et Eleemos._ 8/ 380.4; _Ad Fort._ 12/345.3; _De Bono Pat._ 23/ 414.20; _Ep._ 66.5/730.13. The majority of instances obviously fall in the treatises. The references have a somewhat rhetorical flavour. _Penitents_: _Ep._ 55.22/639.8; 55.27-29/644.7. _Catechumens_: _Ep._ 73.22/795.16; 8.3/488.2; _Test. III_, 98/178.5. _Widows_: _Test._ III, 113/181.20; _Ep._ 7.1/485.8-9; _Ep._ 8.3/487.20. _Virgins_: _De Hab. Virg._, _passim_; _Ep._ 4 _passim_.
2. Pontius, _Vita_ 5.1: "quod iudicio Dei et plebis favore ad officium sacerdotii et episcopatus gradum...electus est".
3. _Ep._ 14.4/512.19.
4. _Ep._ 67.5/739.12.

Decian Persecution. Putting his confessor, Aurelius, forward for the position of reader, Cyprian quoted divine evidence for Aurelius' suitability for the post - in view of the fact that Cyprian was taking the initiative without consultation. The letter opens with an admission that in clerical ordinations it was the custom to consult both clergy and people, and to weigh the merits of each individual with a common council.[1] The people were present at the final council on the rebaptism question, on September 1, 256.[2] Cyprian allowed them to be present at councils, in addition to attending elections.[3] Other bishops may not have been so ready to consult the laity on important questions. The earliest evidence we have for the presence of the laity at councils is in Cyprian, and he had a special relationship to the lay community at Carthage.[4]

The diffusion of Christianity in Africa may have been conditioned by special factors. Though Christianity was primarily urban in nature, the first recorded appearance of Christians in Africa already indicates their widespread dispersion in the countryside.[5] The answer to this phenomenon has been sought in the particular nature of the pre-Christian religion of the area.

The native cult of Saturn contained a monotheistic element, combined with the presence of a divine will which demanded

---

1. Ep. 38.1/579.16-8.
2. SE Episc. Proem. 435.7-8.
3. Ep. 19.2/525.12-526.
4. Supra, p. 19, n. 2.
5. Infra, p. 26.

absolute obedience to itself.[1] Certain practices persisted which had been attached to various pagan cults and were carried over into Christianity.[2] But some such carry-over is a phenomenon common to the development of Christianity everywhere and is more than understandable. Many saints were later to take the place of earlier pagan deities. That piety should be expressed, particularly on a popular level, through established practices, is common all over the area over which the Christian Church extended. This does not indicate, however, that there is any necessary intrinsic connection between the two religions.

The particular flavour of African Christianity has been cited as evidence for a connection between the dour religion of Saturn and its Christian successor.[3] In the Apologeticum, Tertullian paints God as a judge who will reward men for following his laws or punish them for their transgressions. The true Christian will be repaid with eternal life, but those who have been heedless will suffer eternal fire and damnation.[4] At the end of the De Spectaculis, Tertullian again exults in the bloodbath that the Day of Judgment will bring. How many great men of this world will we meet – magistrates who had once persecuted others now themselves liquifying in the flames of a just reward.

---

1. This is the hypothesis of S. Gsell, Histoire ancienne de l'Afrique du nord (8 vols. Paris 1913-28) Vol. IV, p. 498, adopted by Frend, DC, p. 97.
2. For details, see Frend, DC, pp. 97 ff.
3. See Gsell, Histoire ancienne, IV, p. 498; Frend, DC, p. 97.
4. Apol. 18.3.

21

Those who had been idolaters or who had transgressed God's laws delight Tertullian with their terrifying fate.[1] Cyprian's view is similar.[2] And early in the fourth century, Lactantius continues the tradition of taking delight in describing the horrible death of Galerius and others who had persecuted the Church of Christ.[3]

Eagerness for martyrdom in Africa contrasts with a more even-tempered view of a Christian's duty in persecution. So Tertullian's De Fuga in Persecutione forms a strong contrast to the instructions of Peter, bishop of Alexandria, in the Great Persecution.[4] Cyprian followed Tertullianic tradition in his approach to martyrdom at first, but circumstances necessitated a change in attitude.[5] Thus Tertullian seems to have expressed the key concept of African Christianity, when he remarked that fear was the basis of salvation.[6] But rigorism was not peculiarly African. Novatianus, though influenced by Cyprian,

---

1. De Spect. 30.
2. Particularly the Ad Dem. 24.1/ 368.13 ff. and 9/356.25 ff.
3. De Mort. Persecut. 24 ff.
4. There exists no critical text of the Canonical Epistle of Peter. The most accessible version is the corrected text of M.J. Routh, Reliquiae Sacrae[2] (5 vols. Oxford, 1846), Vol. IV, pp. 23 ff., to which should be added the Syriac fragments translated into Greek by E. Schwartz, Gesammelte Schriften III (1959) pp. 90 ff.
5. For a general view, see the Ad Fort., passim. The change in attitude will be discussed, infra p. 217.
6. De Cult. Fem. 2.2.

developed a rigorism of his own.[1]
Ignatius' attitude towards martyrdom had a
compulsive horror to match any of the blood-
thirsty sentiments of the Africans.[2]

In a world hostile and permanently
threatening, visions of the destruction of
the enemy and severe demands on one's
followers are part of the growth of any such
non-conformist group.[3] Christianity always
contained such elements, but the literary
remains from Africa prior to the third
century are so poor that generalizations
should not be made.

In the De Lapsis, Cyprian points to
African laxity, and his own handling of the
question of the lapsed at various councils
shows efforts at conciliation and leniency
rather than uncompromising rigour.[4] While
Tertullian had a strong streak of rigour,
the result was disharmony within the African
Church; it drove him outside a church which
he considered to be lax.[5] But the equation
of rigour with an easy transition of worshippers from a fierce Saturn to a fiercer
Christ will not hold. Christianity has
always had its rigorists, irrespective of
geographical location.

The instability and insecurity of life,
as well as the proximity of Rome, seem more

---

1. For Novatianus, infra p. 221.
2. Particularly Eusebius, HE 3.36.7-10.
3. For later Christians, see especially
N. Cohn, The Pursuit of the Millenium,
Revolutionary Messianism in Medieval and
Reformation Europe and its Bearing on Modern
Totalitarian Movements[2] (New York, 1961),
pp. 283 ff., on Thomas Müntzer.
4. Infra pp. 214 ff.
5. On this, see Barnes, Tert.,
especially pp. 131-42.

potent factors. Rather than in rigorism, the influence of the Punic cult of Saturn may be traced in the concept of sacrifice, which strongly flavours African Christianity. The readiness for martyrdom and the high value placed on personal confrontation and death exceed what we would expect from the scant evidence available for other regions.[1]

It appears to be a question more of mood than of direct derivation. Human sacrifice had been ended in the reign of Tiberius; but the disposition to translate the older view, that God could be placated by the forfeiture of human life, persisted.[2] In essence, however, what happened remains mysterious, and no hypothesis is satisfactory. The nature of sacrifice in African Christianity is the result of a multiplicity of causes, of which insecurity was certainly an important one.[3]

In connection with the supposed expansion of Christianity during our period, a question arises as to its relationship to the different linguistic groups present in North Africa. The traditional classifi-

---

1. Tertullian, De Fuga 2.1, and Cyprian, Ad Fort., praefatio.
2. On the end of human sacrifice, Barnes, Tert., pp. 15 ff.
3. Ad Don., especially 6/8.9 ff. Another hypothesis has been proposed by Picard, Civilisation, p. 110, that the Romanization of native cults may have helped to drive Africans to the Church. But the Church as it is shown to have been operating in Cyprian's work, had its own unmistakable Roman flavour. In any case, this would explain a turning away from native cults, but not the turning to Christianity in preference to other cults.

24

cation divides the population into three groups: the immigrant Roman colonists, the Punic element, and the Libyan native peoples.[1] Caution should be used in any equation between the Libyans of antiquity and the Berber people of modern North Africa.[2] The Libyans only come into the picture as adversaries of the Romans, except for a reference by Tertullian to conversions of barbarian tribes in Mauretania.[3] Though Libyan practices are mentioned by Christian apologists, there is no indication of any particular Libyan mark on the culture of Christian North Africa.

The survival of the Punic language is well attested in the period, particularly in inscriptions.[4] The references to the use of Punic as a legitimate language for fideicommissum indicate that the language was spread over more than the lowest social class of the population.[5] Translations of sermons from Latin into Punic were still required in

---

1. Picard, Civilisation, p. 103.
2. The assumption of a relationship between the Berber of today and the Libyan of antiquity is tenuous, but not disprovable. Libyan was certainly not a language of culture, and there remains a question as to whether it was a living language in the period under study. For a reference to the sources and a discussion of the problem, see F. Millar, "Local Cultures in the Roman Empire: Libyan, Punic and Latin in Roman Africa", JRS 58 (1968), pp. 126-34.
3. E.W. Benson, Cyprian: His Life, His Times, His Work (London, 1897), p. 324.
4. For a collection of the references, see Millar, "Local Cultures", pp. 130-3.
5. Millar, "Local Cultures", p. 131.

Augustine's time.[1] This applies to the area of Hippo; it does not seem legitimate to extend the need all over Africa. With its urban background, Christianity might seem open to influence by Punic speakers. The old network of Punic colonial foundations around Carthage, where presumably a fair size population existed which could trace its origins back to the eastern settlers, might be thought to have required the Christian mission to use Punic. It may have provided the soil for a Punic Christian literature, but of this there is no record.

The language and thought-world of African Christianity is Latin. Cyprian's correspondence shows no knowledge of the existence of any other language or culture. The ungrammatical reply of Lucianus, a confessor in Carthage, to a request of another Carthaginian, Celerinus, betrays a lack of education, but no evidence that he knew any other language than Latin.[2] So on the most routine matters dealt with in his correspondence with Carthage during his exile, Cyprian never raised a question about the need of translation into Punic; nor did he betray the slightest knowledge of its existence.

The evidence of inscriptions may be useful here. Extended Punic inscriptions died out at the beginning of the second century, while formulaic inscriptions of brief extent continued up to the beginning

---

1. On this subject, see P. Brown, "Christianity and Local Culture in Late Roman Africa", JRS 58 (1968), pp. 85-95 = Religion and Society in the Age of Saint Augustine (London, 1972), pp. 279-300. See also Aug., Ep. ad Rom. Incoh. Expos. 13.
2. Ep. 21 and 22.

26

of the third century.[1] The period of Christian expansion fell in the third century, as we have seen, and perhaps predominantly in the second half. It may be that the evidence of Augustine cannot be used to make inferences for all of the African countryside. The first evidence we have of Christianity or the Latin Bible, the Acts of the Scillitan Martyrs, betrays the extent of Latinization in the countryside in 180. The martyrs appear to have been of lower-class origin, and two of them possess native names. There is no reference, however, to any other language but Latin.[2] It may be that the evidence of Augustine is misleading and that sufficiently large pockets of Punic speakers survived to warrant Ulpian's statement that Punic was valid for the fideicommissum process, but that it was a dying phenomenon. The inscriptions would indicate that it was being abandoned in the period of Christianity's rise. But while occasional translation may have been required, Christianity used Latin as its almost exclusive vehicle. Its expansion took place when Punic was ceasing to be used, at least in inscriptions. African Christianity was a Latin phenomenon and remained so.[3]

For the secular world in which the church structure was embedded, the first 50 years of the third century was a period of

---

1. Picard, Civilisation, pp. 104, 109, and 295.
2. Barnes, Tert., p. 63. The two names are Cittinus and Nartzalus, or perhaps the latter should be Nartialus.
3. This is to ignore the Greek evidence of Christianity, but it is not relevant. See Millar, "Local Cultures", pp. 130-3, on the subject.

27

both political and economic vicissitudes. The Church was not unaffected. After the local persecution which Tertullian recorded in the Ad Scapulam, the absence of material complicates any attempt at assessing the situation before the great outbreak of persecution at mid-century. The evidence would indicate that there was no 38-year period of tranquillity for the Church, starting at the beginning of the third century.[1] In a letter recommending Celerinus for ecclesiastical advancement, Cyprian mentioned the death of his grandmother, Celerina, and his paternal and maternal uncles, Laurentius and Egnatius, in the cause of the Church. It is impossible to discern whether one or more outbreaks of persecution were responsible for these martyrdoms. But the deaths of the uncles would probably not have taken place earlier than the year 230, while that of the grandmother was probably after the reign of Caracalla.[2]

The Octavius also refers to persecution, but whether local difficulties in Africa are meant or whether Octavius was involved with them perhaps at Rome, cannot be decided.[3]

---

1. On the whole problem, see Barnes, Tert., pp. 155 ff. The real culprit is of course Eusebius, who set up the framework.

2. Barnes, Tert., p. 158, would place the death of the grandmother possibly under Severus Alexander, and of the uncles under the Gordians. Perhaps Christians perished for their faith in the aftermath of the troubles of 238, which would account for the uncles. If the grandmother died in a different period, there is little hope of locating it.

3. For persecution, see Oct. 9.5;28;37.

This is the sum total of evidence for persecution in Africa during this period. The evidence of Cyprian points to the fact that the persecution of Christians under Decius was to be a radically new experience for them. The disorganization which followed the Emperor's actions also points in the same direction, though the new and systematic approach further complicates the situation. In the De Lapsis, Cyprian explains the disaster of the persecution as a result of the testing of God. Long peace had corrupted the divine discipline which lay sleeping.[1] But the inexactness of Cyprian's use of temporal expressions makes calculation impossible.[2] During the reign of Maximinus, traditionally one of persecution, we only know of the local persecution described by Firmilian in his letter to the African bishop in the year 256.[3]

By the year 250, persecution had become the exception, and its absence had seriously affected the ability of North African Christianity to meet it without profound internal upheaval. The difficulties of the Church are also reflected in the troubles that the period 200-50 brought to North African society at large. The complaints of pagans against Christians seemed as if they had some basis.[4]

The prosperity of first century Africa

---

1. De Lapsis 5/240.8-9.
2. Supra p. 2, on Privatus of Lambaesis.
3. Ep. 75.10/816.17 ff. On this reference, see Barnes, Tert., p. 157; and Barnes, "Legislation Against the Christians", JRS 58 (1968) pp. 32 ff.
4. For a discussion of the Ad Dem., infra p. 275.

29

had been almost totally based upon cereal cultivation.[1] Africa supplied the needs of Rome for grain for two-thirds of the year.[2] Egypt supplied the grain for the remainder of the year.[3] Writing in the 70's of the first century, Pliny the Elder cites grain as almost the exclusive crop of North Africa.[4] With the expansion into regions not suitable for cereal culture, African agriculture became more diversified. African oil became an important part of agricultural export. The cultivation of the olive expanded as the area of colonization was extended towards the south in the second century, particularly in the high plains. The olive began in fact to take over land which had formerly been used for grain production.[5] Viticulture also expanded to become the third major crop during the second century, though African wine was not considered to be of the first grade.[6] Africa was a rich and flourishing province.

1. Juvenal, Satires 8.117-8.
2. Josephus, Bellum Judaicum 2.383.
3. Ibid.
4. NH 15.8. See R.M. Haywood's comment on this passage, Roman Africa, in T. Frank (ed.), An Economic Survey of Ancient Rome (6 vols. Baltimore 1933-40) Vol. IV, p. 45.
5. See Haywood, Roman Africa, pp. 45 ff. for a detailed description of olive-producing areas from 43 B.C. to 235 A.D.; see also Rostovtzeff, SEHRE, pp. 158-63.
6. For a good short introductory sketch, see E. Albertini, L'Afrique romaine, revised by M.L. Leschi (Algiers, 1950), pp. 57 ff. For Roman comments on African wine, see Haywood, Roman Africa, pp. 51 ff.

Agriculture in the period to 250 was basically represented by the same products - oil, cereals, and wine. But decreasing prosperity is reflected, as in the rest of the Empire, particularly in the period following 235.

Under the first two Severan emperors, the African origin of the ruling house and a visit by Septimius in 202/3 contributed towards a large-scale building programme.[1] The first two Severi renamed Carthage, which became Colonia Iulia Aurelia Antoniniana Karthago.[2] Together with Utica, it received the Ius Italicum. Lepcis Magna, the home of Septimius' family, also received the same coveted grant.[3]

Macrinus, successor of Caracalla, could trace his origin to North Africa. He was from Mauretania Caesariensis, but of obscure

---

1. For the constructions of Septimius Severus in Africa, see A. Birley, Septimius Severus. The African Emperor (London, 1971), pp. 218 ff., and n. 1 on p. 218. For the question of Septimius' attitude towards Africa, see T.D. Barnes, "The Family and Career of Septimius Severus", Historia 16 (1967), pp. 87-107, especially p. 106 on "Africitas".

On the repair of roads, see Haywood, Roman Africa, p. 66, though there is some question as to the origin of the work. Municipalities may have restored roads on his orders, but it fits well with his military outlook. The temple of Hr Khina, dedicated to Mercury, may well be a construction of Caracalla. See P. Romanelli, Storia delle Provincie Romane dell'Africa, Studi Pubblicati dall'Istituto Italiano per la Storia antica, fasc. 14 (Rome, 1959), p. 439.

2. CIL VIII, 1220, suppl. 12.522.
3. Romanelli, Storia, pp. 418 ff.

31

birth. Dio comments on the pierced ear that betrayed his origin.[1] His short reign left little time to honour his place of birth; his only memorials are many milestones in Mauretania, one from Proconsularis.[2]

Elagabalus had little to his credit but milestones.[3] But under his cousin and adopted son, Roman expansion in Africa reached its greatest extent. Besides military constructions, several temples owe their origin to the reign of Severus Alexander. Thugga was graced with a temple of Caelestis and Fortuna, in addition to an arch.[4] In addition, a temple of the gens Septimia was raised at Cuicul.[5] A new

---

1. Dio, 78.11.1-2.
2. But none in Numidia; for references, see Romanelli, Storia, p. 437. On the limes in Numidia, see J. Baredez, Fossatum Africae, Arts et métiers graphiques (Paris, 1949), pp. 358 ff.
3. All of them in Numidia and Mauretania - military preparations? See Romanelli, Storia, pp. 437-8, who thinks more numerous constructions of Elagabalus may be an attempt to stress descent from Septimius Severus, but this seems a mistaken hypothesis. The majority of building cited by Romanelli is of milestones, which may have had military functions. The bureaucracy was functioning, even if the Emperor was involved in religious matters. His conduct with the Dea Caelestis of Carthage would indicate that the sympathies of Elagabalus were with his god, rather than with his imperial relation. See Herodian, 5.6.4 ff. and SHA Elagab. 7.3.
4. CIL VIII, 2657, 26551; ILAf 528; cf. CIL VIII, 26549.
5. See Romanelli, Storia, p. 447.

aqueduct was built in Lambaesis.[1] Other constructions also bear witness to the renewed interest of the government in North Africa.[2] But economic support and construction financed by the central government – as well as by private individuals – fell sharply after the end of the reign of Severus Alexander. Private building in Africa on any scale disappeared after 235. The process was not sudden; even during the period of building under Septimius Severus and his less generous son, Caracalla, the number of private dedications had fallen off sharply.

Municipalities still continued to produce dedications, but at a reduced rate.[3] Under the emperors who followed, there was no building by private individuals. The cities took the entire initiative.[4] The causes of this apparent decline in public spirit are somewhat of a mystery. Certainly after 235 the political situation adversely affected economic enterprise.[5] Barbarian invasions also contributed to Africa's economic stagnation, but their effects were not spread equally, and the area around Carthage was not affected. Cyprian's gift of 100,000 sesterces to succour captured Christians is evidence that at least the Church of Carthage possessed some financial resources. Why did not the pagans as well?[6] To some extent the devastations of 238 and the barbarian incursions geographically overlapped. The revolt covered the area most lightly affected by the barbarian

---

1. CIL VIII, 226, 2659, 2662, 2685.
2. Romanelli, Storia, pp. 445-52.
3. Haywood, Roman Africa, p. 119.
4. Ibid.
5. On the revolt of 238, infra p. 38.
6. Ep. 62/698-701.

33

menace. Natural disasters, which seem to purposely occur at times of difficulties of human origin, may have been of some importance.[1]

The policy of the central government contributed to sapping the economy of the cities, but the exact chain of causation cannot be discerned.[2] The absence of private initiative in building is not sufficient evidence for a crisis beyond the class of men involved. Cyprian's complaint about the secularity of African bishops before the persecution of Decius should be a warning against overestimating the economic decline discernible after the year 235.[3] More is involved than simply a falling off in production. The increased demands of the central government meant that a conspicuous display of wealth could be dangerous; the man who drew attention to himself might lose his wealth, or at least

---

1. The charges of the Ad Dem. will be discussed, infra p. 276. The effect may be similar to the dust bowls and droughts in the United States in the 1930's, which added materially to the devastation caused by the economy's failure in those years. The same phenomenon also occurred in Canada's prairie provinces at the same time and under similar circumstances.

2. For a good brief sketch, see R. Rémondon, La crise de l'Empire romaine[2], Nouvelle Clio (Paris, 1970), pp. 109 ff.

3. De Lapsis 6/240.13 ff. The best work on the general economic decline is still Rostovtzeff, SEHRE, especially p. 453. R. is correct in not positing a quick financial decline, but certainly the psychological situation shifted. The display of wealth could be dangerous.

34

make its extent obvious to the officials of the imperial bureaucracy. The question of Africa's financial condition at the middle of the third century is still unsolved. The burdens of the _annona_ and the extension of the border to the south must have been contributing factors to lowering production and increasing pressure on the lower classes of the population.1 The increased needs of the imperial government exerted pressure on every social and economic group in North Africa. The demands increased under men perhaps less responsive to senatorial demands and styles of life, like Maximinus. But it was a problem that transcended personalities.2 The political disturbances which arose in the years after the death of Severus Alexander merely deepened an already existing problem.

Before the revolt of 238, Africa Proconsularis enjoyed a period of peace that had lasted since the troubles that racked her in the civil wars of 68/9. The other provinces of Roman Africa, however, were less

---

1. For some of its consequences, see Rostovtzeff, _SEHRE_, pp. 483-5. For more recent bibliography, see C.R. Whittaker's edition of Herodian (Cambridge, Mass., 1970) Vol. II, _Loeb Classical Library_, p. 179;also Rémondon, _La crise_, pp. 111-2 and 129.

2. Romanelli, _Storia_, p. 445, exaggerates the influence of Maximinus. Much of the problem is the universally hostile press that this emperor has received, which was possibly the result of the involvement of a large section of the senatorial class against him in the revolt of 238, as well as from his assassination of Severus Alexander, which may well have influenced the portrait of him by Eusebius.

35

fortunate. The nomadic tribes on the fringes of the area of Romanization were a source of constant difficulty for the administration. The major source of documented trouble lay in the far west, in Mauretania Tingitana.[1] But there was also trouble in Numidia, though the documentation is sparse. Cyprian was moved to send a letter of condolence and an offer of financial aid to the bishops of Numidia whose congregations had suffered from the inroads of the barbarian tribes.[2] The letter has been traditionally dated to 253, in connection with inscriptions which record troubles that began in that year.[3] There exist, however, no indications of date within the letter, and it may well deal with troubles at the beginning of Cyprian's office, before the start of the persecutions.[4] Such disturbances may not have been rare. Cyprian asked the Lord's help that other Christians would not fall into the same situation.[5] The Roman borders in the western provinces were never safe in the first half of the third century. Warfare probably alternated between minor raiding and large-scale operations. The impact on Carthage and

---

1. For the troubles of this period, see Romanelli, Storia, pp. 447 ff., and M. Rachet, Rome et les Berbères. Un problème militaire d'Auguste à Dioclétien, Collection Latomus, 110 (Brussels, 1970), pp. 223 ff.
2. Ep. 62/698 ff. For the bishops, see Von Soden, "Prosop.", index.
3. See Rachet, Rome et les Berbères, pp. 238 ff.
4. Pointed out by G.W. Clarke, "The Barbarian Disturbances in North Africa of the Mid-Third Century", Antichthon 4 (1970), pp. 76-84.
5. Ep. 62.5/700.20 ff.

its inhabitants when events were taking place in the extreme west in Tingitana and Caesariensis was probably small. The great distance that separated Proconsularis from the western provinces must have dampened the effect; but occasionally, as in the affair of the Numidian bishops, the insecurity on the borders of the area of Romanization would make itself felt. Under Marcus Aurelius, the Moors had penetrated to Spain.[1] The factors that led to insecurity were always present.

The military pressures of the first third of the century opened bright and unprecedented prospects for army personnel. The year 235 saw the elevation of a military emperor of undistinguished origin.[2] But this was no anomaly in the age of Macrinus and Adventus.[3] Maximinus made strategic mistakes. Ready to deal with military problems, he failed to heed the necessary principles of internal politics. In his three years of reign, he never once visited the capital, and he failed to show proper respect for the senatorial class.[4] Though

---

1. See Romanelli, Storia, pp. 366 ff.
2. Primus e militaribus, Aurel. Vict., Caes. 25; e militaribus, Epit. de Caes. 25; "ex corpore militari primus ad imperium accessit sola militum voluntate", Eutrop., 9.1. For a reappraisal favourable to Maximinus and against the consensus of ancient sources, see R. Syme, Emperors and Biography. Studies in the Historia Augusta (Oxford, 1971), pp. 179 ff. Zos., 1.13 is not so specific: genous gar on aphanous.
3. For these and other examples, see Syme, Emperors, p. 190.
4. Syme, Emperors. But the hate generated seems to betoken more than just

37

he had been subject to conspiracies before, the fatal impetus for the overthrow of the military emperor came from Africa.[1]

The revolt found its origin in fiscal oppression by a procurator from the district of Carthage. Maximinus' need for money was a spur for any official who needed quick advancement.[2] The imperial agent attempted to extort funds from some young men of noble birth and, after having them fined in the courts, to strip them of their property.[3] Asking for a delay of three days

---

4. (cont'd) neglect. The wars of Maximinus in Germany must have required heavy expenditure, and Maximinus was not backward in obtaining it in any manner possible. This is certainly a major charge against him: Zos., 1.13; Herodian, 7.3.1. The Latin sources stress the lack of education and his hostility to the senators: Epit. de Caes. 25; Aurel. Vict., Caes. 25; Eutrop., 9.1; SHA Max., passim.

1. Herodian, 7.3.1. For the conspiracy of Magnus, see Herodian, 7.1.5-8 ff.; for the conspiracy of Quartinus, Herodian, 7.1.9-10. The SHA Max. 10-1 also deals with the conspiracies, though they are only faulty cribs from Herodian.

2. Herodian, 7.3.5-6 and 7.4.1 point to an ever-increasing attempt to gain money from an ever-widening circle of victims. For further statements on Maximinus' avarice, supra p. 37, n. 4; Zon., 12.16. As Whittaker, Herodian, II, p. 176, says, Africa presented easy pickings; but this was late in the reign.

3. Herodian, 7.4.3. In his commentary Whittaker, Herodian, II, pp. 176-7, adds that Gordian had cultivated the organization of iuventutes, of which there is evidence at the time in Africa. He derives part of his

38

before payment, the young men formed a conspiracy of all who had suffered under the
procurator or who feared they might be his
victims in the future.[1] Rich supporters
were ordered to come in from the countryside
armed with clubs and axes. Their tenants
and underlings also came, in obedience to
their masters' commands and similarly
armed.[2] The plot succeeded. The avaricious
procurator met his death at their hands.
But his end now threatened the safety of the
conspirators. They decided that the only
way to survive was to call out the whole
province in revolt, bringing in on their
side the aged proconsul, M. Antonius

---

3. (cont'd) evidence from SHA Gord.
4.6, but the passage does not state this; it
merely says that he gave horses in his
consulship to the factions, and that Gordian
endeared himself to the people by presenting
stage plays and juvenalia. But the author
quoted therein is Cordus, a standard SHA
fiction, and the rest of the passage is
typical SHA fälschung. Whittaker is wrong.
No such hypothesis can be accepted without
further information.
    1. Herodian, 7.4.3. SHA Gord. 7.2 is
merely a fictional embellishment of Herodian's
account. The account in SHA Max. 14 is less
expanded.
    2. Whittaker, Herodian, II, p. 179, and
others use the participation of the agricultural workers as evidence for rural dissatisfaction, but the story in Herodian makes clear
that the pressure was on the rich not the poor
and that the workers responded to their
masters' orders not their own initiative.

Gordianus Sempronianus.[1] Gordian was residing in Thysdrus when the conspirators approached him. Tradition makes him hesitant to accept the dangerous position of leader, but the opportunities for his son and the quick acceptance and energetic response of the Senate point to the possibility that he was not entirely unaware that dissatisfaction in Africa might lead to violent action against Maximinus.[2]

All Proconsular Africa immediately joined the revolt.[3] After a few days at Thysdrus, Gordian arrived at Carthage and set out to win support outside of Africa and to do away with political opponents at Rome. The news of the revolt was followed by a rising in Rome, and the growth of

---

1. For Gordian's career prior to his proconsulate of Africa, see Syme, Emperors, pp. 166 ff., and Whittaker, Herodian, II, pp. 180-2.

2. As Syme, Emperors, p. 163, points out, the idea of refusal is a standard component in the treatment of usurpers. So Decius under Philip. See Zos., 1.22. Whittaker, Herodian, II, pp. 186-7, opts for a planned revolt also and reviews the African connections of some of the senators involved. The chronology of the revolt is hopeless, but it probably started in March of 238; see Whittaker's note to Herodian, 7.5.7. The eclipse of the sun accepted by Whittaker seems permissable. This section of the Vita is explicitly assigned to Dexippus, and the proximity of the consular date at 234 bears him out. But the exact chronology is still not ascertainable.

3. Herodian, 7.5.8 uses Libya, but the context points to the old province of Africa.

organized opposition by the Senate, which organized a "committee of twenty" to see to the defense of Italy against Maximinus.[1] The fortunes of the revolt outside Africa are not germane to our subject; but its course in our area was fraught with important political and economic consequences.

The response to Gordian was not universal. Capellianus, the legatus Augusti pro praetore of Numidia, did not join in the general approbation of Gordian's action.[2] At first it seems that the soldiers of Numidia recognized the rebel, but that their commander brought them back to allegiance. But the case is dubious. It is an inference from certain inscriptions of Numidia which have the name of Maximinus erased. There are, however, other possible explanations for this. Herodian asserts that Capellianus had an old grievance against Gordian, and therefore opposed him immediately. The inscriptions may have been the work of locals who had given their immediate support to Gordian, or they may have been erased after the death of Maximinus, as an act of revenge

----

1. See ILS 1186; SHA Max. 32.3; and Herodian, 7.10.3 with Whittaker's note, Herodian, II, pp. 226-7.
2. For Capellianus, see B.E. Thomasson, Die Statthalter der römischen Provinzen Nordafrikas von Augustus bis Diocletianus, Acta Instituti Romani Regni Sueciae, 8° IX:2 (2 vols, Lund, 1960), Vol. II, p. 214. See also PIR[2] C 50; and Romanelli, Storia, p. 453. The Historia Augusta mistakenly assigns Capellianus to one of the Mauretanias, probably misled by Herodian, SHA Max. 19.1 and SHA Gord. 15.1. See Herodian, 7.9.1 where he refers to barbarian raids as a daily feature of life.

41

on an area over which his rule had been particularly costly.[1] At any rate, Capellianus marched against the main base of the rebels - Carthage.[2] The only troops available to the aged proconsul were the Carthaginian urban cohort, and a cohort detached from the legion stationed at Lambaesis under Capellianus.[3] But these troops were not sufficient to oppose Capellianus' disciplined legionary force. At the news of his advance, the populace of Carthage was thrown into consternation. A large undisciplined force marched out and formed up ranks, trusting to numbers rather than to discipline to win the engagement.[4]

---

1. Romanelli, Storia, pp. 454-5, thinks it may have been the work of locals. Whittaker, Herodian, II, p. 215, opts for the inscriptions as showing initial support for Gordian. The old grievance of Capellianus is recorded by Herodian at 7.9.2.

2. Herodian, 7.9.2-3. SHA Gord. 15.2, having wrongly located Capellianus in Mauretania, has him march against Carthage with an irregular force. Herodian, who is to be preferred, plainly points to the troops of Capellianus as the regular legion stationed in Numidia. SHA Max. 19.1 is an extremely compressed version of SHA Gord. 15.2.

3. On the military forces of the proconsul, see R. Cagnat, L'armée romaine d'Afrique et l'occupation militaire de l'Afrique sous les Empereurs[2] (Paris, 1913), pp. 57 ff., 211 ff. On the question of whether these troops were loyal to Gordian, see Whittaker, Herodian, II, pp. 190-1. Herodian, 7.6.5 implies that at least some were.

4. For what it is worth, SHA Gord.

42

They were led by the proconsul's son. Unused to war, the Carthaginians were completely routed.[1]

The consequence for Carthage was lamentable. Herodian reports that after the battle, when Capellianus entered the city, he began a reign of terror. Any prominent person who had escaped the battle was murdered by the enraged legate. Funds were robbed from temples and from public and private sources.[2] Other cities which had thrown down their dedications to Maximinus were attacked by Capellianus, their leading citizens killed, and the lower classes expelled from their territory. Fields and villages were given over by the legate for his soldiers to plunder.[3] The funerary inscription of a man of apparently humble condition testifies to some of the damage wrought by the revenge of Capellianus:

L. AEMILIUS SEVERINUS QUI ET
PHILLYRIO V(IXIT) A(NNIS) LXVI
P(LUS) M(INUS) ET PRO AMORE
ROMANO QUIEVIT AB HOC CAPELLIANO
CAPTUS[4]

---

4. (cont'd) 15.1 states that the entire citizen body supported Gordian, but this may simply be an inference from Herodian, though the actions of Capellianus support this. See Herodian, 7.9.4.

1. Herodian, 7.9.4-9.

2. Herodian, 7.9.10; SHA Gord. 10.1. SHA Max. 19.4 mentions the murder of principes civitatum.

3. Herodian, 7.9.11.

4. ILS 8499 from Theveste, indicating the extent of sympathy. See Romanelli, Storia, p. 457; Whittaker, Herodian, II, p.222.

43

The damage to the economy and social relationships of North Africa is likely to have been extensive. Certainly Herodian shows no love for the Africans as a people, and there would have been little advantage in overestimating the destruction caused by the revolt.[1] It is probably no coincidence that the total lack of building by the curial class in the cities dates from around this period – though it had been falling off thirty years earlier. The concentrated pogrom of Capellianus against those prominent in the cities who opposed him would naturally have fallen on the decurions, further damaging the economy of the cities, while the looting of the countryside would have added to the general impoverishment. The price paid for supporting the revolt was high for so short a reign.[2]

The reign of Gordian III resulted in the disbandment of the legion that had opposed and overcome his uncle and his grandfather. The erasures of its name on inscriptions testify to its disgrace.[3] The legion was not restored until the beginning of the reign of Valerianus and Gallienus. There is a record of a return of a vexillatio of the III Legio Augusta from Raetia, dated October 22, 253.[4] The loss of

---

1. See Herodian's comments on the Carthaginians at 7.9.4.
2. On the length of the reign of Gordian I and II, see Whittaker's note, Herodian, II, p. 221.
3. Cagnat, L'armée romaine, pp. 47 and 155; and Romanelli, Storia, pp. 459 ff.
4. ILS 531 from Gemellae. See T.D. Barnes, "Some Persons in the Historia Augusta", Phoenix 26 (1972), p. 140.

44

the legion as a protective force must have opened up parts of North Africa not affected by the devastation of the revolt, further exposing those areas to destruction.[1]

Political effects of the revolt were enduring. In 240, the Carthaginians raised a pretender against Gordian III. The disbandment of the army, which left them open to attack, may have played a part in motivating the movement. Zosimus portrays the revolt as started by the Carthaginians themselves. The year 238 may have left a legacy of desperation.[2] The revolt was put down when the pretender, Sabinianus, was deserted by his supporters after the governor of Mauretania or Numidia had been sent against him. The Carthaginians sought and obtained pardon.[3]

The unprotected state of North Africa, with the withdrawal of the III Legio Augusta, offered a golden opportunity for the nomadic tribes of the interior in Mauretania Tingitana to plunder their sedentary neighbors under Roman influence. They did not hesitate to take advantage of

---

1. For a discussion of possible arrangements for defense in the interim, see Romanelli, Storia, pp. 459 ff.

2. The revolt is described in Zos., 1.17 and SHA Gord. 23.4. The Vita at this point may go back to Dexippus. Note the annalistic opening of 24.1 which supplies the date. Zosimus only dates the occurrence soon after the opening of the sole reign of Gordian III.

3. Zos., 1.17; SHA Gord. 23.4. Nothing else is known of Sabinianus, though he may have been a proconsul of the province. See PIR[1] S 13. The revolt may have been put down by the governor of Mauretania Caesari-

45

the situation.[1] The next extant evidence
of a peace treaty dates from 277-80.[2] The
troubles which began in Numidia and Mauretania Caesariensis in 253 involved tribes
other than the Baquates. The southern
areas of the western provinces were
sources of constant uneasiness for the
Roman authorities. The instability of the
situation may explain the lack of progress
of Christianity, particularly in the
provinces of Mauretania. Internal
problems may have had an effect on the
urbanized province of Proconsularis.
Numidia too was harassed by nomadic tribes.
The climate was one to breed chronic
insecurity among the Romanized inhabitants
of the cities. Protection in this world
was hard to come by, as the anti-Roman
feelings of the Octavius possibly illustrate.[3]

    Christianity offered refuge in a
rather battered world. In Carthage, one man
made the choice of giving up a career and
wealth to join the barely tolerated religion
of Christ. His choice was well-rewarded.

---

    3. (cont'd) ensis, perhaps Faltonius
Restitutianus. For Faltonius, see PIR[2] F
109 and Thomasson, Die Statthalter, II,p.276.
    1. Given the absence of the Third
Legion, Rachet, Rome et les Berbères, p. 234,
may place too much emphasis on this.
    2. Rachet, Rome et les Berbères, at
p. 237.
    3. Infra p. 81.

Chapter II: THE OCTAVIUS
AND THE LEGACY OF TERTULLIAN

The economic and social crises in the African provinces in the first half of the third century created an atmosphere of instability and, for some, the questioning of established views and received traditions.[1] Christianity offered an alternative whereby through conversion a man could learn to cope with this new and hostile world.[2] But how attractive was this alternative to the upper classes of the Roman world?

The evidence for the penetration of Christianity among the upper classes is slight prior to the reign of Constantine. As late as the end of the fourth century, Jerome replied to the attacks of the rabidi adversus Christum canes that the Church had

> "nullos philosophos et eloquentes, nullos...doctores".[3]

The early third century presents only fragmentary and discontinuous indications of the social diffusion of Christianity. Vibia Perpetua, who underwent martyrdom with her companions on the 7th of March, 203, at Carthage, may have been of curial rank.[4] Outside Africa, Christian wives are attested for the governors of Cappadocia and Syria. Writing against Celsus in the middle of the

---

1. See Chapter I, pp. 34 ff.
2. See Chapter III, p. 116.
3. Jerome, Vir. Ill., prologus.
4. Pass. Perpet. 2. And Barnes, Tert., p. 70.

47

third century, Origen claims that Christian teachers are eagerly received in the best social circles.[1]

Eusebius' contribution towards clarification of the situation is small. His apologetic tendency results in an overestimation of the spread of Christianity. The individuals he cites as examples of Christians of high status are freedmen of the imperial household.[2] The single senatorial example, Astyrius, is dated to the 260's.[3]

---

1. Contra Celsum 3.9 and 3.30. Unfortunately the evidence is late and relates to the situation in the East rather than the West. G.W. Clarke, "The Historical Setting of the Octavius of Minucius Felix", JRH 4 (1966/7), p. 275, is correct to stress the Eastern orientation of Origen, but as far as his Severan connections, this is an inference from Eusebius, 6.21.3 ff., which is probably an exaggeration. The well-known interest of the Severan women in Eastern philosophy will suffice to explain Origen's summons, without postulating any further connection with the imperial house.

2. Clarke, "Historical Setting", pp. 274 ff., for a list with references.

3. HE 7.16.1. PIR[2] A 1269, possibly identified with M. Bassaeus Astur; see also G. Barbieri, L'Albo senatorio de Settimio Severo a Carino 193-285, Studi pubblicati dall' Istituto Italiano per la Storia antica, fasc. 6 (Rome, 1952), n. 1486. PLRE, p. 120, s.v. Astyrius, does not hazard a conjecture. More recently, see W. Eck, "Das Eindringen des Christentums in den Senatorenstand", Chiron I (1971), p. 388, n. 5, who thinks that the identification is unlikely.

48

Inscriptional material is even more disappointing. Liberalis is cited as consul and martyr, but his date and identification are uncertain.[1] The majority of extant inscriptions refer to liberti rather than to Christians of curial or senatorial rank.[2] For Africa, evidence is entirely lacking.[3]

Further evidence for Carthage is forthcoming in the pronouncements of the most important figure in the intellectual development of early African Christianity, Tertullian, who claims that Christians now beset the State. Every age, sex and rank is filled with people who have adopted the true religion, even if the pagans lament it as a gross injury.[4] Addressing the proconsul of Africa in the autumn of 212, Tertullian proclaims that to extinguish the Christian sect in Carthage would be to decimate the population of the city. But more telling is his statement that to destroy the Christians would entail the slaughter of persons of Scapula's own social standing. Kinsmen and friends of those in the proconsul's own class would be condemned to death.[5]

Many have distrusted the claims advanced by Tertullian, accusing him of gross exaggeration.[6] But Tertullian's own

---

1. ILCV, 56-7, not listed in PLRE.
2. Clarke, "Historical Setting", pp. 275 ff.
3. The conjectural identifications of Dessau will be discussed below.
4. Apol. 1.7.
5. Ad Scap. 5. For text, see CSEL 76 (1957), 9-16.
6. Clarke, "Historical Setting", p. 272 refers to Tertullian's "heavy penchant for

49

social background provides support for his assertion.[1] Numerous exhortations to refrain from holding office were directed at Christians by their own authors from this period, implying that if Christians did not hold office, they were certainly of the wealth and rank to be capable of doing so should they choose. Certainly the widespread reiteration of such exhortations would imply that the rule was observed at least sometimes in the breach.[2]

Tertullian himself provided the bridge for the reception of the Christian message by the cultivated sections of Roman Africa.[3] By conforming to the rules of the Latin literary culture of his contemporaries, he removed an obstacle that prevented an appreciation of the content of Christianity.[4] Tertullian rejected, however, the basis for accommodation which he himself had established. His insistence upon drawing rigid and logical deductions from the principles of Christianity had not only alienated him from many of his fellow Christians, but had increased his hostility towards the government that persecuted both him and his co-religionists.[5] Tertullian could claim that the prayers of Christians on behalf of the Empire made an important contribution to its defense.[6] But as persecution continued and Tertullian re-thought his view of church and

---

6. (cont'd) forensic hyperbole", in Apol. 37.4.
1. Barnes, Tert., p. 195.
2. For the contrary inference, see Clarke, "Historical Setting", p. 275.
3. Infra pp. 75 f.
4. Infra pp. 75 f.
5. Infra p. 88.
6. Apol. 33 ff. is instructive.

50

state, the half-hearted acceptance of imperial authority gave way to a more pronounced hostility which culminated in the abuse and threats of the De Corona Militis and the Ad Scapulam.

Others were willing to follow in the direction in which a strand of his thought pointed. Christianity could seek accommodation with the pagan world. A synthesis would be formed in which the Christian message was clothed in pagan literary dress, thus reaching the members of the population at whom it was aimed.

The Octavius of Minucius Felix adopted this approach. It forms the intellectual background for the milieu that led Cyprian to adopt Christianity as an alternative to what seemed a disintegrating and shattered pagan world view. Tertullian formed the most potent influence on his thought, outside of the Bible.[1] But the absence of Tertullian's erratic brilliance in the Octavius allows it to construct a more representative introduction to the transition of African Christian thought into a form which would find acceptance among the educated Roman classes of the province.

The central difficulty in using the Octavius as representative of the intellectual milieu of the first quarter of the third century has been the question of its date. A heated and prolonged controversy has grown up about its relationship to the Apologeticum of Tertullian.[2] Resemblances

---

1. Jerome, Vir. Ill. 53. For further discussion of this passage, see infra pp. 100f
2. For a summary of the earlier literature, see B. Axelson, Das Prioritäts-problem Tertullian-Minucius Felix, Skrifter utgivna av Vetenskaps-Societeten i Lund, 27

51

in style and content are too close to represent the results of chance alone. The composition of the _Apologeticum_ is firmly dated to the autumn of 197, or slightly later.[1] Thus the question resolves itself into the problem of which work is first and served as the basis for the second.[2]

The problem has been decided in favour of the priority of the _Apologeticum_. The _Octavius_ contains resemblances not only to the _Apologeticum_, but also to the earlier version of that work by Tertullian, the _Ad Nationes_. But careful analysis has revealed that the earlier work contains fewer resemblances to the _Octavius_ than the finished version which became the _Apologeticum_.[3]

---

2. (cont'd) (Lund, 1941), pp. 10 ff. Later literature is summarized in J. Beaujeu's excellent edition and commentary, _Minucius Félix: Octavius_ (Paris, 1964), to which should be added C. Becker's important article, "Der _Octavius_ des Minucius Felix", _SBBayer_, hft. 2 (Munich, 1967).

1. _Apol._ 35.9, 35.11 and 37.4. See also Barnes, _Tert._, p. 55.

2. M. Sordi, "L'apologia del martire romano Apollonio, come fonte dell' _Apologeticum_ di Tertulliano e i rapporti fra Tertulliano e Minucio", _Rivista di Storia della chiesa in Italia_ 18 (1964), pp. 169 ff. has argued that both the _Apologeticum_ and the _Octavius_ are dependent on a third work by Apollonius. But the use of Greek in Rome in the late second century, as well as the direct resemblances in thought and expression of the two works, tell against such an hypothesis.

3. Axelson, _Das Prioritätsproblem_, p. 66, on the relation of the two works. Also Barnes, _Tert._, pp. 49, 104-6.

But such an argument can cut both ways. It could be argued that the _Octavius_ appealed more to Tertullian as he revised, resulting in its greater utilization in the _Apologeticum_. Further detailed analysis led to the false view that Minucius Felix was simply a compiler and that his dialogue was a mosaic.[1]

Recently this view has been abandoned, and a decisive argument has been brought forward to establish the priority of the _Apologeticum_.[2] A careful analysis of the use made in the _Octavius_ of Cicero and Seneca has revealed that the author adopted and changed them for his own purposes. The dialogue is more than a mere patchwork of classical commonplaces. A comparison reveals that the works of Tertullian are utilized in the same manner by Minucius Felix as the others. Thus the question of priority has been resolved in favour of Tertullian.[3]

With the establishment of the _terminus post quem_, the problem of the _terminus ante quem_ assumes new importance. The _Octavius_ is badly represented in Christian literature. Only Lactantius, Jerome, Eucherius and the author of the disputed treatise, the _Quod Idola Dii Non Sint_, mention or utilize the _Octavius_. The earliest approximately datable reference is that of Lactantius in the _Divinae Institutiones_.[4] This was probably composed between the years 304 and

---

1. Beaujeu, _Minucius Félix_, xliv ff., where these are cited.
2. Becker (1967).
3. Ibid.
4. The _Divinae Institutiones_ contains two references, 1.11.55 and 5.1.21, but only the second is of any consequence for the question of dating.

53

313.[1] Lactantius lists Minucius Felix, Tertullian, and Cyprian in what has been taken to be chronological order. But as earlier discussion has shown, this is not correct. Lactantius is listing these apologists in order of literary merit, without chronological reference.[2]

Jerome's notices are more illuminating. In the De Viris Illustribus, Tertullian is listed as number 53, Minucius Felix as 58, and Cyprian as 67.[3] In the list of the De Viris Illustribus, chronological mistakes abound. Jerome's statements cannot be used except with further evidence. The reference to Minucius Felix provides no information that could not have been inferred from the Octavius itself. It presupposes no other

1. Altaner-Stuiber, Pat., p. 186.
2. As a careful reading will confirm. Div. Inst. 5.1.21:

"eo fit ut sapientia et veritas idoneis praeconibus indigeat. Et si qui forte litteratorum se ad eam contulerunt, defensioni eius non suffecerunt. Ex iis qui mihi noti sunt, Minucius Felix non ignobilis inter causidicos loci fuit. Huius liber, cui Octavio titulus est, declarat quam idoneus veritatis adsertor esse potuisset, si se totum ad id studium contu- lisset. Septimius quoque Tertul- lianus...Unus igitur praecipuus et clarus exstitit Cyprianus..."

3. Jerome,Ep.49 (48),13,60.10,70.5; Comm.in Isaiam proph.8, praefatio; PL 24.

54

sources.[1]

The only treatise in antiquity which makes extensive use of the _Octavius_ is the _Quod Idola Dii Non Sint_. The work is simply an abstract of Minucius Felix and Tertullian. The first nine chapters are directly based on chapters 18-23 of the _Octavius_; while the last six are abstracted from the _Apologeticum_ 21-23. Obviously if the date of the treatise could be established, a secure _terminus ante quem_ would emerge. Attempts have been made to ascribe the work to Cyprian but without success. Some have even claimed to find traces of the _Divinae Institutiones_ in it; but though evidence for dependence on Lactantius is tenuous, so much dispute surrounds the _Quod Idola_ that it is useless for any chronological purposes.[2]

Resemblances to authentic works of Cyprian provide another possibility, but Cyprian's style is very much a personal quantity. Direct dependence can be established between several of the treatises of Cyprian and Tertullian, and they establish the fact that Cyprian never borrowed directly but that he extensively reworked

---

1. G.W. Clarke, "The Literary Setting of the _Octavius_ of Minucius Felix", _JRH_ 3 (1964/5), p. 195, stresses this.
2. The text is printed in _CSEL_ 3, part 2, pp. 19-31. Koch attempted to prove its Cyprianic authorship in _CU_, pp. 1-78. See H. Diller, "In Sachen Tertullian-Minucius Felix", _Philologus_ 90 (1935), pp. 98-114, 216-39, who tried to establish traces of Lactantius in the _Quod Idola_. M. Simonetti successfully questions traces of the _Div. Inst._ but fails to establish Cyprianic authorship, in "Sulla paternità del _Quod Idola Dii Non Sint_", _Maia_ 3 (1950)

the sources which he used.[1]

Certain verbal similarities exist, however, and while they do not decide the question, they add weight to the argument that Cyprian was familiar with the Octavius.[2] In its final attack on the pagan philosophers, the Octavius stresses their duplicity: they clothe loathsome action with fine phrases, but with Christians noble action accompanies fine character:

"Nos non habitu sapientiam sed
mente praeferimus, non eloquimur
magna sed vivimus, gloriamur nos
consecutos quod illi summa in-
tentione quaesiverunt nec invenire
potuerunt."[3]

In 256 Cyprian exhorts his audience to recognize the virtue of patience for a Christian. In so doing he contrasts the false patience of the philosophers with the true patience of Christians. They are philosophers in fact and not merely externally:

"...nec vestitu sapientiam sed
veritate praeferimus qui virtutum
conscientiam magis quam iactantiam
novimus, qui non loquimur magna
sed vivimus."[4]

---

2. (cont'd) pp. 265 ff.
1. Infra p. 288.
2. For a full listing of such passages see Beaujeu, Minucius Félix, lxix. Note that 341.18 should read 361.18. The only one with any basis is discussed here.
3. Oct. 38.6.
4. De Bono Pat. 3/398.19-21 for this. Also Beaujeu, Minucius Félix, lxxii. For

56

Not only is the striking phrase nec vestitu sapientiam sed veritate found with slight variation in Minucius' non habitu sapientiam sed mente praeferimus; but the passages in both continue with sharp resemblance: non eloquimur magna sed vivimus is equivalent to qui non loquimur magna sed vivimus - so perhaps Cyprian's own unconscious reference to Christians who live in consciousness of the virtues is based on Minucius' account of the pagans who have sought the virtues but nec invenire potuerunt. The striking effect of the passage is in the sustained resemblance of thought and expression. More than simple verbal reminiscences are evidenced.[1] There is a basic parallelism of thought.

Of the resemblances posited between Cyprian and Minucius Felix, nine of twenty are found in the Ad Donatum. Probably the first extant work of the Carthaginian bishop, it has special value for establishing the relationship between the Octavius and the Cyprianic corpus. The Ad

---

4. (cont'd) date, see Appendix II.
1. This is the problem with the majority of the passages cited by Beaujeu, Minucius Félix, lxix. They are simply verbal similarities. Given the highly rigid nature of ancient education, they would form the stock and trade of almost any Latin author. For an instructive example, see his note to 4.6, and G.W. Clarke's discussion in "Minucius Felix: Octavius 4.6", CPh 61 (1966), pp. 252-3. See also note to 4.1 referring the phrase vultu fatebatur to Juvenal, 2.17, qui vultu morbum incessuque fatebatur. How many other ways can this be expressed in Latin? Similar actions require similar expressions.

Donatum purports to be a dialogue, like the Octavius; but whereas the Octavius actually is one, the Ad Donatum is merely a Scheindialog.[1] There are traces of the dialogue form both at the beginning and the end of the work. Cyprian addresses Donatus directly, recalling the promise he had once made to meet with him and pass the day pleasantly in conversation which would instruct the soul with divina praecepta. He begins with Donatus, whose eyes are fixed upon him alone, forgetting the pastoral pleasures of their surroundings.[2] Cyprian then launches into his discourse. Donatus almost disappears, and all pretense of a dialogue disappears with him. Though the fiction of a discourse is at times maintained, Donatus does not even have an opportunity to nod his agreement in the Platonic manner.[3] At the end he emerges and the pretense of the dialogue form is somewhat restored. Cyprian advises Donatus that though the conversation is extremely pleasant, it is a holiday and they should be on their way to eat and sing heavenly praise.[4] The complete absence of any dialogue has led some editors to class the Ad Donatum with the epistles, where it apparently belonged.[5] The strange appearance of the supposed dialogue was striking. The style is rich and mature, but the opening is

1. Becker (1967) p. 95.
2. Ad Don. 2.1-2. For text, see CSEL 3, part 1, p. 316.
3. Ad Don. 9-10/10.24 - 12.14.
4. Ad Don. 16/16.4-14.
5. For instance, Pamelius. See Hartel, praefatio, lxxxii. So also Rigaltius in his edition of 1648. See Hartel, praefatio, lxxxiv.

58

strangely clumsy. The work begins like a dialogue, but turns immediately into an epistle.[1] The problem of the opening of the Ad Donatum finds its solution in the Epistula Donati ad Cyprianum, which had first been removed from the main text by Rigaltius in his 1648 edition. Hartel printed it in the Cyprianic appendix, judging it spurious.[2] A reasonable case has been presented for the manuscript tradition of the fragment, and its place at the beginning of the Ad Donatum fits in coherently with the rest of the work.[3] The fragment breaks off and may have been part of a longer introduction which gave some balance to the respective participation of Cyprian and his friend.

Aside from the fact that both works are dialogues, other areas of similarity emerge. Both are set during the vintage holidays of the autumn.[4] Both stress the healthful climate that autumn brings.[5] In their catalogue of pagan sexual immorality, both stress homosexuality.[6]

---

1. The epistulary form beginning with carissime occurs frequently in Cyprian, e.g., Ep. 34 and 35.
2. Hartel, praefatio, lxv.
3. For a reasoned and successful argument for the authenticity of this fragment, see C.G. Goetz, "Der alte Anfang und die ursprüngliche Form von Cyprians Schrift Ad Donatum", TU N.F. 19, hft. 1c (1899)1-16.
4. Oct. 2.3, Ad Don. 1. For these legal holidays, see Suetonius, Divus Julius 40.1; SHA Marc. Aurel. 10.10; Corp. Jur. Civil., Dig. 2.12; Cod. Just.III, 12.6(7).
5. Oct. 2.3, Ad Don. 1/3-4.5.
6. Oct. 28.10-11, and Ad Don. 9/26.9-27.5

(The point is a commonplace even among pagans, however. While the stress in Cyprian is on simple homosexuality, Minucius Felix concentrates on fellatio.) The _Octavius_ and the _Ad Donatum_ also emphasize the flowing periods and eloquence of the pagan assemblies and law courts as not necessary for the exposition of divine matters. Only simplicity and truth are needed.[1] But again, this is a topic found in Cicero.[2]

The most common features of the two works - the utilization of the dialogue form and the fall vacation setting - point to a high probability of dependence of one author upon the other; but the question remains as to which deserves priority.

The relationship has been the subject of assumption. But curt dismissal of Cyprian's talents as an innovator does not guarantee the priority of Minucius Felix.[3] Other factors, however, indicate this. In his references to persecution, Minucius Felix indicates sporadic action on the part of government officials rather than anything widescale and consistent. Referring to his earlier pagan phase, Octavius contrasts his defense as an _advocatus_ of those guilty of terrible crimes, while he regarded Christians as not worthy of a hearing. He could torture them not to elicit truth but rather to make them deny their religion and thus commit falsehood. If they foreswore their

---

1. _Oct._ 16.6 and _Ad Don._ 2/4.5-17.
2. Cicero, _De Nat. Deor._ 1.5.10.
3. Beaujeu, _Minucius Félix_, lxxi, characterizes him as "maladroite pour inventer un genre litteraire nouveau". So also Becker (1967), pp. 94-5.

60

nomen, pardon was granted.[1] Later, comparing the Christian with the soldier, Octavius mentions the smile on his face as he boldly went forth to the torture of execution.[2] Earlier, Caecilius, Octavius' pagan antagonist, berates the Christians for being easily deceived by promises of some glorious future life. They neglect the present, suffering torments of cold, hunger and want. Racked with pain but locked in deception, they remain impervious in their stupidity. Besides the normal horrors of existence, they seek punishments, torture, and crosses: non adorandae sed subeundae. Yet if their God could not deliver them from these cruelties, how could He provide for them in the next life?[3] This is certainly not a period of peace and freedom from persecution.[4]

The period from the Ad Scapulam to Decius has traditionally been seen as one of freedom from persecution, but evidence is accumulating that this was not in fact the case.[5] In a letter to the clergy and congregation of Carthage, Cyprian, justifying his selection of Celerinus for a position in the clergy, hymns the merits of the confessor's ancestors in addition to his own as

---

1. Oct. 28.3 ff.
2. Oct. 37.1-6. For the miles Christi, infra p. 202.
3. Oct. 12.1-5.
4. Clarke, "Historical Setting", p. 170, thinks this was composed in a period of peace and dismisses the remarks of the Octavius as merely part of the apologetic genre.
5. For the traditional interpretation, cf. Frend, M&P, p. 254. Also Monceaux, HAC, p. 18, and Baus, HCH, pp. 220-1.

further justification for his choice. Celerinus' grandmother had been crowned with martyrdom for the faith, as had his paternal and maternal uncles, Laurentinus and Egnatius, who before their glorious exit had been soldiers in the service of a secular lord.[1] Chronologically these deaths would seem most reasonably to fall in the period of the Great Peace.[2] So also persecution fell upon the Christian community in Cappadocia in the last year of Severus Alexander.[3] But the actions reported in Firmilian's letter (75) point only to local trouble with the Christian community. There is no reason to believe it can be used as evidence for action on the part of the central government. Further, the schema advanced by Eusebius, which equated evil emperors with those emperors who persecuted, is undermined by the occurrence of the persecution in the reign of an emperor "friendly" to Christianity and not under the "tyrant" Maximinus. Though the Exhortation to Martyrdom of Origen points to harassment of the Christian community at Alexandria, its failure to refer to present trials instead of Biblical examples of martyrdom indicates that the situation was far less dangerous than indicated by Origen, and that there again was no direct connection with Maximinus but that it was a local conflict.[4]

---

1. Ep. 39.3.
2. For greater detail, see Barnes, Tert., p. 158; also his "Three Neglected Martyrs", JThS N.S. 22 (1971), p. 159.
3. Firmilian, apud Cyp., Ep. 75.10.
4. Not in Lactantius, De Mort. Persecut., who has a period of peace extending from Domitian to Decius. This should be a

Though the period of the Great Peace was not an era of perfect felicity for the Christian community, it lacked the concentrated effort of the emperors from Decius on. The Octavius portrays the earlier sporadic form of persecution which finds classic expression in Pliny's letters to the Emperor Trajan and apparently continued to the reign of Decius.[1] This would be a strong probability for dating the work of Minucius Felix to before 249/50.[2]

Other elements also converge on this time period. Inscriptional material containing the names of the participants in the dialogue has come to light.[3] For Minucius Felix, inscriptions have been preserved from Tebessa, Carthage, Cirta,

---

4. (cont'd) warning about the schema of persecuting emperors put forward by Christian sources, e.g., HE 6.28.

1. Ep. 10.96-7.

2. On persecutions before Decius, see Barnes, Tert., pp. 149-62; also Barnes, "Legislation", pp. 32 ff.

3. H. Dessau, in a series of articles in Hermes, tried to show that Caecilius Natalis of the dialogue was the same as the municipal triumvir of Cirta in 210, and to identify him with the Natalios of Eusebius, HE 5.28.8, who flourished shortly after the ninth year of Septimius Severus, i.e., 201, until the end of the pontificate of Zephyrinus, 201-17. On Eusebius and his lists of the bishops of Rome, see Lawlor and Oulton, Eusebius, pp. 44 ff. Dessau's identifications can be nothing more than conjectures. See his "Über einige Inschriften aus Cirta", Hermes 15 (1880), pp. 471-4; also his "Minucius Felix und Caecilius Natalis", Hermes 40 (1905), pp. 373-86.

63

Bulla Regia and Ostia.[1] Octavius Januarius occurs on material from Neferis, Gasr, Mezuar, Thubursicum Bure, Capua and Pisaurum.[2] The most discussed of all are the inscriptions of Caecilius Natalis from Cirta.[3] Attempts have failed to identify the man named in the inscriptions with the pagan friend of Minucius Felix. The name is rare and confined to Africa.[4] Especially significant is that the inscriptional material dates from the reign of Caracalla. The single appearance of the name does not allow the Caecilius Natalis of the dialogue to be identified with the character in the Octavius; however, the similarity in name and the rarity of its occurrence lend weight to a date of sometime in the first half of the third century.[5]

---

1. CIL VIII: 9208; 22547 (Tebessa) 12449 (Carthage) 19600 (Cirta) 25584 (Bulla Regia); XIV: 1359 and 5028 (Ostia).

2. CIL VI: 232846; VIII: 12393 (Neferis) 14428 (Gasr Mezuar, a colonia in the reign of Caracalla) 15320 (Thubursicum Bure); X: 4253 (Capua); XI: 6430 (Pisaurum).

3. CIL VIII: 6996; 7094-8 dating from the reign of Caracalla. The name on the inscription is MARCUS CAECILIUS Q(UINTI) F(ILIUS) Q(UIRINA TRIBU) NATALIS.

4. The only Caecilius Natalis in the PIR is the man in PIR[2] C 65; for Minucius Felix, PIR[1] M 432. An inspection of the indices of CIL, in addition to PIR[2] and PLRE has revealed only this one instance of the name Caecilius Natalis.

5. See Beaujeu, Minucius Félix, xxvii-xxviii, on the possibility that the father of the triumvir, Quintus, may have been the character in the Octavius, as first suggested by E. Baehrens in his Teubner edition

64

These indications, though not compelling in themselves, cumulatively point to a period between 197 and 250. The exact period cannot be ascertained. The absence of specific references to Christians as imperial officials in the entourage of the Emperor, which is stressed by Tertullian in the Ad Scapulam, might point to a period when these events had receded into the past.[1] But since the majority of these references are to Caesariani, their low social station may have excluded mention in the Octavius, because of its appeal to a higher social class. The dialogue is also too unspecific in its references to events for it to be inferred that it is an answer to a particular pagan literary piece. For a long time scholars have attempted to view the dialogue as a specific answer to the charges made against Christians by Fronto in the oration mentioned in the dialogue; but at close examination, the oration dissolves into what perhaps were merely comments made in a speech on another subject.[2]

Unsuccessful attempts have been made to link a section of the Noctes Atticae of Gellius with the Octavius. The short section in the Noctes Atticae in which Favorinus is portrayed as a judge between a Stoic and a Peripatetic can hardly be conceived as the background to the Octavius. The fact that the form of the dialogue is similar, in that both works contain a judge and two disputants

---

5.   (cont'd) of 1886, vi.
1.   Ad Scap. 4.
2.   For this view, see Schanz-Hosius, p. 267.

65

is not decisive.[1] The loss of so much ancient literature leaves the question of filiation open. There is no reason to believe that Gellius was original in his approach to the dialogue form; there is in fact reason to believe the opposite in the case of the Noctes Atticae. The work is a miscellany and not the place for innovation.

Another similarity between the two works is that both take place at Ostia. One must bear in mind, however, that Ostia was a famous seaport of Rome and provided an obvious location for an author. For Minucius Felix, Ostia seems chosen for artistic considerations which would allow him to indulge in numerous descriptive scenes. The location at Ostia in itself does not justify any hypothesis of literary filiation. Nor can the fact that Caecilius enunciates sceptical positions in his refutation of Christianity, as does Favorinus in Gellius' dialogue, be used as evidence for a link between the two works. Caecilius is not a Sceptic but a defender of the traditional religious practices of the pagan empire. Both Sceptics and Stoics supported the

---

1. Aulus Gellius, Noctes Att. XVIII, 1.2-3. Beaujeu, Minucius Félix, xxi ff., who advances this argument, recognizes that the parallel is weak and tries to bolster it by citing the fact that both Favorinus and the Octavius are concerned with the seductions of argutiae. But the attraction of rhetoric and its ability to distort the truth are a commonplace. The weakness of this argument is also seen by B.R. Voss, Der Dialog in der frühchristlichen Literatur, Studia et testimonia antiqua, 9(Munich, 1970) p. 42.

practice of traditional rites.[1] The model, if one were needed for the character of Caecilius, is Cotta in the De Natura Deorum.[2] Sufficient models are provided by Plato and Cicero. Though Minucius may have known of the section of Gellius, there is no direct proof that this was the case, nor can the Octavius be viewed as a simple refutation of or allusion to the dialogue in the Noctes Atticae. The only information that provides a terminus ante quem for the Octavius, then, is its relationship with Cyprian's Ad Donatum.

The dispute about the date of the Octavius has also been accompanied by disagreement about the place of its composition, which is generally thought to be Rome or Carthage.[3] But any attempt at arguing for a particular place is fruitless without an explicit statement by the author or other explicit evidence. It is more profitable to try to determine for what audience and in pursuance of what ends Minucius composed his dialogue.

Jerome only states that Minucius practiced law at Rome, not that the dialogue took its inception there.[4] The mise-en-scène is Rome, but the African origin of the participants and certain African interests would indicate that the work was primarily

_____

1. Epictetus, Diss. 4.6.7; Sextus Empiricus, Adv. Phys. I, 49.
2. Becker (1967), p. 86.
3. Quasten, Pat., p. 155, assigns the Octavius to Rome. So also Axelson, Das Prioritätsproblem, p. 94. Clarke, "Historical Setting", p. 270, calls it a document of Severan Rome; likewise Beaujeu, Minucius Félix, p. 23.
4. Jerome, Vir. Ill. 58, possibly an

directed to an African audience in Cirta rather than Carthage. Caecilius' origin in Cirta is noted several times in the dialogue. So Caecilius mentions Fronto as Cirtensis noster.[1] In his reply to Caecilius Octavius condemns Fronto's discussion of the Christians as mere abuse and refers to tuus Fronto. The fact that the only other Caecilius Natalis known in the whole of antiquity is domiciled at Cirta suggests that Caecilius has Cirta as patria, and it is a suggestion difficult to resist.

Octavius' arrival at Rome on a visit, leaving his home, wife, and children behind, provides the occasion for the dialogue. But where did he leave them? As the three friends walk along the open beach, Octavius and the others discuss stories of his sea adventures. Surely this must refer to Octavius' arrival at Rome by sea.[2] Also, the majority of the inscriptional evidence points to an African origin for Octavius Januarius.[3] The same is true of Minucius Felix.[4] The dialogue points to a long friendship which had started before the dialogue took place, and Africa would have been the most likely place for the relationship to have formed.[5] There are references to what appear to be points of interest,

---

4. (cont'd) inference from Oct. 2.1.
1. Oct. 9.6. Beaujeu, Minucius Félix, p. 28
2. Beaujeu, Minucius Félix, p. 89, and note to 3.4; Clarke, "Historical Setting", p. 273, thinks that no conclusions can be drawn as to a sea voyage, but the context leads to the opposite conclusion.
3. Supra p. 64, n. 1.
4. Supra p. 63, n. 3.
5. Oct. 2.2-3.

68

particularly directed towards an African audience; for example, to the deification of Juba, King of Mauretania, by vote of his countrymen.[1] Julius Caesar's crossing to Africa is singled out as an example proving the inefficacy of augury.[2] Other examples are from the early Republic. The reference to Africa may have drawn the author to cite Caesar's successful disregard of religious proprieties. Again at the discussion of infant sacrifice, Africa comes into the picture. Octavius, using retorsio to defend the Christians on this point, refers to the sacrifice of young children to Saturn: parents smothered their children's tears with kisses and endearments so that the sacrifice could proceed.[3] The name of Saturn, the major deity of Africa, occurs throughout the work.[4] A reference is made to Juno as Poena.[5] Juno was equated with Tanit, the Punic deity, and worshipped as Dea Caelestis. There are other references to Juno in the Octavius, but none specifically African.[6] Though these references may be drawn from a literary source, the use of this channel does not exclude a real interest. The choice of literary selection is dictated by interests of author and audience.[7] More

---

1. Clarke, "Historical Setting", p. 268, incorrectly cites this passage as 24.1.
2. Oct. 26.4.
3. Oct. 30.3.
4. Oct. 22.5; 23.9-11; 27.6; 30.3-4.
5. Oct. 25.9. The same chapter gives further examples of similar analogues, e.g., Mars Thracius and Diana Taurica.
6. Oct. 19.10; 22.5; 23.4; 24.3.
7. It is time that the postulate "literary derivation equals unreality" was abandoned.

importantly, why did Minucius select Octavius and Caecilius as the other personages in the dialogue? In the opening section of the work, Minucius praises the upright and noble character of his old friend, Octavius, who at the time of writing had died. He had been the author's guide towards the truth, dispelling dark gloom and leading him into the path of light and knowledge, wisdom and truth.[1] Caecilius was also intimately related to Minucius, having long been a friend of his.[2] The relationship must have had its origin in Africa, but the questions of when and how cannot be answered.[3] Thus the dialogue, besides being an apology for Christianity, is also a loving memorial to a departed friend, and to his success in converting a pagan to Christian truth. For apologetical purposes at Rome, this was a strange choice.

It has long been remarked that the dialogue is directed towards an upper-class social milieu.[4] But if it was directed to upper-class pagans at Rome, the choice of characters is curious. The De Natura Deorum of Cicero, which is a major source for the Octavius, uses characters who are well-known, as do all the dialogues of Cicero. The only other Christian dialogue extant by this date is Justin's conversation with Trypho the Jew, written in Greek. While this may at first appear to utilize obscure

---

1. Oct. 1.
2. Oct. 3.1.
3. Beaujeu, Minucius Félix, xxix, conjectures that they met in Carthage while studying, while Minucius met Caecilius at Rome in "les milieux africains". But such speculation is fruitless.
4. This will be discussed below.

70

personages, Justin himself was a figure of some reknown in the Christian community at Rome, and the dialogue is set in Ephesus, directed to the Jewish and Christian communities there who could be expected to be acquainted with both figures of the dialogue.[1]

Of what importance was Caecilius or Octavius at Rome, or even at Carthage? What direct impact would his conversion have had on an élite pagan audience? Such dialogues tend to take place soon before the leading participant's death. The De Oratore of Cicero takes place soon before the deaths of Antonius and Crassus. The evocation of the dead Octavius would be especially telling in a milieu in which he was well-known. Cirta, rather than Rome or Carthage, is the likely candidate.[2]

The apologetical tendency of the Octavius would be little served by such an obscure conversion. More persuasive is the contention that the Octavius was written during a period of provincial retirement for Minucius in Africa. The dialogue may perhaps have been directed at a Cirtan audience, Cirta possibly having been the patria of all three characters. The inscriptional evidence points to the importance of a Caecilius Natalis and his father, Quintus, at Cirta.[3] The conversion of either would

1. See Altaner-Stuiber, Pat., p. 67. Trypho is perhaps identical with the well-known Rabbi Tarphon, a contemporary of Justin. See also Eusebius, HE 4.18.6.
2. Supra p. 67 f. So Macrobius wrote the Saturnalia in memory of Praetextatus, see Sat. 1.17.1.
3. Supra p. 63, n. 3.

71

have been a Christian coup of the first order, a conversion important for apologetic purposes and likely to influence other members of the local aristocracy.

Other considerations also point to the conclusion that in the first instance the work was directed to the Cirtan upper-classes. The only extensive use of the Octavius in antiquity is in the Quod Idola Dii Non Sint, a work of African origin.[1] The only extant manuscript of it is Codex Parisinus Latinus 1661 (Saec. IX) where the work is mistakenly preserved as the eighth book of Arnobius, Adversus Paganos, again pointing to the fact that whatever small interest it later retained for a Christian reading public was centered in Africa. The Christian environment at Rome during the early third century was predominantly Greek. The first production we have in Latin is Novatianus' De Trinitate, which is purely theological in character - though it draws heavily on Tertullian, as does Minucius. The Octavius does not fit into this context. It is out of place in Rome.[2] The Africa of

---

1. The absence of Latin Christian literature elsewhere in the West than Africa prior to Novatianus strongly suggests an African origin for the work, as do the extensive parallels cited by Koch, CU, pp. 1-78, to Cyprian's work. Koch's intention to establish Cyprian's authorship of the Quod Idola is not successfully carried out, but his work does point fairly conclusively to the fact that the Quod Idola was composed in Africa, probably in the second half of the third century.

2. For the linguistic environment of Rome at the opening of the third century, see G. Bardy, La question des langues dans

Tertullian corresponds more to the atmosphere of the dialogue.

In considering the purpose and aim of the Octavius, a distinction must be made between the primary and secondary audiences for whom the work was composed. The characters, with their local associations, would be particularly striking in a Cirtan milieu. The characterizations would then have particular and personal effect. This is not to argue that the work was intended solely to be read in such a context. As with Cicero's dialogues, the reader personally acquainted with the characters would be especially affected, as the dialogue utilized his own recollections and feelings. This would not preclude a dialogue from also having been written to portray and discuss particular philosophic or, in the case of the Octavius, religious problems, and thereby being effective for a wider audience as well.

The Octavius can therefore be used to establish the intellectual milieu in Christian Africa in the period between the death of Tertullian and the conversion of Cyprian. The arguments used by Minucius are derivative and well-known; but they point to the particular views of provincial Africans of the curial and educated sections of society who had embraced Christianity and now desired that the path to salvation be opened for others.

But one particularly difficult obstacle hindered the attainment of this goal. Opening his attack on Christianity, Caecilius reproaches the Christians for being an

---

2. (cont'd) l'église ancienne,I: Etude de théologie historique (Paris, 1948)pp.81ff

73

ignorant and common herd.[1] They pretend to
answer questions which experts realize tax
the limits of human knowledge and intelligence and perhaps lie beyond them.[2] The low
status of Christians, and particularly their
ignorance, is a reproach constantly hurled
against them.[3] This objection extended more
importantly to the Scriptures as well. For
an educated man, they formed an insuperable
barrier creating strong aversion. Tertullian
recognized that for a pagan, the Scriptures
could only be read after one had found
faith, but would never serve as an introduction to the faith.[4] By the last quarter of
the second century, at least one translation
had been made of a part of the Bible into
Latin. The Acts of the Scillitan Martyrs
mentions Speratus as having libri et epis-
tulae Pauli viri justi.[5] Tertullian also
employed a Latin translation at times.[6]
But if anything, the Latin of the translations was even more objectionable than the
original Greek, being full of irregular and
foreign usages.[7]

If Minucius was to reach his audience
of educated listeners, another approach was

---

1. Oct. 5.4.
2. Oct. 5.3-5.
3. On status, see discussion supra p.
47 ff. So Celsus, in Origen's Contra Celsum
3.9; and Clarke, "Literary Setting", passim,
who localizes the document at Rome, see p.
202.
4. Tertullian, De Anima 1.
5. Pass. Sanc. Scillitan. 12.
6. Barnes, Tert., p. 277.
7. For a text of the African Bible in
Cyprian's time, see H. Von Soden, "Das
lateinische Neue Testament zur Zeit Cyprians,"
TU 33 (Leipzig, 1909).

required. In his De Testimonio Animae, Tertullian had called upon the soul to deliver its witness to the existence of the Christian God. He invoked not the educated and Attic spirit, but rather the soul of the crude and unlettered artisan and peasant. The approach had possibilities. Pagans and Christians both shared the concept, and it could form a common premise for discussion. In the Apologeticum, Tertullian had outlined the basic approach of the De Testimonio Animae. Perhaps this gave Minucius his impetus.[1] He utilized different elements of his pagan tradition, but pursued the basic idea of attempting to convert, or to at least influence, his audience favourably by employing a form of argument that both could share. Moreover, Minucius' pagan education provided the skill and necessary elements for him to deploy, persuading his listeners through his use of Cicero, Seneca, and Plato. Specifically Christian elements are kept to a minimum. The name of Christ is entirely absent, though referred to by paraphrase.[2] Every attempt is made to meet the pagans on their own ground.

A partial source for Minucius was Plato's Phaedo. Additions from Seneca and

---

1. This is an hypothesis. Whether the earlier forms of Christian apologetic had any effect is not ascertainable. At least we know that Minucius actually read the Apologeticum.

2. Oct. 9.4, ipsius antistitis; 29.2, hominem noxium et crucem eius. There are certain Christian Latin usages in Minucius Felix. For these, refer to Beaujeu, Minucius Félix, p. 41, n. 1.

75

especially Cicero are utilized and reshaped to fit the author's purposes.[1] Cicero, probably most familiar to readers of the dialogue, is used to shape and supply stylistic material for the work. By setting the action of the dialogue at Rome, the magnetic attraction of the capital could be utilized; reference could be made to the routes of success open to the provincial man, even if he became Christian. So with all his animosity towards Christians in general, Caecilius constantly remains at Minucius' side in Rome.[2] This co-existence of Christian and pagan ends with the arrival of Octavius, who decides that the favour of conversion is owed to a friend as close as Caecilius. Certainly his conversion would influence their fellow provincials in Cirta. A dispute ensues with Caecilius presenting the pagan point of view, Octavius the Christian, and Minucius as the rather partial judge.[3]

Caecilius opens the argument with a profession of scepticism. Man's intelli-

---

1. The view of the dialogue as a patch-work has been successfully refuted by Becker (1967). Refer supra p. 51. On the Phaedo as source of the dialogue's structure, see Becker (1967) pp. 71 ff.
2. Oct. 3.1.
3. Beaujeu, Minucius Félix, lxxiv, sought a model in Favorinus; see also note 4.6 with special reference to North African practice as shown by Sallust, Jugurtha 11.3. He has been refuted successfully by Clarke, "Octavius 4.6", pp. 252-3. Also Becker (1967) p. 71. But the basic impetus was no doubt the typical controversiae of the schools. On these, see H.-I. Marrou, Histoire de l'éducation dans l'antiquité6

76

gence is a weak and limited instrument. Real wisdom consists in following the ancient Delphic oracle in searching and discovering the self, rather than in theological and cosmological speculation. But granted that we engage in such speculation, at least let us do so as educated men. The Christians are a rabble of lower-class and illiterate people who come to fixed conclusions about points that philosophers have endlessly debated, displaying only their ignorance in advancing arrogant conclusions.[1] The influence of the New Academy and Cotta of the De Natura Deorum is evident.[2] Caecilius continuously attacks the notion of providence in the formation and order of the world.[3] This, however, is merely a preparation for the shift in his position to the defense of tradition. Since all is basically idle speculation, the best solution is to adhere to the traditions of our ancestors and to adore the gods we have known from the cradle and whom our ancestors worshipped.[4] Thus Caecilius enunciates a position which was probably most common among educated pagans who resisted Christianity. Writing later in the East, Origen replies to the same intellectual stance.[5] The attack was particularly effective against the Christians, who were constantly reproached as

3. (cont'd) (Paris, 1965), p. 415.
1. Oct. 5.1-6.
2. Beaujeu, Minucius Félix, note ad loc., p. 85.
3. Oct. 5.7.
4. Oct. 6.1-2.
5. Origen, Contra Celsum 8.45. Also Beaujeu, Minucius Félix, note ad loc., p. 81; and Clarke, "Literary Setting", passim.

innovators who had deserted their ancestral cults, and who further perverted the already perverted Jewish religion. But at least Jews could claim an ancestral tradition for their activities, which was closed to the Christians.[1] Thus what may be taken as the typical eclectic position of the pagan aristocracy is established. It depended in part on arguments from the arsenals of various schools of philosophy and in the last instance on upper-class conservatism.

Caecilius then turns to the argument from utility. While each area worshipped its ancestral gods, the Romans worshipped one and all. This is the reason for their expansion, so that they now hold empire sine fine. They raised altars to all gods, and maintained the hallowed rites without interruption. This is the source of their dominion over all.[2]

Caecilius focuses on those aspects which appeal to upper-class pagans. The arguments, whatever the philosophical trappings, are directed towards class prejudice and political success. But the resumé of charges that Caecilius hurls at the Christians concentrates on their strange and evil practices, their low social class, and their lack of a proper notion of their place in society.[3] Octavius' answer to the indict-

---

1. The best ancient discussion is the Contra Celsum. For this concept of the Christians as a "new people", see Harnack, M&A, pp. 240-78. On this point, see also Oct. 8.3.
2. Oct. 6.2-3. For references to this locus classicus of pagan defense, see Beaujeu, Minucius Félix, pp. 81-2.
3. Oct. 8.4, an extremely important section for the real trend of the argument.

ment is prepared by Minucius, who inveighs against the deceptive tricks of rhetoric. Words fascinate; arguments are unpleasant fare. The educated must take care in their responsibilities so that the common people are not duped by the abilities and blandishments of a persuasive orator. Truth is obscure. Wordy subtlety can carry the day, so acute judgment must be exercised.

Caecilius protests the prejudiced position of Minucius, who in turn protests that he only points the argument back towards a solid basis. He does not let the hints of the "judge" escape him. Minucius insists he is only adding to the common stock:

> "ut examine scrupuloso nostram
> sententiam non eloquentiae
> tumore, sed rerum ipsarum soli-
> ditate libremus."1

After protestations in a vein similar to Minucius, Octavius begins a short _ad hominem_ attack on Caecilius. But he manages to temper the accusation by ascribing the weak and erratic argument of his opponent not to purposeful malice but rather to his inability to see the truth. Octavius will set him free from his anxious tossing by refuting the arguments and establishing the single and only way that leads to truth.

He first attempts to refute Caecilius by defending the economic and social position of the Christians. Wisdom is a natural commodity. All men have it regardless of sex or social position. Even the philosophers, before they earned their reputation, were considered as ignorant and of base rank. Riches are a hindrance to the search

---

1. _Oct._ 15.2.

79

for wisdom. The sheen of gold often eclipses the light of the truth. Attention should be directed to the validity of the argument, rather than to the person of the disputant.[1] No attempt is made by Octavius to refute the contention that Christians are generally from the lower ranks of society. Instead, he attempts either to make this a virtue, or at least to show that this is no hindrance in the search for truth. For an audience to whom rank and position mattered, there was no alternative for him to pursue. There could be no appeal to transcendent revelation as a basis for discussion.[2]

The shared human capacity for truth becomes the framework for a major part of the remainder of Octavius' argument. One of the most damaging sections of the sceptical argument of Caecilius was his contention that the world, miserable as it is, had no marks of a divine providence or of divine concern.[3] Firstly, he marshalled one of the oldest and most enduring of all proofs, the argument from design. Octavius points to the order of the heavens, the sea ebbing and flowing with startling regularity. Animals display the hand of the Maker. Beauty of form is combined with an assortment of protective features that betray design. So the body of man displays not one portion which was not made for either use or beauty. Surely all this is not the product of chance[4] The argument is full of Stoic commonplaces, and all the more effective for that. Octavius

---

1. Oct. 16.5-6.
2. For citations, Beaujeu, Minucius Félix, p. 98.
3. Oct. 6.1 ff.
4. Oct. 17.3-18.5

80

studiously avoids any Christian dogma or overtones. The terms of reference are pagan. In fact, the basic idea is that Christianity is inherent in the best of paganism.[1] Poets also add their voice to the Christian consensus. All recognize the existence of God, or at least gods. Either the philosophers were Christian or Christians are philosophers.[2] Cyprian would later find use for this commonplace.[3] The attempt to fuse Christians with the intellectual élite of pagan society is one of the dialogue's constant themes.

Central for a provincial and pagan audience was the question of the attitude that a Christian must take with respect to the ruling power. The condemnation of Christians by Roman magistrates was a fact of life. Before Octavius converted to Christianity, he shared the prejudices of Caecilius unquestioningly. He thought that the Christians ate babies, participated

---

1. For the sources of this basically Stoic argument for the connection and design of the cosmos, see Beaujeu, Minucius Félix, ad loc.. The most developed use of pagan philosophical argument by Christians can be found in the Contra Celsum of Origen. See especially H. Chadwick, Early Christian Thought and the Classical Tradition. Studies in Justin, Clement, and Origen (Oxford, 1966). The connections with Tertullian are indeed much too evident to warrant further comment.

2. Oct. 19.3-20.

3. De Bono Pat. 2. It is also common in the Greek apologists, i.e., Justin and Athenagoras. Clement recognized the need of Christianity for philosophy, e.g., Strom. 7.35-46.

81

in incestuous banquets, and worshipped monstrous deities. He did not regard Christians as worthy of a hearing when on trial.[1] But conversion forced upon him one of the central problems for a Christian attempting to obtain a hearing, that is, how to regard Rome. Caecilius stressed that the success of the Romans in warfare and conquest was due to their piety in honouring the gods of the entire world.[2] Given the position of the Romans with respect to the Christians, Octavius can only reject them and their success. He points out that this talk of the majestic world empire is mere fraud. In origin the Romans were nothing but a band of criminals. Their empire grew not from piety but from cruelty and rapine. Romulus, their founder, murdered his own brother so that he might reign. From this characteristic start, they grew by destroying the homelands of others. Whatever the Romans held or possessed was merely the booty that they had savagely wrenched from the property of others.[3] As for their pretended piety, what manner of piety was it to worship the very deities you have first desecrated and then captured? Roman greatness was a product not of true devotion but of open sacrilege. Even the native gods of the Romans were shameful. Who else numbers prostitutes and diseases among their divinities? If any of the Roman oracles or auguries had some effect, it was due to the action of demons who attempted to lead others to their ruin, to gain some compensation for their own depravity. The demons themselves admitted that this was true

1. Oct. 28.
2. Oct. 6.2.
3. praeda, Oct. 25.1-5.

when driven out of men's bodies by exorcism and prayer. Upon hearing the name of the one true God, quailing and shaking in misery they flee. Christians can easily put them to flight. It is demons who inspire these false charges against us.[1]

In spite of the attempt made by the Octavius to come to grips with the problem of provincials and Christianity, its synthesis breaks down on this point. As long as Rome was opposed to Christianity and prepared to take measures against it, there could be no final and successful rapprochement. With the conversion of Constantine, Eusebius could effect a successful ideological meeting of state and church.[2] In the early third century, both groups found themselves in a situation of mutual suspicion, with each side at times acting as the antagonist. Christian views varied from one extreme to the other. Clement of Alexandria sought the way of rapprochement. Military service was to be performed by Christians, Roman law recognized, and taxes paid. If the magistrates persecuted them, this was to be viewed as an act of Providence and a fact of life. But there were limits to obedience, and idolatry and the imperial cult could not be permitted.[3]

At the other extreme, Hippolytus saw the Empire as the Kingdom of Evil. It was the beast of the Apocalypse (13:1) and the fourth beast in Daniel (7). The Empire had satanically imitated the Church by gathering

---

1. Oct. 25.6-27.8.
2. e.g., Origen, Contra Celsum 2.30.
3. Clement, Paed. 2.14.1; 3.91.3; 2.11.2; 3.91.2. On this see also Strom. 1.171; 4.79.1.

83

together all the peoples of the earth. For Hippolytus there was no way to come to terms with Rome.[1]

Origen's view was far more comprehensive. Using the Epistle to the Romans (1:13 ff.) as his authority, he derived the power of the Roman State from God.[2] Persecutions were an abuse on the part of magistrates who would, on the Day of Judgment, have to answer for it.[3] In fact, the assembling of people under the aegis of the Roman Empire at the time of Augustus had providentially prepared the way for the Christian mission.[4] Laws should be obeyed, and a Christian should manifest his loyalty to the State unless demands were made which conflicted with the allegiance he owed to a higher power, the imperial cult being an obvious case in point.[5] The Church was really the City of God on earth. It exists along with the secular state, and its laws are in harmony with the established constituion of all peoples.[6] Christians should devote themselves to doing good for all, especially by making available the Word of God to all peoples, until the day when God will allow the conversion of the entire Empire.[7] Origen's position is a mean between the extremes of Hippolytus and Clement. He would allow that Christians be exempt from military service, just as pagan priests were, for they aided the Empire with their prayers. But the major trend of his

---

1. Origen, In Dan. Comm. 4.9 and Hippolytus, De Antichr. 25.
2. Origen, In Rom. Comm. 9.26.
3. Origen, Contra Celsum 2.30.
4. Origen, In Rom. Comm. 9.26.
5. In Jerome, Hom. 9.2 and In Jos. Hom. 8.7; Origen, Contra Celsum 4.22.
6. Origen, Contra Celsum 8.69.
7. Origen, Contra Celsum 5.35-7.

thought was that peaceful co-existence was a necessity until the time of Christian victory.

The viewpoint of Latin Christianity is more ambiguous. Tertullian has been interpreted as a loyal subject, while others find that he totally rejects all that is Roman.[1] His attitude cannot be divined. His works abound in both negative and positive reactions to Rome.[2] It is impossible to determine whether any of his statements are the result of genuine feeling or merely dictated by the audience addressed and the point to be made.[3]

Perhaps because Minucius Felix has only one extant work his attitude lacks the ambiguity of Tertullian. Its relationship to the Apologeticum will illustrate the point. Tertullian found it necessary to reply to the contention that the Romans owed their Empire to their piety. His attitude is distinctly less hostile, however, than that of Minucius, who utilized his chapter as a major source for his reply in the Octavius. Tertullian's reply abounds in irony, not rancour and hate. The Romans owed their prosperity to the gratitude of their native gods. No doubt Sterculus and Mutunus have shown their beneficence to their worshippers[4]. Foreign gods would certainly have preferred to aid their own worshippers. Juno would

---

1. Loyal, in Sherwin-White, The Roman Citizenship (Oxford, 1939), p. 268. Anti-Roman, in Frend, M&P, p. 365.
2. Positive, in Tertullian, De Pall. 2.7 and De Anima 30.3. Negative, in Tertullian, De Cult. Fem. 2.13.6.
3. So rightly Barnes, Tert., p. 219.
4. Apol. 25.3-4. Sterculus is the god of dung and Mutunus of coitus.

have chosen Carthage over Rome and Jupiter his grave in Crete to a temple on the Capitol.[1] After this flight into irony, Tertullian attacks the thesis by claiming that the gods were once human beings in any case. From whom did Jupiter and Saturn draw the gift of empire? Perhaps it was from Sterculus. It is obvious that they could not have bestowed kingship when they themselves reigned before they were gods.[2]

In addition, religion had failed to make headway until the Empire had been established. Native Roman religion was a poor thing. Their images and temples owed their existence to the ingenia Graecorum atque Tuscorum. Thus the Romans were not religious before they were great, from which it follows that they were not great because they were religious. In fact their greatness is a product of piety's opposite: they owed their triumphs to sacrilege. Their spoils were the captured gods of other peoples. After all, the conquered had religion as well as the conqueror.[3]

Tertullian's repudiation centres around the absurdity of the gods. The functions of the native Roman pantheon are held up to ridicule by attributing the growth of empire to the gods of dung or sexual intercourse. He stresses the inexplicability of foreign deities deserting their own worshippers for the Romans. He utilizes the Euhemeristic explanation of the origin of the gods, to show that the Empire existed before the gods themselves. More importantly, he demonstrates that Roman sanctity was the fruit of conquest and not its cause,

---

1. Apol. 25.7-8.
2. Apol. 25.11.
3. Apol. 25.12-17.

86

and that this very conquest results in impiety because of the need for looting shrines and temples in the process of winning dominion. But the major point of Tertullian's attack is directed against the pagan gods and not their human worshippers.

Though dependent upon Tertullian, Minucius has shifted the point of his argument towards a more hostile assessment of Roman religion. He argues against the Romans and not their gods. The Roman State was born in crime and murder; conquest is simply an extension of it.[1] The process continued with the continued expansion of the Empire. All is the product of looting and plunder. The Romans worshipped gods they themselves had conquered. The absurdity of their own deities is apparent. Take the Vestal Virgins, for example, who submerge themselves in lust. Empire existed before the Romans. The eastern monarchies had none of Rome's religious paraphernalia, yet they were mighty states.[2]

Some obvious points are made by both authors: the absurdity of the Roman pantheon and of foreign gods who preferred the Romans over their own native worshippers, and the charge that conquest is sacrilege by nature. But the differences are more striking than the similarities. Minucius attacks the Roman State, pointing out that its origin was in bloodshed and its growth through pillage and sacrilege. He stresses that all that they have is but the property of others, appropriated as booty by the conquerors. They disregard their own religious obser- vances as well - witness the behaviour of the Vestal Virgins. Minucius considers the

---

1. Oct. 25.1-4.
2. Oct. 25.5-12.

auspices also, and shows them to be the work of corrupt demons.[1]

The general trend of the _Octavius_ is towards rapprochement. Tertullian oscillated; but the entire thrust of Minucius' thought is directed towards reducing the evident differences between Christian and pagan in so far as possible. The hostility of this section demands explanation, if it is to be brought into line with the rest of the work. The rancour may stem from persecution of the Christians, of which the author claims personal acquaintance.[2] Though this may have provided the fuel for Minucius' indignation, such a tactic can only be regarded as a blunder in view of his general purpose. Alienating one's audience does not lead to their conversion; but if the local nature of the primary audience is accepted as a reasonable postulate, then the reaction towards Rome can be explained. The exactions of the procurator in Carthage under Maximinus led to a revolt in 238.[3] Though the sources do not reveal that this incident had any nationalistic overtones, it still may have given rise to anti-Roman sentiment, for the extinction of the revolt was followed by harsh and widespread devastation in Africa Proconsularis.

Even though the theme of Rome's injustice in the passage is a _topos_, this does not necessarily deprive it of genuine feeling nor of the possibility that it was directly motivated by the events that had occurred in Africa Proconsularis.[4] The use

---

1. _Oct._ 26 ff.
2. _Oct._ 28.
3. Herodian, 7.4.2.
4. H. Fuchs, _Der geistige Widerstand gegen Rom in der antiken Welt_ (Berlin, 1938),

88

of such a theme by pagan authors who were writing as members of a common cultural and literary milieu, and its employment by an individual who had placed himself outside that milieu and was now attempting to integrate his adopted creed which had long met opposition among educated pagans, is of a different order. Though effective on an intellectual level, and in demonstrating a common literary heritage, the strong anti-Roman flavour exemplified the very separateness that Minucius Felix was trying to overcome.

The absence of a large corpus of Latin Christian literature between Tertullian and Cyprian allows no deductions to be drawn as to the effect of the Octavius. Lactantius mentions it only to criticize its inadequacies with regard to his own standard of apologia.[1] His mentor, Arnobius, shows no acquaintance with it, though it was its inclusion as the eighth book of the Adversus Nationes that guaranteed its preservation.[2] But the traces of the Octavius found in Cyprian would indicate that it was at least part of the Christian intellectual heritage

---

4. (cont'd) pp. 85 ff., who thinks Octavius 25 may derive from Cicero's De Republica 3.20, rather than from Tertullian's Apologeticum 25.14. There is no doubt of its being a topos, as Fuchs points out, but this does not prevent its use by Minucius to express genuine convictions.

1. Lactantius, Div. Inst. 5.1.21.

2. Parisinus Latinus (Paris, Bibl. Nationale, ms. lat. 1161), represents the only manuscript tradition that we have. Bruxellensis (Brussels, Bibl. Royale, ms. lat. 10847) is only an 11th century copy of the 9th century Parisinus.

available for Cyprian to draw upon. Its attempt at accommodation must have seemed ludicrous to African Christians in the second half of the third century. The conditions of truce that had existed between the State and the Church had broken down in the reign of Decius. The conflict of Christianity and paganism was to take other forms than those envisioned by Minucius Felix.

Cicero had ended the De Natura Deorum without completing the discussion. After Cotta's slashing attack on Stoic doctrine and traditional religion, Lucilius, pleading the lateness of the hour, asks for the apportionment of time on some future day to defend the doctrines which Cotta attacked. More than acquiescent, Cotta claims that he had only expounded his point of view for the sake of discussion, and he offers himself gladly to Lucilius for refutation. But Velleius interposes a last jibe at the Stoics with a snide remark on their faith in dreams. Cicero rounds out and ends the discussion by expressing his own preference for the exposition of the Stoic Balbus, but essentially leaves the discussion with no fixed conclusion.[1]

The Octavius ends on a more triumphant note. Caecilius and Minucius stare in wonder at Octavius after the conclusion of his argument. In his awe, Caecilius claims that both he and Octavius are the victors. For Octavius had vanquished him in argument, and Caecilius himself had defeated his own error. Caecilius admits that Octavius has established his case for the action of Providence in the world and his belief in God's existence. He admits that Octavius has

---

1. Cicero, De Nat. Deor. 3.40.

90

also convinced him of the sincerity of the latter's sect which he now makes his own. But the note of triumphant Christianity is tempered. Caecilius says that he has not been fully convinced; there still remain some minor points, aliqua consubsidunt, which demand elucidation, although they are not fatal to the truth. As in Cicero's dialogue, final certainty is not offered. The setting of the sun brings an end to the day's discussion, and the following day is set aside to clear up Caecilius' doubts. Minucius stresses his satisfaction with the outcome of the discussion, and he renders thanks to God who has inspired Octavius. Man's testimony is weak and needs God to complete it.[1]

The finale of the dialogue owes something to Cicero, though Caecilius' conversion appears due more to friendship than to superior philosophical principles.[2] He acknowledges three propositions as generally proved by Octavius: Providence, God, and Christian sincerity. But Minucius' attempt to skirt the dogma of Christianity had proved fatal in the end. The absence of dogma meant that only specific philosophical points were discussed, not beliefs which were germane or peculiar to Christianity. Except for demonstrating the sincerity of Christianity, Minucius has been too general in his approach. The propositions that Caecilius assents to would be equally at home in Stoic philosophy as they would be in

---

1. Oct. 40.3.
2. As Voss, Der Dialog, p. 42, points out, the ending is a topos which may be an imitation of the De Natura Deorum of Cicero in the case of Minucius.

91

Christianity.[1] Minucius found the result of his attempt to approach the upper-classes within their own intellectual framework was a serious adulteration of Christianity. The sterility of the approach is demonstrated by its lack of imitation. In his refutation of Celsus, Origen was to produce an apologia using traditional arguments culled from the philosophical schools with more effect and without sacrificing the unique religious qualities of Christianity.[2] In his famous question, "What has Athens to do with Jerusalem, the Academy with the Church?", Tertullian had pin-pointed the root of the problem.[3] As early as the Apologeticum, he was aware of the essential difference. A Christian was not simply a member of another school of philosophy. In a series of neatly contrasted antitheses, he made the difference obvious. The philosopher is busy with his refutation, while the Christian is concerned with his own salvation. The philosopher is essentially a man of destruction, who seeks truth through analysis, while the Christian is the builder of truth. The follower of Christ is the foe of error; the philosopher is its friend. One is the guardian of

---

1. R. Hirzel, Der Dialog, ein literar-historischer Versuch (2 vols. Leipzig, 1895), Vol. II, p. 369, sees its importance in the absence of the fanatical element and the use of the philosophic approach. But this approach in the Octavius is so diluted that Christianity loses its own form and its message as well.

2. See H. Chadwick's introduction to his translation of the Contra Celsum (Cambridge, 1953) p. xiv.

3. Tertullian, De Praescr.Haeret. 7.

truth; the other is the purloiner of it.[1]
The Christian Sophist recognized the truth,
that Christianity without some form of
mediation was alien to the mentality of the
Greco-Roman upper-classes.[2]

---

1. *Apol.* 46.18.
2. Fuchs, *Der geistige Widerstand*, pp.
19 ff., rightly stresses the difficulty
that the Christian creed, with its demand
for unconditional acceptance, created for
the thought-world of Rome. Fuchs rightly
sees that the section of the *Octavius* that
deals with Rome's growth through pillage
and rapine (85) shows its continued existence
as a Christian theme. But his general view
of the opposition between Christian and
Roman is different from the one presented
here. He states that the initial opposition
of the Christians to Rome was not a necessity, as their "other worldly" orientation
presented no danger to the Roman world.
But this is to ignore the actual ramifications of the Christian view of life. The
unconditional demand to worship a particular
god must inevitably manifest itself in
action and thought. Christian procedure,
once the Empire had officially become Christian, is the clearest manifestation of such
a demand and its consequences. As long as
the State was intimately bound up with
religion, Christianity and Rome remained in
basic opposition. The Jews, with their
nationalistic direction, presented less of
a problem to the State; but the spread of
Christianity threatened Rome with its universal claims. The opposition which Minucius
Felix was trying to overcome was only dealt
with by changes in both the Church and the
Empire which eventually allowed a coalescence
of the two.

Though he contributed to the founding of a rapprochement between the new religion and its pagan environment, Tertullian was aware of an irreducible minimum of opposition which no amount of borrowing could efface. In his efforts to further bridge the gap, Minucius had given away the very position whose defense he had undertaken. But for a Christian, there were other means of dealing with the pagan world. The upper-classes of third century Africa were to offer at least a few recruits to the Christian camp.

Chapter III: FROM RHETOR TO BISHOP

Biography has always been popular. The subject presents an easy unity, and the personalities of great men are of compelling interest. Tacitus essentially closes an epoch in Latin literature. With Suetonius, history becomes biography for a period of over two hundred years. Not until Ammianus Marcellinus at the end of the fourth century does the annalistic framework reappear in the literature of the West.[1]

Christians too desired records of their heroes. The Acts of the martyrs attest their desire to preserve the record of the ultimate act of Christian heroism for the benefit of future generations.[2] Martyrs were important for their deaths; with the expanding church structure of the third century, other Christians became important

---

1. The standard work on Greco-Roman biography remains F. Leo, Die griechisch-römische Biographie nach ihrer litterarischen Form (Leipzig, 1901). For a more recent work, see A. Momigliano, The Development of Greek Biography (Cambridge, Mass., 1971).

2. See Pass. Perpet. 1. The question of the relation of the biographical content of the four Gospels to Christian biography is especially difficult. The position of Christ is such that the re-telling of his life in the Gospels can hardly be called biography. See M. Goguel, La foi à la résurrection de Jésus dans le christianisme primitif (Paris, 1933), pp. 41-3. The Acts of the Apostles is a more likely ancestor of Christian biography.

95

for their lives. The kernel of the passio could be expanded. The deeds of bishops in times of stress, and the need to defend them against the accusations of enemies, provided the first Christian biography.[1]

The need for defense seems to be the genesis of the Vita Cypriani, the first specimen of Christian biography.[2] The work falls into two parts after the exordium (1.1-6). The first (2-10) is the Vita itself, the conversion of Cyprian and his work as bishop. The second section begins with the second exile and ends with the death of Cyprian and the reflections of Pontius (11-19).[3]

---

1. For a more detailed sketch of Christian biography in antiquity, see M. Pellegrino's introduction to his edition of Pontius' biography of Cyprian, Vita e martirio de San Cipriano, Verba Seniorum, 3 (Alba, 1955), pp. 8-34, where he characterizes it definitely as a biography. So A. von Harnack, in his important study of the Vita, "Das Leben Cyprians von Pontius: die erste christliche Biographie", TU 39, hft. 3 (Leipzig, 1913), p. 33. Monceaux, HAC, p. 190, calls it "au fond un éloge de Cyprien", but in so doing he does not pay attention to the genres of pagan biography. See Polybius' comments on the biography of Philopoemen, Hist. 10.21.8, and Plutarch, Alex. 1.

2. See Appendix IV. The title adopted here is an abbreviated form. For the manuscript titles, see Pellegrino, Vita, p. 88.

3. This is the schema rightly accepted by Harnack, "Das Leben", from whom Pellegrino, Vita, pp. 75 ff. has adopted it. However, P. Corssen, "Das Martyrium des

Thus the biography is composed of the older form of passio with the addition of a vita. The Vita of Cyprian was necessitated by imputations on the conduct of the bishop. So this first form of Christian biography arises from the immediate context of events in Carthage soon after Cyprian's execution by the Roman authorities in 258.[1] His life

3. (cont'd) Bischofs Cyprian", ZNW 18 (1917/8), p. 205, would begin the second part of the Vita with chapter 7. But as Pellegrino had observed, the discourse continues with a list of Cyprian's works and a further justification for the delay of his martyrdom. The real break is Vita 11.1:

"His tam bonis et tam piis
actibus exilium supervenit."

1. This seems to leave the actual relation between pagan forms and Pontius' biography as a secondary problem. H. Delehaye, Les passions des martyrs et les genres littéraires[2], Subsidia hagiographica 13B (Brussels, 1966), p. 71, is essentially correct, that the model for Pontius is Passion literature such as that of Perpetua. The relationship to pagan genres is secondary. R. Reitzenstein, "Die Nachrichten über den Tod Cyprians", SBHeidel, Phil.- hist. Kl. (1913), Abhand. 14, pp. 52 ff., posited a connection with the exitus virorum illustrium such as the work of Titinius Capito mentioned by Pliny, Ep. 8.12.4-5. Pontius shows evidence of rhetorical training, see Monceaux, HAC, p. 192; but if the account given here is true, the genesis does not lie in that direction. Exitus literature concentrates on the death of the hero. The sections of Tacitus' Annales

97

before his conversion is almost a complete blank; it is the spiritual rather than the physical birth of this homo Dei with which Pontius has chosen to begin.1

Until the start of this century, even the name of Cyprian was not correctly given.2 The future bishop's actual name was composed of nomen, cognomen, and agnomen. His full name was Caecilius Cyprianus qui et Thascius.3 The use of the

---

1. (cont'd) which deal with the deaths of various major figures in his narrative illustrate the difference between the genre of exitus literature and the technique employed by Pontius. See Tacitus on Seneca (XV.61-4); Thrasea Paetus (XVI. 21-35); see also Plutarch, Cato Minor. Both Plutarch and Tacitus deal at length with the deaths of these individuals. The main concern was with the death of the protagonist not his life. The first part of the Vita should dispose of this connec- tion, though formal rhetoric may have been influencial. Corssen's attempt to relate it to the laudationes funebres is no more successful. It may be that Passion literature in general had some connection with this genre, but the only discernable similarity is that they are both located within the context of death.
    1. "Unde igitur incipiam?...nisi a principio fidei et nativitate caelesti?" (Vita 2.1)
    2. Monceaux, HAC, pp. 202-3, first handled it accurately. Unfortunately, some have paid no attention to his demonstration. See S. Colombo, "S. Cipriano di Cartagine: L'uomo e lo scrittore", Didaskaleion N.S. 6 (1928), p. 2.
    3. For the agnomen in Christian names,

name varies appreciably. The edict confiscating his property as bishop during persecution calls him Caecilius Cyprianus, while the proconsul Galerius Maximus addresses him as Thascius Cyprianus.[1] The heading to letter 66 is given as Cyprianus qui et Thascius, but the usual form is Cyprianus.[2]

The cognomen Cyprianus is portentously rare in African inscriptions. The only examples are posterior to Cyprian and are Christian. They are in honour of the bishop and give no information on filiation.[3] The agnomen Thascius, or the variant Tascius, is equally absent in inscriptional material. But a male or female martyr of that name is mentioned by the Martyrologium Hieronymianum on September 1.[4] Jerome reports that

---

3. (cont'd) see I. Kajanto, Onomastic Studies in the Early Christian Inscriptions of Rome and Carthage, Acta Instituti Romani Finlandiae, 2, no. 1 (Helsinki, 1963), pp. 61 ff. The phenomenon among pagans is well demonstrated by the inscription of C. Helvius Honoratus qui et Pontius. See Appendix IV.

1. For the edict of confiscation, see Ep. 66.4/729.15-16. The citations of the proconsul are to be found in AP 3.3 and 4.3.

2. The use of the agnomen here may be ironical, as Cyprian's correspondent who has opposed the bishop is addressed as Florentius qui et Puppienus.

3. Examples are CIL VIII: 455, 2291, 10539, 13426, 13588-600, 13602, 13937; "Kuprianos", 13601.

4. H. Delehaye and H. Quentin (ed.), Martyrologium Hieronymianum, Acta Sanctorum, collecta...a Sociis Bollandianis Nou., ii, 2 (Brussels, 1931):

Cyprian took his _cognomen_ from the presbyter, Caecilius. Caecilius had been
instrumental in his conversion and had
commended his wife and children to Cyprian
on his death.1 The _Vita_ reports the name as
Caecilianus, which Jerome misread. In any
case, a _nomen_ is never derived in this
manner. Jerome must have thought the full
name was Thascius Caecilius Cyprianus.[2]
Cyprian's nomenclature is composed of
elements either too rare or too common to
yield any results.

Augustine confessed his ignorance of
Cyprian's birth date, and we share the same
position.[3] The year of birth is equally

---

4. (cont'd) "In Africa civit(ate)
Tunizia Natale s(an)ctoru(m) Tascie
(or) Tasciae (or) Tasci."
Monceaux, _HAC_, p. 203, n. 6, hypothesizes
that this name was given to Cyprian by his
pagan friends prior to his conversion. But
this is a groundless hypothesis. The lack
of consistency in nomenclature is obvious
from the Cyprianic corpus. One would hardly
think that an official sentence of death
would be passed using a familiar nickname.
The passage in _Vita_ 4.30 gives no indication
of irony. The _nomen_ Caecilius is extremely
common in Africa, as a glance at the index
of _CIL_ VIII will confirm.

1. Jerome, _Vir. Ill._ 67. For
Caecilianus, _infra_ p. 137.

2. For this name, _Vita_ 4.1. The
apparatus of Hartel and that of Pellegrino
report no variants in the manuscripts, but
Jerome may have had a variant reading or
simply read the name incorrectly.

3. Augustine, _Sermo_ 310.1: "Quando
natus est ignoramus. Et quia hodie passus
est, natalem eius hodie celebramus."

100

unknown, but there are some indications for the approximate period. In discussing Tertullian, Jerome asserts that he heard from Paul of Concordia, who had known Cyprian's notarius, that Cyprian would ask for Tertullian every day by saying Da Magistrum. The relative clause is "qui se beati Cypriani iam grandis aetatis notarium Romae vidisse diceret", leaving the meaning of iam grandis aetatis uncertain.[1] It may refer to Cyprian, but the Latin is unclear, and Cyprian's secretary must surely have been of advanced age for Paul of Concordia to have seen him.

Jerome mentions that Cyprian taught rhetoric and had earned a reputation before he converted to Christianity.[2] In his letters, Jerome repeats this.[3] Augustine also mentions his prowess in oratory.[4] Pontius writes that Cyprian was devoted to the study of the bonae artes.[5] Pontius provides no further indication of date, however, nor does the Ad Donatum.[6]

---

1. Jerome, Vir. Ill. 53. The examples of the use of grandis in the Thesaurus Linguae Latinae do not allow a strict application of the term to be inferred. It seems, however, to point to an age of at least 50. For example, see Pompon., Dig. 1.2.2.50.
2. Jerome, Vir. Ill. 67.
3. Jerome, Ep. 84.2.
4. Augustine, Sermo 312.4.
5. Vita 2.1: "fuerint licet studia et bonae artes devotum pectus imbuerint, tam en illa praetereo: nondum enim ad utilitatem nisi saeculi pertinebant."
6. Harnack, GAL, p. 368, argues from the fragment of the beginning of the Ad Donatum, at Hartel, CSEL 3, part 3, Ep. 1/

101

We can only infer that Cyprian was old enough in 246/7 to have gained some experience as a rhetorician and therefore was not a youth.

The bishop's relation to Tertullian provides no further evidence as to his age. The passage in Jerome only implies the great respect with which the first major writer of African Latin Christianity was held by Cyprian, but whether there was any personal contact between the two men is not known.[1]

Beyond his fame as a teacher of rhetoric which implies at least some time being spent as a pagan prior to conversion, little other help is available. Pontius provides some, indicating his sources for the biography.

---

6. (cont'd) 272, which mentions the singular agreement of Donatus and Cyprian apud oratorem, that Cyprian was young at the time of writing. But the reference is to the past and cannot be so used.

1. Monceaux, HAC, p. 203, infers no personal contact with Tertullian, as does Harnack, GAL, p. 367, but this is not a necessary consequence of any evidence that we have. Monceaux uses this as an argument for his dating of Cyprian's birth, using the traditional date for Tertullian's death of the year 220, so that Cyprian would only be 10 years old at the time. But Barnes, Tert., pp. 51-2, has shown that the De Pudicitia, which was traditionally dated to the year 220 and formed the usual terminus of Tertullian's life, has been wrongly dated. The last work we have which is datable from his pen is the Ad Scapulam, from the autumn of 212. Given Tertullian's constant output, he may well have met his death in that year or soon after.

102

He states that he was present at certain of the events in the _Vita_, while he heard of others _de antiquioribus_.[1] But Pontius' position in the bishop's entourage is not clear. The absence of any mention of him in the letters would probably indicate that he was in the company of the bishop. It was not until soon before the exile that Pontius became an intimate member of Cyprian's circle.[2] It is a presumption, but a reasonable one, that the _antiquiores_ that Pontius drew upon were the contemporaries of the bishop. These were men like Donatus, who had known Cyprian closely in the period of his conversion. If this was the case, we can probably place Cyprian in the generation before Pontius. An age of thirty would seem reasonable to postulate for the writing of the _Vita_, giving Pontius a birth date of 220-5.[3] If we place Cyprian in the previous generation, his approximate date of birth would be about 200 A.D. The election of Cyprian after so short a period as a Christian would also suggest he was not particularly young.

This is the sum total of information relevant to Cyprian's time of birth. The results are insubstantial, but the information would suggest a man no longer young at the time of his conversion. Beyond that we cannot venture.[4]

---

1. _Vita_ 2.3.
2. _Vita_ 12.3.
3. See Appendix IV.
4. The estimate presented here would make Cyprian slightly older than is normally accepted. Harnack, _GAL_, pp. 367-8, would have him at about 30 when he converted. But so young a man would probably have had more

Jerome calls Cyprian Afer.[1] The term seems confined to what had been Proconsularis at Cyprian's birth. But where in Proconsularis was he born? Carthage would be an obvious possibility, but Cyprian's rhetorical interests would have drawn him to the capital, as they later drew Augustine.[2] Gregory Nazianzus reports that Cyprian was of great and illustrious birth in the capital of Proconsularis, but the statement is of no independent worth.[3] Augustine is more explicit, citing Carthage as the bishop's

---

4. (cont'd) difficulty in controlling the Church than did Cyprian, even with the prestige of the Carthaginian see. Monceaux, HAC, p. 203, because of his views on the relation of Cyprian and Tertullian, places the date of birth "vers 210". Altaner-Stuiber, Pat., p. 172, opts for 200/210 which is more likely correct. Colombo, "S. Cipriano", p. 14, rightly argues that the election shows he was a mature Christian dating his birth to around 200.

1. Jerome, Vir. Ill. 67. Monceaux, HAC, p. 203, interprets this as specifying Proconsularis. The use of the term by a contemporary source supports this. Thus the Tripolitanian birth of Clodius Albinus attested by the SHA: "Albino ex familia Ceioniorum Afro quidem homini", SHA Cl. Albin. 10.7. See also SHA Sept. Sever. 2.8 and SHA Cl. Albin. 12.8. Monceaux is right.

2. Augustine, Conf. 4.7.12.

3. Gregory Naz., Oratio xxiv. Also xxiv.6. Unfortunately, Gregory fails to temper his panegyrical aspirations with historical fact. The Oratio mixes charac-teristics of Cyprian bishop of Carthage with Cyprian magician of Antioch. For the text of Oratio xxiv see PG 35.

home. The reference does not seem to refer only to Cyprian's ecclesiastical office.[1] The _Vita_ provides some indication that Carthage was the place of his birth and the focus of his entire life. After his return from exile at Curubis, Cyprian took up residence in the gardens that Pontius notes he had sold at the beginning of his conversion for the sake of the poor, but which later were restored by the _indulgentia Dei_.[2] The _Acta Proconsularia_ also mention that while waiting to be brought to trial, Cyprian remained in _suis hortis_.[3] Thus at least part of his patrimony is certain to have been in Carthage. It must surely be a major part, from the emphasis laid upon its disposal for the poor. The return of it to Cyprian, though not explicitly stated, may have been the action of a grateful community in reward for the bishop's excellence. This lends further support to a Carthaginian origin, as there is no reference to any other property of such size in any other area. Cyprian also refers to his own property in Carthage from which he retreated to avoid being captured and sent to Utica to be judged by the proconsul.[4] One could hypothesize that the ancestral home of Cyprian's family was in these _horti_.

Carthage seems the most likely _patria_ for him; certainly no evidence points

---

1. Augustine, _Sermo_ 309.2. The reference is more than metaphorical. The context is based on _Vita_ 11.3 ff.
2. _Vita_ 15.1. The _horti_ will be discussed later, _infra_ pp. 348 f.
3. _AP_ 2.2.
4. _Ep._ 81.1/841.5.

105

elsewhere.[1] Nothing is explicitly said about his antecedents, except that they were pagan.[2] But the family was of some wealth.[3] Cyprian's career in rhetoric implies a property of some substance or a wealthy patron. The latter is less probable, in view of the stress of Pontius and Jerome on Cyprian's wonderful generosity in bestowing his property to the poor.[4] Cyprian's family may have possessed curial rank at Carthage. This would explain his quick rise within the Christian hierarchy, which was a source of amazement to Pontius.[5]

1. Benson, Cyprian, p. 9, tries to utilize the notice at Jerome, Vir. Ill. 67, Cyprianus Afer, to show that Cyprian was not a Carthaginian. Presumably Jerome would have said Carthage had he known. But the usage is merely a literary variant, since Jerome uses Carthaginiensis to describe the location of Cyprian's episcopate. A short survey of the other notices will confirm that urban designations are usually confined to the city of ecclesiastical office, and at times not even the origin is given. See Origen, no. 54 and Lactantius, no. 80.

2. Vita 3.1, de imperitis sentibus.

3. Infra n. 4 on his property.

4. Vita 2.7; Jerome, Vir. Ill. 67; Jerome, Chron., ad annum 2273; Jerome, Comm. in Iohan. 3.6. Monceaux, HAC, p. 204, cites Augustine, Sermo 312.4 for his personal wealth, but the passage concerns Cyprian's oratorical prowess.

5. Vita 2.7. Pontius says that in selling his possessions for the poor, he obtained two goods, pity and the avoidance of secular ambition...this might mean the traditional curial responsibilities of a family of Cyprian's standing.

106

It would also accord with the increasing social status of Christian converts in the third century in the West, of which the Octavius of Minucius Felix is a sign. But there is no evidence of higher rank.[1] Most telling of all is that during his exile at Curubis, Cyprian was visited by many of senatorial and equestrian status, because of their previous friendship with him.[2] Certainly the importance of a Christian bishop would not alone account for the establishment of such ties. The friendships as the Vita states were a product of Cyprian's pagan phase and point to his own station in life.[3] Certain ancient sources state he was a magician; as for his real profession, this is less obvious.[4] Pontius

---

1. For the curial class of Carthage, see Audollent, Carthage romaine, pp. 325 ff. Benson, Cyprian, p. 4, cites Gregory Naz., Oratio xxiv, which states that Cyprian was a member tēs Boulēs. But Gregory cannot be used in isolation. C.E. Freppel, Saint Cyprien et l'église d'Afrique au IIIe siècle (Paris, 1865) p. 63, gives Cyprian senatorial rank, but there is no evidence for this. The whole work is strongly Catholic in prejudice. Altaner-Stuiber, Pat., p. 172, avoids the question. Monceaux, HAC, p. 204, is essentially right when he states that Cyprian "devait appartenir à la haute bourgeoisie locale".
2. Vita 14.3.
3. An argument could be made that it was the product of his career rather than family ties that resulted in these contacts. But in connection with the other information available, positing curial rank would seem the most reasonable solution.
4. For the confusion with Cyprian of

fails to be specific, and only adds that Cyprian was devoted to secular studies.[1] Lactantius is more explicit, but the purely literary context of his information creates the suspicion that he might have been suppressing other aspects of Cyprian's career to stress his importance as a pagan rhetorician. One could, after all, teach rhetoric and still practice it as an advocate.[2] In fact the general practice, as

---

4. (cont'd) Antioch, supra p. 104, n. 3. This also occurs in Prudentius, Peri Steph. 13. Similar charges of magical practices were levelled against Apuleius and some Greek Sophists. For the Greeks, see G.W. Bowersock, Greek Sophists in the Roman Empire (Oxford, 1969), p. 116. A major part of Apuleius' apology is devoted to the refutation of a charge of magical practices.

1. Vita 2.2. The usual interpretation is that Cyprian was a rhetor and a lawyer. See Benson, Cyprian, pp. 46 ff. See also Monceaux, HAC, p. 204. Quasten, Pat., p. 341, avoids the problem by not being specific. But L. Bayard, St. Cyprien: Correspondance[2] (2 vols. Paris, 1945), Vol. I, p. x, and Altaner-Stuiber, Pat., p. 171, regard Cyprian as a rhetor only. So P. de Labriolle, Histoire de la littérature latine chrétienne[5], Collection d'études anciennes (2 vols. Paris, 1947), Vol. I, p. 203.

2. Lactantius, Div. Inst. 2.1. See G.W. Clarke, "The Secular Profession of St. Cyprian of Carthage", Latomus 24 (1965), p. 635, in his excellent collection of the evidence points out that previous scholars have failed to notice the difference between an advocatus and a juris consultus. The

108

indicated by the Greek Sophists in the East, would indicate that practice as a rhetorician was normally combined with some sort of work in the courts, even if only as an occasional event.[1]

Jerome speaks only of the bishop's rhetorical career.[2] He states that Cyprian obtained glory as a speaker and that he taught rhetoric at Carthage.[3] In his re-working of Eusebius' chronicle, he notes again that Cyprian was a rhetorician but

---

2. (cont'd) latter would be hard to combine with a career as a rhetor, while the former has such precedents. For the difference, see F. Schulz, History of Roman Legal Science (Oxford, 1946), p. 71. If Cyprian was a lawyer, he was an advocatus. Clarke, "Secular Profession", argues that the edict of Diocletian shows the difference between rhetors and members of the legal professions. (For the edict, see S. Lauffer (ed.), Diokletians Preisedikt, Texte und Kommentare, 5 (Berlin, 1971), pp. 124-5, items 71-2.) But two mistakes vitiate Clarke's inferences. The edict represents a situation of retrenchment after a long period of anarchy. Cyprian's career falls before it, so that inferences to his career from the edict are not necessarily true. Secondly, the edict sets fees for profes-sionals. Presumably, further information would be necessary to exclude the practice of law by a rhetor. All the edict does is set his fees if he does take a case, it does not exclude his practice as an advocatus. Arnobius, Adv. Nat. 2.5 adds nothing to this problem's solution.

1. On the practice in the East, see Bowersock, Greek Sophists, pp. 12 ff.
2. Jerome, Vir. Ill. 67.
3. PL 25, 1143.

109

adds nothing regarding any legal activities.[1] Jerome's testimony is of some weight, if we remember his contact with the _notarius_ of Cyprian through Paul of Concordia.[2]

The sources for the legal aspect of Cyprian's career are equally exiguous. Augustine is the only informant. Cyprian had turned that magnificent instrument of his eloquence to the service of the Church. His wonderful voice, which had previously been accustomed to sharpening the contests of forensic mendacity, was now turned to the praise of martyrs and to the destruction of devils.[3] This is a possible hint of Cyprian's activities in the legal sphere. But there is no evidence that Augustine had information now lost to us and unknown to Jerome.[4]

The most difficult evidence of all is the _Ad Donatum_. Written soon after Cyprian's conversion and baptism, this dialogue is a statement of his disappointment in and rejection of the secular world in which he

---

1. Under Olympiad 208.
2. Jerome, _Vir. Ill._ 67. See also _supra_ p. 101.
3. Augustine, _Sermo_ 312.4: "Ut tantae vocis...quae forensium mendaciorum certamina solebat acuere", _PL_ 38, 1421.
4. A good study of the relationship of Cyprian to Augustine is in C.G. Goetz, _Geschichte der Cyprianischen Literatur_ (Basel, 1891). A good selection of _testimonia_ by Augustine on Cyprian is given by Harnack, _GAL_ I, 2nd half-volume, pp. 706-13. Augustine, _Sermo_ 312, consists, for the most part, of generalities which seem based on Pontius, on the writings of Cyprian, and on Augustine's own personal knowledge of the Carthaginian monument to Cyprian.

had played a distinguished part, and an affirmation of his new faith.[1] The setting is modeled on that of the _Octavius_. Since we know that Minucius was a _causidicus_ for at least part of his career at Rome and that this enters into the setting of the dialogue, this raises the question as to whether formal imitation resulted in Cyprian consciously changing his own circumstances to conform to the pattern set by the _Octavius_. The answer would seem to be negative. Where other models can be found for Cyprian's treatises, he always utilized their elements in his own way.[2] Thus we can take the statements of the _Ad Donatum_ as relevant to Cyprian's own career, and not simply reflections of the _Octavius_.

Unfortunately the _Ad Donatum_ presents little information on Cyprian's activities. The opening of the treatise refers to the autumn vacation when the vintage festival invites relaxation.[3] This has been taken as a reference to the legal recess, but rhetorical schools also closed during the same period and so no deduction can be

---

1. It may even have taken place in the gardens that are mentioned in the _Vita_ as his property. For a more detailed discussion, see _infra_ pp. 127 f.

2. The reference is to Tertullian. For a discussion of this relationship, see _infra_ p.289. Clarke, "Secular Profession", p. 633, calls the _Ad Donatum_ a highly stylized _apologia_ for his conversion, and he dismisses its evidence as vague and consisting of rhetorical generalities.

3. _Ad Don._ 1/3.4-6.

111

made.[1] Further, in his prologue contrasting the simplicity necessary for discussing the Word of God with the false eloquence of secular pursuits, Cyprian couples the law courts and the rostrum as centres of secular eloquence. The context places the expressions in iudiciis and pro rostra closely with Cyprian's statements about the extent of his own eloquence. This is thin, but nevertheless possible, support for some oratorical display in the Carthaginian law courts. Though in the last instance the passage is based on the Octavius, the chain of association may at least point in the direction of some legal activity on the part of the future bishop.[2] The only other hint that the treatise supplies is in Cyprian's discussion of the evils of the pagan world. Among them he cites the corruption in the law courts. In the presence of the Twelve Tables, injustice displaces fair dealing and equity is sold. This is the one reference we have to the presence of the ancient Roman legal code in the Carthaginian Forum. The references are more detailed than other Cyprianic condem-

---

1. For the legal recess, see p. 59, n. 4. For the closing of the schools of rhetoric, Augustine, Conf. 9.2. But notice the close connection with the legal recess which Augustine himself makes. This reference, plus Sermo 312.4, led Monceaux, HAC, p. 204, to his deduction about Cyprian.
2. Ad Don. 2.4/10. Hartel rejects the reading of contione, which is not in manuscript S and breaks the rhythm of the construction. The passage is most likely based on the Octavius (14.3-4) though this section does not include mention of iudicia and the rostra.

nations dealing with private vice, mainly sexual in nature, and the gladiatorial games.[1] The treatise is highly rhetorical, and these statements can be interpreted as part of a general condemnation; but its greater detail points in the direction of some legal activities, though as a rhetor Cyprian's connection would have been close without his actual participation in legal proceedings. Cyprian certainly taught rhetoric, but the question remains open as to whether he took part in judicial proceedings.[2]

The uncertain details of Cyprian's life before his conversion may take on some life by a comparison with the similar career of another great African bishop. Though falling a hundred and fifty years later, Augustine's rhetorical career may provide some flesh for the skeletal evidence we have for the bishop of Carthage.[3] Augustine was born of a poor family in 354 at Thagaste in the old province of Numidia. His father turned to the patronage of a local notable, Romanianus.[4] The contrast in means and social status with Cyprian is apparent. But if a patron could be found, education provided a ticket to a

---

1. <u>Ad Don.</u> 10/11.11 ff.
2. This undermines the position of A. Beck, <u>Römisches Recht bei Tertullian und Cyprian</u>, <u>Schriften der Königsberger gelehrten Gesellschaft</u>, Geisteswiss. Kl., 7, hft. 2 (1930), pp. 22-9.
3. The main source of information is, of course, the <u>Confessiones</u>. The standard biography is by P. Brown, <u>Augustine of Hippo</u> (London, 1967). An extensive bibliography on Augustine may be found there.
4. His father was Patricius, a <u>tenuis municeps</u>, <u>Conf.</u> 2.3.5.

113

career in teaching and perhaps administration. Cyprian abandoned a promising career.[1]

Augustine's early career at the lower levels in Thagaste concentrated on the Latin classics. Cicero, Virgil, Sallust and Terence were the only authors to whom great attention was paid.[2] The curriculum was devoted to the imitation of classical style and literary subjects. All else was neglected.[3] The education resulted in a facility and felicity of expression hard to equal by any other method. Most importantly it firmly tied the pupil into the antique literary traditions and severely subordinated innovation to the interest of preservation and perfection.

At the age of fifteen Augustine had finished his preparation and was installed at a provincial university at Madauros, the home of Apuleius. His education contrasted strongly with that of Apuleius, the African representative of the Second Sophistic. Augustine knew no Greek, while Apuleius served as a mediator for Greek literary fashions in North Africa and was himself bilingual.

Finally in 371 at the age of seventeen, Augustine arrived in the metropolis of Roman Africa to continue his education in rhetoric. The city which Augustine characterized as a "hissing cauldron of lusts" could still vie with Alexandria for second place among the cities of the Empire. In the West, outside of Rome it had no

---

1. _Vita_ 2.7.
2. For standard curriculum, see Marrou, _Histoire de l'éducation_, pp. 389 ff.
3. See Marrou, Ibid., p. 407.

114

rival.[1]

Augustine's ambition was like that of Cyprian, to excel in the art of speaking; but among the authors prescribed for the course it was Cicero, in his Hortensius, who made the most singular impression on him.[2] The effect of Cicero's exhortation to philosophy on the young Augustine was immense. No records preserve evidence that classical philosophy served as a preparation for Cyprian's conversion.[3]

From his nineteenth until his twenty-eighth year, Augustine gravitated towards rhetoric as Cyprian had before him. The search for honour and distinction plagued his mind and the minds of his fellow academics. They competed for prizes for poetry - presumably wreathes won in oratorical competitions - and for the applause of an audience.[4] Teaching gave the young rhetor qualms. Rhetoric taught success in debate, but success did not always equal the justice of a case.

Though separated by a large gap in time, the two African rhetoricians and future bishops cast some light upon each other. The academic curriculum of both would have been similar. Each was a product of an antique tradition of pagan rhetoric which deeply influenced his style in his Christian productions. The affinity is evident in the comments of the bishop of

---

1. A cauldron of lust: Conf. 3.2.1. For a judicious summary to the background of Augustine's statement, see Brown, Augustine of Hippo, pp. 38-9.
2. Augustine, Conf. 3.4.
3. Ibid.
4. Ibid, 4.1.

115

Hippo on his earlier counterpart.[1] Each shared a feeling of unfulfillment, though Cyprian, not having the Christian atmosphere that Augustine had been nurtured in, took far longer to realize the insufficiency of his manner of life. Each differed in temperament and in intellectual direction. Augustine was a thinker, a man searching to solve the problems of life and existence. Cyprian was an administrator; once he had discarded the system of values in which he had been reared, he found in Christianity a creed which basically answered his questions. Existence and its justification were no longer a problem for him. Augustine, however, found in Christianity a starting point on which to base future speculation. But the resemblances between the two will allow us to use Augustine as a guide to give substance to a portion of Cyprian's life which is almost totally absent from the sources.[2] The preoccupations of Cyprian as bishop effaced his success as rhetor.

What makes a man convert, give up a promising career, and join a sect that is despised and disturbing to his former friends? Why did Cyprian in particular

---

1. See the _testimonia_ in Harnack, _GAL_, I, 2nd half-volume, pp. 706-13.
2. The _Confessiones_ of Augustine is an example of the difference. The closest thing we have to an autobiographical statement for Cyprian is the _Ad Donatum_, but the contrast in the handling of the author's own thoughts and feelings is remarkable. Augustine's is a personal statement of a man's search for faith and understanding. The _Ad Donatum_ preserves little but generalized and highly stylized expressions of emotion.

116

convert? The answers involve certain contradictions in our sources.[1]

Pontius records little of the actual
conversion. He presents Cyprian's transition
as a smooth one: first the reading and study
of the sacred writings; then the break-
through from darkness into light.[2] The aged
presbyter, Caecilianus, aided in the process.
This man, himself of exemplary piety,
became for Cyprian the parent of his new way
of life.[3]

Jerome portrays the transition just as
simply as Pontius: Cyprian, who had
previously been an adsertor idolatriae, was
so moved by the story of Jonah that he
immediately converted from his past form of

---

1. The best study of the phenomenon of
conversion is A.D. Nock, Conversion. The Old
and the New in Religion from Alexander the
Great to Augustine of Hippo (Oxford, 1933).
E.R. Dodds, Pagan and Christian in an Age of
Anxiety. Some Aspects of Religious
Experience from Marcus Aurelius to Constantine (Cambridge, 1965) pp. 133 ff., leans
too heavily on psychological method and
Jungian presuppositions. The conditions
for conversion listed are neither compelling
nor, as Dodds admits, confined to Christianity. In Cyprian's case, conversion
brought him into intense contact with the
world, not withdrawal from it.

2. Vita 2.3.

3. Vita 4.1. The passage has been
successfully changed from the old reading of
de nobis to de novis by L. Bayard, "Notes
sur la Vita Cypriani et sur Lucianus", RP
N.S. 38 (1914), pp. 206-10, and adopted by
Pellegrino in his edition, p. 108.

117

life.[1] The context may be supplied by Jerome to emphasize the contrast in Cyprian's conversion, and there may be little substance to it. His commentary is, after all, on Jonah. Both Jerome and Pontius have an ulterior purpose in their portrayal of the important convert. The Ad Donatum supplies a more convincing explanation of Cyprian's renunciation of his past.

Composed soon after his baptism, around 245, and probably set in hortis suis, the treatise is a dialogue with an old friend who had been educated with Cyprian and had remained his close friend as Cyprian's career progressed.[2] Both men had become Christians, perhaps at the same time. Cyprian claims in his exposition that Donatus knows the cleansing effect of Christianity. The death of evil and the birth of virtue were experiences shared by both.[3] Donatus

---

1. Jerome, Comm. in Iohan. 3. As Clarke, "Secular Profession", p. 637, has pointed out, it is illegitimate to use this phrase of Jerome as an indication of profession. The theme of this section of the commentary tells against such an interpretation.

2. They had been pupils together apud oratorem, Hartel, CSEL 3, part 3, Ep. 1/272.

3. Ad Don. 4/6.11-2. L.A. Lenain de Tillemont, Memoires pour servir à l'histoire ecclésiastique des six premiers siècles (Venice, 1732), IV, pp. 601-3, had long ago noticed the discrepancy between the seemingly effortless conversion registered by the Vita and the soul-searching one in the Ad Donatum. Also from this Audollent, Carthage romaine, p. 43, n. 7, had hypothesized a slow conversion. Monceaux, HAC, p. 205, simply neglects the question, as does Benson,

118

must now keep to the way of innocence placing all his trust in God. Now a celestial warrior, Donatus must maintain his contact by prayer and reading.[1] The advice and precepts with which Cyprian instructed Donatus would surely indicate the superior position of the former as a convert to the new faith. There may have been mutual interchange while the two pagans converted, but it appears that Cyprian was spiritual instructor to Donatus.[2] Pontius makes no mentions of Donatus. His stress upon purely Christian inspiration explains this: pagan associations are better glossed over or omitted when defending a Christian against other Christians.[3]

---

3. (cont'd) Cyprian. A more original explanation is given by Freppel, Saint Cyprien, p. 67, who sees the action of Providence. Pellegrino, Vita, p. 97, in his notes to Vita 2.4, tries to harmonize the account of the Vita with that of the Ad Donatum, by showing the similarity of expression between Ad Don. 4 and Vita 2.3, but the reference is too general. Pontius, in fact, omits any detailed discussion of the conversion, and concentrates instead on the fidei suae prima rudimenta - perhaps a hint that all was not smooth passage for Cyprian.

1. Ad Don. 3/5.1-20; 5/7.3-8.8; 15/15.15-16.3; 16/16.4-14.

2. Donatus was probably a fellow rhetorician, as Schanz-Hosius, p. 340, conjectures.

3. The question arises as to whether Donatus can be identified with any of the other Donati mentioned in the Cyprianic corpus. The name is frequent among Christians in Africa and was to be used widely in the next century; it occurs on six occasions

Cyprian portrays his conversion as the result of a long and arduous disillusionment with the world of paganism. He had, as have many men since, lost his bearings in life. The accustomed satisfactions and pleasures no longer held appeal. The attractions of public life, the crowds of clientes, the banqueting - all of the material pleasures which he had once highly valued - began to feel like endless meanderings.[1] But intense as·was his dissatisfaction, so was its remedy seemingly impossible to obtain.[2] Cyprian stresses the carnal, but not neces-

---

3. (cont'd) in Cyprian's works. The bishop preceding Cyprian can be safely ruled out (Ep. 59.10/677.17). The name also occurs among the bishops mentioned in the headings of Ep. 57 and 70. Again a bishop at the council of September 1, 256, Donatus from Cibaliana (SE 55); an enemy of Cyprian's election who was a presbyter (Ep. 14.4/512. 16); the last a martyr in the Decian Persecution (Ep. 22.2/534.20). Monceaux, HAC, pp. 260-1, accepts the five contemporary references as representing five separate individuals. But the reference to the bishop in SE 55, and the headings of Ep. 57 and 70, may point to the same individual. If so, his bishopric in Cibaliana would rule out his having been identical with the addressee of the Ad Donatum. The martyr died at Rome, so that his identification with our Donatus is extremely unlikely. Donatus is not referred to elsewhere in the Cyprianic corpus. The reason why, if it were known, might tell us more about the bishop. The correspondence is incomplete, however, and nothing should be deduced from his absence.
1. Ad Don. 3/5.1-21.
2. Ad Don. 4/5.21 ff.

120

sarily the sexual aspects of life: the world is covered with a cloud of obscurity that obliterates the truth through the veil of the flesh. This was done by evil spirits and impure demons that confound and confuse a man's soul.[1] To display better the evils of a world gone mad, Cyprian asks his friend to imagine himself transported to a high mountain peak so that he might see comprehensively the evils of the world. Lucianus had used the device effectively.[2] Below all is chaos, a world in confusion. Land and sea are beset with piracy and robbery. Blood flows wholesale; a single murder is a crime, but murder on a grand scale brings reward and honour.[3]

After a general execration, Cyprian turns to specific types of so-called pleasurable pursuits. The gladiatorial games, particularly reprehensible to a Christian, come in for their share of abuse. Tertullian had given the history of their development and condemned them as a cultured form of cruelty.[4] What offended Cyprian was that the art of murder was taught. Men of

---

1. Ad Don. 5/7.15-16.
2. Ad Don. 6/8.9-10; Lucianus, Icar.. For a discussion of his historical significance, see Bowersock, Greek Sophists, at p. 116.
3. Ad Don. 6/8.14 ff.
4. Tertullian, De Spect. 12. For his sources, Barnes, Tert., p. 95, and references there. But dislike was not a Christian monopoly, and pagans registered their disgust as well, see Seneca, Ep. Morales 7.3-5. For gladiators in the East, see L. Robert, Les gladiateurs dans l'Orient Grec, Bibliothèque de l'Ecole des Hautes Etudes, 278 (Paris, 1940).

121

adult age, well-clothed, and presumably of high station came forward willingly to participate.[1] Worse yet, the natural ties of family bonds were violated. The father of the contestant, his sisters and brothers, would look on enjoying the spectacle while forgetting the bloodshed.[2] Other aspects of pagan life carry their own contagion. The theatre renews the lessons of crime for each succeeding generation. Pagan gods are portrayed as models of lust, adultery and crime. Jupiter, supreme in power and dominion, is also supreme in vice. Such a religion can only lead to degradation. Men imitate the deities they worship and adore.[3]

---

1. Ad Don. 7. Even Christianity, with its emphasis on brotherhood, failed to break the structure of a society which was rigidly tied to class distinctions. Like Stoicism, it found the means to accomodate a basically egalitarian ideal with an unegalitarian social milieu. The defense against the low status of Christian recruits found in Origen, Contra Celsum 3.15 and Oct. 9 ff. shows Christian acceptance. One would expect a man of Cyprian's background to be sensitive on this point.
2. Ad Don. 7/8.22-29.
3. Ad Don. 8/9.15-10.23. See also Tertullian, De Spect. 10 on this topic. A treatise, perhaps contemporary with the Ad Donatum, is the De Spectaculis, which Hartel included in his appendix, CSEL 3, part 3, 3-13. For manuscripts, see Harnack, GAL, I, 2nd half-volume, p. 717. The work is strongly dependent on the De Spectaculis of Tertullian, especially the opening sections. There is also some resemblance with the Ad Donatum, see O. Bardenhewer, Geschichte der altkirchlichen Literatur

But the decay of morals was not confined to the gladiatorial games or to the theatre. Vice flourished behind walls and locked doors.[1] With such degradation, surely the Forum, the centre of justice, would be preserved untouched. But even here evil is rampant.[2] Judicial decisions are sold by the judge. Guilt is so common that innocence is now considered a crime. Law has come to terms with crime: as long as the deed is public, it is not a crime, Shame and integrity have fled.[3]

Even the things that pagans value are basically of no worth, or, at worst, positively harmful. High honour and position bring with them care and fear. Power engenders fear, and fear affects the man who uses it. Even the presence of bands of satellites does not bring true protection.[4] Cyprian is here pursuing a topic found

---

3. (cont'd) (5 vols. Freiburg i.Br., 1913-32), Vol. II (1914) p. 493. At any rate, it is simply a derivative work and adds nothing to the Christian discussion of the theatre and its distractions, even if Novatianus is the author. See B. Melin, Studia in corpus Cyprianeum, Commentatio academica (Uppsala, 1946), pp. 67-122. But proof of authorship is almost impossible to establish, and the case is certainly not decisive.

1. Ad Don. 9/10.24-11.10. This reference appears in the Oct. 28.11: libidinoso ore inguinibus inhaerescunt. As Beaujeu suggests, there may be direct borrowing by Cyprian from Minucius, Minucius Félix, lix.

2. Ad Don. 10; Cyprian's career p. 101.

3. Ad Don. 10/11.11-12.14.

4. Ad Don. 13/14.12-23.

123

widespread among the Epicurians. Juvenal had accurately summed up the terrible demands of high office in his <u>Fourth Satire</u>. The insecurity of high position, particularly tyranny, has a long history stretching far back into Greek literature.[1]

For Cyprian, none of the forms of success or pleasure considered part of a normal life had any attraction. The <u>Ad Donatum</u> points to at least part of the answer: success could not bring Cyprian the one quality that makes all else worthwhile. He had failed to obtain security.[2]

> "Things fall apart; the centre
> cannot hold;
> Mere anarchy is loosed upon the
> world...
> The best lack all conviction,
> while the worst
> Are full of passionate intensity."[3]

Only that which is greater than the world can provide the refuge from which man can look upon the vortex of life with safety. If God provides such a refuge, then man is free from all shocks. Man is loosed from the grasp of the mortal and made ready for immortality.[4] A basic theme of the philosophical schools that had dominated

---

1. For references to the Greek material, see T.A. Sinclair, <u>A History of Greek Political Thought</u> (London, 1951).
2. <u>Ad Don.</u> 14/14.24-26. This is the central and most important section for understanding at least part of the reason for Cyprian's conversion.
3. W.B. Yeats, "The Second Coming", in <u>The Collected Poems</u> (New York, 1956).
4. <u>Ad Don.</u> 14/14.24-26 - 15.5.

124

both Greek and Roman thought since Hellenistic times was the question of man's relation to the world around him. How could pain be avoided and virtue practiced when existing conditions were so unpropitious? The Stoic and Cynic answer had been the attainment of apatheia, freedom from evil passions and the absence of disturbance from external events.[1] But such an answer was of little use to those who could not disengage their personalities from the events of their lives. Even the deification of nature added nothing for the devotee. It still resulted in the same essential helplessness.[2] The message that the schools offered admitted the misery of existence without solving its problems.[3]

Christianity offered an answer to helplessness by making endurance into a

---

1. For a discussion, see L. Edelstein, The Meaning of Stoicism, Martin Classical Lectures, 21 (Cambridge, Mass., 1966) pp. 1-19. Dodds, Pagan and Christian, p. 18, would ascribe the terrible wave of pessimism that swept over the West to a Gnostic tendency that had non-Hellenic roots. But the leading Hellenistic schools of thought had already developed the basic concept of withdrawal. The first centuries of the Empire intensified the scope and ramifications of this feeling, but withdrawal does not lie outside the Hellenic tradition.

2. See A.M.J. Festugière, Personal Religion Among the Greeks, Sather Classical Lectures, 26 (Berkeley and Los Angeles, 1954), pp. 104-9, on some of the implications of the Stoic concept of nature for the individual. See also Marcus Aurel., Med. 12.36.

3. See Marcus Aurel., Med. 2.17.

positive program. While the Stoic or Cynic could expect little after faithfully following his creed, the Christian could look forward to eternal life and blessedness. Christianity offered a less austere path to salvation.

What motivated the feelings of anarchy and meaninglessness in Cyprian that made chaos of the values of his past life?[1] No attempt is made here to seek a simple equation between the events of 238 and Cyprian's conversion; rather, the combination of his own dissatisfaction, the troubles of 238, and the influence of Minucius Felix and Tertullian seem to have acted together as catalysts on a man trying to escape the bonds of mortality and the physical world. An instructive parallel in the opposite direction is Voltaire, who found that his Deism could not endure the test of the Lisbon earthquake of 1755. His poem on that event marked his transition from the typical rational Deism of the 18th century to a position which can only be characterized as atheism.[2]

The influence of Minucius Felix and Tertullian may have directed Cyprian to the

---

1. Nock, Conversion, p. 5, recognizes that conquest or invasion, i.e., external circumstances, may have great effect on man's attitude toward religion and in setting the stage for the phenomenon of conversion. As he points out (p. 15), the desire to escape from mortality and the unbending will of fate are important ingredients. Thus, the drive to bring into being a "new man" is the striking feature of the Ad Donatum.

2. See Theodore Besterman, Voltaire (New York, 1969), pp. 351 ff.

126

new religion. They may even have set him on the course leading to conversion. To a man with rhetorical training, the Christian Scriptures could have little attraction.1 For while the evident feeling of chaos that drove him from his past may explain his ultimate rejection of the world, it will not make clear why Cyprian chose Christianity as his particular solution. The Octavius might explain how a man with his background could arrive at a Christian solution. More importantly, the anti-Roman colouring might have appealed to a man who had suffered loss from the actions of an imperial legate.2 From Minucius Felix, the road turned to Tertullian. The ancient evidence, and Cyprian's own works, point to his great familiarity with Tertullian.3 The articles of belief that the Octavius glosses over, insinuating rather than stating, would have been plainly presented to Cyprian together with attacks against unorthodox Christians like Marcion or followers of Valentinus. After this essential grounding in the apologetic and disciplinary treatises, the way was open to approach the Bible with less repugnance.

During his period of study, friendships would be made with Christians eager to help smooth the path of a convert of such importance and talent. Caecilianus may have become acquainted with Cyprian at this time, perhaps guiding him and Donatus in the new

---

1. See Augustine, Conf. 3.5, where the rhetor found that the language of the Bible suffered in comparison with Cicero. See also supra p. 74.
2. Oct. 25-26.
3. Jerome, Vir. Ill. 67. See also Ep. 84.2.

literature and instructing them in the dangers which lay hidden in Tertullian's tortured and brilliant rhetoric.[1] The exact impact of Caecilianus upon Cyprian remains a subject for conjecture. Pontius may have been inclined to exaggerate his impact, being a member of the clergy and interested in stressing the perfect Christianity of his subject. He may have been something less than "amicum animae coaequalem...tamquam novae vitae parentem".[2] The Ad Donatum is directed towards a different purpose. It is essentially an apology for Cyprian's conversion and baptism.[3] Though filled with Christian terminology and ideas, it is directed to Cyprian's former pagan fellows. It displays the thought and the increasing disillusionment of men of the author's own class leading a pagan life. The long sections on the horrors of honour and office are most sensibly aimed at men for whom these were possibilities.[4]

Cyprian's attitude towards his

---

1. Cyprian never mentions Tertullian by name. Perhaps Caecilianus warned him to beware the Montanist emphasis of Tertullian. Using him as a source without naming him would give comfort to the Montanist cause.

2. Vita 4.2.

3. Ad Don. 3/5.6, for reference to Cyprian's baptism as already having taken place when the treatise was written.

4. Monceaux, HAC, p. 261, shows an awareness that the major purpose of the treatise was to detach the reader from the world. So also M. Pellegrino, Studi su l'antica apologetica, Ed. di storia e letteratura (Rome, 1947), p. 110.

128

conversion was passive. The major propulsion towards his new way of life came from God. The act of baptism was like a second birth brought about by the infusion of a light from above. The clouds of darkness were dispelled by the spirit infused from God.[1] Later, when discussing the security brought about by union with God, Cyprian emphasized that it is a gift of God: et gratuitum de Deo munus. In the same way that nature bestows its gifts on all, so the spirit that brings a new life holds out its gift of salvation for all.[2]

Augustine again provides a parallel with the Ad Donatum, as others have already seen.[3] In an agony of indecision, struggling within himself, he left his friend, Alypius, and went to sit alone underneath a tree in the garden. In his inner anguish, he heard the voice of a child nearby repeating the refrain: "Take it and read, take it and read". Augustine took up the Bible, believing that the child's voice had been a divine command and that the answer to his doubts would be found in the first passage he should read. A passage in Matthew put an end to his turmoil and marked the essential turning point in his life.[4]

---

1. Ad Don. 4/6.3-7. On the expression secunda nativitas, see Pellegrino, Vita, p. 94, n. 1. Pontius may be drawing on the Ad Donatum, at Vita 2.3.
2. Ad Don. 14/24-15.14.
3. For example, Monceaux, HAC, p. 263.
4. Augustine, Conf. 8.12. The passage was Matthew 19:21. The method is still followed, and a curious almost contemporary reference to a similar process is the Virgilianae Sortes of the Historia Augusta.

At his own conversion, Augustine manifested the same basic pattern of passivity as Cyprian. Each was heavily influenced by the faith and by the persuasion of an individual heavily committed to Christianity. Caecilianus and Ambrose have at least that much in common. But the early household memories of Augustine, as well as the strong personality of his mother Monica certainly played a part in the process for which there is no parallel in the life of Cyprian.[1] For each, the adoption of Christianity ended a period of doubt and led to the beginning of a new and fruitful career within the Church.

The conclusion of the Ad Donatum is a tribute to the new sense of integration that the former rhetor felt. Cyprian asks Donatus to return home with him, now that the day is almost over.[2] He asks him to join him in a meal temperate but graced with the singing of psalms by Donatus, so that the evening should not lack heavenly grace. The strong sense of peace and contentment would not be lost on readers of the work.

The date of Cyprian's conversion is uncertain. His career as a Christian before his election to the episcopate was extremely short; a date around 245 would

---

4. (cont'd) See for example SHA Hadr. 2.8. On the sortes, R. Syme, Ammianus and the Historia Augusta (Oxford, 1968), p. 127.

1. See Nock, Conversion, p. 266, on this facet of Augustine's conversion.

2. Ad Don. 16. The descent of the sun is a common device on which to end dialogues. So Cicero, De Nat. Deor. 3.40 and Macrobius, Sat. 6.4.8.

130

seem to be approximately accurate.[1] The baptism may have occurred at Easter. According to Tertullian, Easter was the usual time for this ceremony, and Easter 245 or 246 would seem reasonable.[2] How long Cyprian hesitated in study before he took the final step can be conjectured as having been of some duration. His deep knowledge of Tertullian manifested in his first treatise, as well as his free use of the document and his extensive quotations would imply a period of some study. The revolt of 238 may have started the reaction against pagan society which culminated in baptism seven or eight years later.

Cyprian's break was not total. The Vita reports that many of his former pagan associates, men of high rank, offered him support and sanctuary should he choose to flee the Valerianic Persecution.[3] The Ad

---

1. The date can only be reconstructed from the terminus for the beginning of Cyprian's episcopate, and the information available from Pontius, Vita 3.4 and 5.1. Jerome, Vir. Ill. 67 seems to depend on Pontius here. Monceaux, HAC, p. 205, is probably correct to assign the conversion to 245 or 246. For the beginning of the episcopate, see infra p. 138.

2. The suggestion of Easter for Cyprian's baptism is Benson's, Cyprian, p. 13. The only problem is Cyprian's later career in the clergy. The extraordinary speed with which he passed through the various grades may indicate that ordinary practice, even in baptism, did not apply to him. Perhaps for such an important convert, procedures could be modified by request.

3. Vita 14.3. Monceaux, HAC, p. 205, tends to overestimate the impact of Cyprian's

131

Donatum may certainly be viewed as his _apologia_ for the conversion.

Even before his baptism, he decided that the most efficacious means of pursuing divine favour was renouncing all the allurements of the flesh.[1] He felt that if continence was observed, his faculties would preserve their full capacity for divine illumination. Christian repugnance to sexuality is not unusual in this period. The anti-sexual attitude in the _Ad Donatum_ gives further support to Pontius. To a great extent, this constituted a rejection of the material world in its most evident and personal form.[2] For a man for whom biography preserves no record of family, the sacrifice may not have been so great. Augustine, however, for a variety of reasons, found continence a harder yoke to bear.[3]

To mark the beginnings of his new way of life, Cyprian disposed of a large amount

---

3. (cont'd) conversion. If the scandal at Carthage was so great, surely by 257 and after a decade of separation the behaviour of the local notables mentioned by the _Vita_ would be inexplicable.

1. _Vita_ 2.4-5. That this resolution took place before his conversion is stated by Pontius, who places it "inter fidei suae prima rudimenta...nondum secunda nativitas novum hominem splendore toto divinae lucis oculaverat". The reference at 2.5 must be to baptism. Therefore, the resolution took place, it would seem, prior to that ceremony.

2. _Ad Don._ 9/10.24-11.10. For the rejection, see Dodds, _Pagan and Christian_, pp. 1 ff.

3. Augustine, _Conf._ 10.30.

of his personal property to provide for the maintenance of the poor.[1] However, the *Vita* and the other sources differ on this point. The manuscripts offer a variety of readings. The most recent editor has adopted *tota pretia* which would lead one to conclude that Cyprian sold (all?) of his wealth.[2] But this inference is open to interpretation. The text adopted by Pellegrino (2.1) runs:

> "Distractis rebus suis ad
> indigentium multorum pacem
> sustinendam, tota pretia
> dispensans..."

It may be that Cyprian first sold all his goods (*distractis rebus suis*) and then took the proceeds and gave them to the poor (*tota pretia dispensans*). Jerome seems to have copied the *Vita* stating that Cyprian disposed of *totam substantiam suam*.[3] The question of Cyprian's remaining assets thus depends on the phrase *distractis rebus suis*, which unfortunately is not susceptible to definite interpretation.

---

1. *Vita* 2.7.
2. Pellegrino, *Vita*, p. 98, prints *tota pretia*, whereas the text of Hartel reads *tota prope pretia*, based on his emendation of manuscript T (Reginensis 118 of the 9th century) which reads *tota pro pretia*. Thus Hartel's emendation (*prope* from *pro*) is quite reasonable.
3. Jerome, *Vir. Ill.* 67. Jerome's manuscript of the *Vita* may have read *tota pretia*. So the use by Monceaux, *HAC*, p. 207, and Bayard, "Notes sur la *Vita*", p. 276, of Jerome's reading for support against Hartel's conjecture is justified.

Other sources would indicate that Cyprian retained a portion of his former wealth. At the beginning of his exile during the Decian Persecution, he asked the clergy of Carthage to be especially solicitous for the poor, explaining that he had deposited money from his own resources for this purpose with Rogatianus.[1] Again, in writing to Florentius, Cyprian mentions an edict of prescription against his property: "Si quis tenet possidet de bonis Caecili Cypriani Episcopi Christianorum".[2] If Pontius wrote tota pretia, thereby suggesting that Cyprian sold all his wealth, it would seem that he was exaggerating Cyprian's sacrifice to poverty. He may in fact have corrected himself later. On his return to Carthage, Cyprian took up residence in the very gardens which he had sold for the maintenance of the poor, which had been restored by the grace of God, and which he would have sold again for the sake of the poor had he not been prevented from doing so by the persecution.[3] Pontius' desire to compare his hero favourably with Biblical examples, and perhaps himself slightly jealous over the new convert's high economic and social standing, probably led him to overestimate Cyprian's attractions to poverty.[4]

Cyprian must have faced a problem with regard to his former profession which, though

---

1. Ep. 7/485.11: de quantitate mea propria.
2. Ep. 66.4/729.15-16.
3. Vita 15.1 and AP 2.2.
4. See Corssen, "Das Martyrium", p. 296. Some of the manuscripts preserve the reading praedia, see Hartel, ap. crit., xcii.

involved strictly with literature, still bound him closely to pagan mythology.[1] The evidence points to his general repudiation of this literature with his conversion to Christianity. While citations from the body of pagan literature abound in Tertullian, they are almost entirely absent from Cyprian's writings.[2] This does not mean, however, that Cyprian lost his ability to use secular rhetoric for Christian purposes.

Progress came quickly to the neophyte. Soon after the conversion, he received the office of presbyter.[3] Given his influence and the prize that his conversion was for the Christian community, a short duration before promotion in the ecclesiastical hierarchy is reasonable.[4] Perhaps the

---

1. The difficulty of dealing with pagan literature remained a central problem for Christians down through the Middle Ages. See R.R. Bolgar, The Classical Heritage (New York, 1964), p. 45; E.R. Curtius, European Literature and the Latin Middle Ages (New York, 1953), trans. W.R. Trask, pp. 65 ff.
2. For these, De Bono Pat., 1/397.1-12.
3. Vita 3.3: presbyterium vel sacerdotium statim accepit. Jerome, Vir. Ill. 67: post non multum temporis adlectus in presbyterium.
4. Pellegrino, Vita, p. 104, n. 6, thinks that the statim of Pontius should be taken with discretion, citing Jerome's expression which implies a more gradual rise. But even if Pontius exaggerates, the Vita was composed for an audience that knew of Cyprian's career and the rapidity of his advancement. His position and later election to the episcopate all presuppose a

135

advancement took place in 246 or 247, approximately one year after his conversion.[1]

The _Vita_ stresses the virtues of the presbyter, portraying his exemplary life as a devout Christian.[2] Cyprian would read the Scriptures closely, selecting for special study those who were singled out for approval by God. Then, learning what the individual had done to merit God's pleasure, he would teach that this deed must be emulated. So Job was glorified for his unshatterable faith. No one among the poor or unfortunate was turned away from Job's door without his granting whatever help he could give. Even his possession of a wife did not bend him from his inflexible course of virtue.[3]

---

4. (cont'd) career of quick advancement, and Pontius' notice, while it cannot be entirely checked, should be taken at face value, unless there is a contrary indication. Jerome's source at this point may well have been Pontius, and he should not be accorded preference if he was attempting to state a more leisurely chronology. There is no apparent contradiction, at least, between his information and that of Pontius.

1. Monceaux, _HAC_, p. 208, leaves the date open. Benson, _Cyprian_, p. 22, opts for 247, based on his calculation of the beginning of Cyprian's episcopate.

2. So the paradigms of Philip, at _Vita_ 3.2, from _Tim._ 3:6, and Job, _Vita_ 3.6.

3. _Vita_ 3.4-9. There seems embedded in the _Vita_ at this point a fragment of Cyprian, as had already been recognized as extending from 3.7 to the words _haec debent facere dicebat, qui Deo placere desiderant_. Harnack, "Das Leben", note _ad loc._, thinks this is a stenographic account of a sermon of Cyprian. But it may be an

Sometime during his tenure of the presbyterate Caecilianus, the priest who had been instrumental in his conversion, died.[1] During his last hours he asked that Cyprian be responsible for his family's welfare.[2]

This is sparse detail in which to set the background for Cyprian's rise to the highest grade of the Carthaginian Church. His importance as a convert of high social standing has already been noted, and his

---

3. (cont'd) imitation of Cyprian by Pontius. Pontius' rhetorical techniques are so similar to Cyprian's that any deduction would be hazardous.

1. Vita 4.1 ff. This has been dated here because of its place in Pontius' narrative, but the evidence is not conclusive. Vita 3.4 points to its occurrence at this time, as it marks the end of Cyprian's activities as a neophyte. The end of this period is marked by Vita 5.1. Bayard's suggestion, "Notes sur la Vita", p. 208, to read de novis instead of de nobis may hint that Pontius has misplaced the episode. Pontius implies that Caecilianus made Cyprian tutor in charge of his family (which, however, was forbidden to priests, as Cyprian remarks in Ep. 1.1/30.8-10). But perhaps Pontius does not refer to a strict tutela, merely to a commendation.

2. Vita 4.3. An informal tutela would perhaps not have violated Church regulation. On the tutela, see H.F. Jolowicz, Historical Introduction to the Study of Roman Law[2] (Cambridge, 1952), pp. 249 ff. Benson, Cyprian, p. 1, mistakenly takes Pontius to mean that Cyprian had been adopted by the aged presbyter, but this was inferred from Benson's

137

oratorical powers found new and influential paths for achievement as he preached in his capacity as presbyter. His association with Caecilianus would also point to influence among the Carthaginian clergy. Once the death of the bishop of Carthage opened the episcopate, the way was open to Cyprian to stand for this office.[1]

The election took place sometime after May 248 and prior to May 249. Justifying himself to Cornelius after May 252, Cyprian mentions that he had served his congregation faithfully in a quadriennial episcopate.[2] The quadriennium in the Roman system of counting could signify any period from three years and a day to four years less a day.[3] His election generated great heat in Carthage. Perhaps Cyprian's career had

---

2. (cont'd) incorrect use of the name Caecilius.

1. Supra p. 17.

2. Ep. 59.6/673.10-11: Plebi suae in episcopatu quadriennio iam probatus. The letter is dated by the reference to a council in chapter 10, Idibus Maiis, to sometime after May 15, 252. For a further discussion, see Appendix V.

3. For an interesting analysis of Roman dating, see G.V. Sumner, "Germanicus and Drusus Caesar", Latomus 26 (1967), pp. 413-21. Benson, Cyprian, p. 24, basically agrees with this dating. Monceaux, HAC, p. 208, dates the election to the first months of 249. But there is no warrant for delimiting the quadriennium more than Benson has done. Tillemont, Memoires, pp. 54-5, proposed the year 248, which is still a distinct possibility, but again he tried for too high a level of precision.

138

advanced too quickly for some. In the election a group of five presbyters opposed him.[1] Pontius is astounded at their reconciliation with the bishop, but Cyprian informs us that the feud engendered by the election not only endured but later served to generate new disputes.[2] Pontius does not preserve the names of the five, but some names can be restored from Cyprian's correspondence. In the last letter written in his first exile to his congregation at Carthage, he complains that it was due to the malignity of certain presbyters that he could not return to his see before Easter 251.[3] These men were motivated by their ancient hatred for him. Conscious of their conspiracy against his election, they had retained their hatred for the man elected by the judgment of God and the favour of the people.[4] Cyprian could not resist comparing them to the five men selected to help carry out the recent persecution.[5] He identifies one of the five as the presbyter Fortunatus.[6] Involved along with Fortunatus

---

1. <u>Vita</u> 5.6. For their number, see Ep. 59.9/676.5. These are surely the men meant in the <u>Vita</u>.

2. <u>Vita</u> 5.6 emphasizes the miraculous victory of Cyprian over his past enemies. These men must have either been dead or absent from the minds of the audience when Pontius wrote the <u>Vita</u>. Otherwise, even in a panegyric, such gross distortion would have occasioned negative comment. For the continued duration of feud, Ep. 59.9/676.5; 43.1/591.5-6.

3. Ep. 43.1/591.6-7.

4. Ep. 43.1/591.8-9.

5. Ep. 43.3/592.7 ff.

6. Ep. 59.9/676.1 ff. The name is

139

as an opponent of Cyprian on the question of re-admitting those who had lapsed was Novatus, a priest who was to play an important role in the troubles that plagued the African Church after the Decian Persecution, and who was to involve himself in the election of a bishop of Rome in opposition to Cornelius.[1] It is surely no accident that these two names appear linked in an early letter of the bishop, written soon after his retreat from Carthage and the beginning of the persecution in 250.[2] Cyprian mentions that his fellow priests, Gordius, Fortunatus, Novatus and Donatus had written to him. Though the content of their correspondence is not specifically stated, it may be safely inferred that it concerned the question of the lapsed, for Cyprian states that it was impossible for him to reply, as he had decided at the onset of his episcopate to do nothing without the advice of the clergy and the consent of the people.[3] Surely these are four of the five men who later opposed Cyprian's return from exile, and who had opposed his election at the beginning of his episcopate.[4]

---

6. (cont'd) quite common among African Christians, see Hartel's index.
1. For a full collection of references and discussion, infra pp. 250 ff.
2. Ep. 14.4/512.16 ff.
3. Ibid.
4. Freppel, Saint Cyprien, p. 75, identifies Florentius as Cyprian's fifth opponent, but Ep. 66 offers no indication that he was connected with this group at the time of the election. In fact, chapter 4 would seem to point to Cyprian's behaviour during the Decian Persecution as the cause

140

Pontius singles out the most important factor in Cyprian's election as the support he received from the plebs.[1] The people were inspired by the Spirit of God. Literally surrounding the candidate's home, they besieged him in their desire for his election.[2] Cyprian also stresses the decisive nature of this support.[3] The excitement and backing of the people were invaluable. Nothing is said of a party of clergy who supported the recent convert for such an elevated position. Though there certainly must have been a certain party, perhaps friends of Caecilianus, no details about them can be found. For a new bishop needed the consecration of some of his fellows.[4] Their actions and names are entirely excluded by the Vita, and Cyprian has preserved no record which identifies them.[5]

The emphasis on the people and the judgment of God in both Cyprian's and the Vita's description of the election would indicate that the five presbyters who opposed his election may have had a certain

---

4. (cont'd) of Florentius' withdrawal from communion with Cyprian.

1. Vita 5.1.
2. Vita 5.4.
3. Ep. 59.6/673.9-10 and 43.1/591.8.
4. Ep. 67.5/739.6-740.8.
5. Only conjecture would be possible. But some of the bishops, after acting solely for Cyprian (such as Caldonius and Fortunatus) and who served as his envoys during the controversy between Novatianus and Cornelius, may have taken part in his election. See Ep. 44 and 45.1/599.12 - 600.14.

justification. Though stressing Cyprian's amazing progress in his new faith for apologetic purposes, Pontius was probably aware that the new convert's election would excite the anger of men who, after a long career in the Church, would certainly have expected that they might succeed to the bishopric when it became vacant.[1] Cyprian himself must have sensed the opposition as a strong force. He withdrew in order to yield to those who were more advanced in the Christian faith, considering himself unworthy for episcopal office. But the opposition of the populace to his withdrawal overrode whatever scruples Cyprian felt on that occasion.[2] Whenever challenged as to the authority of his administration, he has constant recourse to the favour of the people which manifested the will of God as his central justification for holding his office.[3] The strong support of the plebs for his election is understandable. Certainly a man of Cyprian's standing and wealth in the pagan community could offer greater protection and support to the Church than any of the rival candidates that

1. Vita 5.1: "adhuc neophytus et ut putabatur novellus electus est".
2. Vita 5.2. Pontius' account obviously interprets the situation in a light favourable to Cyprian. But his earlier acceptance of rapid advancement, plus his later security in his position, would indicate that humiliter was not the precise characterization for Cyprian's action at the time. So the comparison of Pontius to the ordination of Paul, Acts 9:25; II Cor. 13:33.
3. Vita 5.2.

142

the clergy might provide.[1]

Whatever the opposition, Cyprian soon began to perform his duties. The enmity of the presbyters did not end, but the situation during the first years of office provided little opportunity to find any rallying point for the forces opposed to him.[2]

Sometime before the opening of the persecutions which marked the sixth decade of the third century, the new bishop composed a compendium of Biblical passages for his friend Quirinus.[3] The treatise was in response to Quirinus' request for a compendium of divine teaching on the Jews and on the nature of Christ and Christian belief.[4] Cyprian stresses that the work is not a treatise, but rather material that would serve to form a treatise for some future writer.[5] It would be used as a mnemonic device to facilitate familiarity with the contents of the Bible on these issues.[6]

1. The election of Ambrose provides an illuminating parallel, as seen by Benson, Cyprian, p. 25.
2. For continuing discontent despite the rosy picture of Vita 5.6, see Ep. 43.1/591.7.
3. For the dating of this treatise, see Appendix III. The most recent text of the Testimonia will be found in R. Weber (ed.), Opera Cypriani, Corpus Christianorum, Series Latina 3, Pars 1 (Turnholti, 1972). For a bibliography, see Quasten, Pat., pp. 362-3, and Altaner-Stuiber, Pat., pp. 174-175.
4. Cyprian, Test. 35-6, praefatio.
5. Test. 36.5 ff., praefatio.
6. Test. 36.4, praefatio. On Quirinus' identity, no certain result can be obtained. Monceaux, HAC, p. 284, has suggested that

The first book of the _Testimonia_ (or _Ad Quirinum_) assembles Biblical quotations arranged under twenty-six headings, showing how the Jews had lost the favoured position they once enjoyed with God, and that the only means by which they could obtain pardon was to join the Church and receive baptism, thus erasing the stain that had resulted from the murder of Christ.[1]

Tertullian had handled the Jews harshly. They were the first opponents of the new religion, and their synagogues were the springs from which persecution flowed.[2]

---

6. (cont'd) Quirinus is identical with the Christian mentioned as ministering to the needs of those condemned to the mines during the Valerianic Persecution, Ep. 77.3/835.19 and 78.3/837.18. This is the only Quirinus mentioned in the corpus, and the possibility is strong but less certain than Monceaux implies. The corpus is too incomplete for positive identifications of most of these men. Labriolle, _Histoire de la littérature_, I, p. 230, suggests that the use of _Fili Carissime_ indicates that Quirinus might have been a bishop. But in his first few letters to fellow bishops, Cyprian's most usual term for the salutation is _frater_; see headings of Ep. 2 and 3. Occasionally he will use _filius_ as in his letter to the bishop Magnus. More decisively the _praefatio_, xxxvi to Books 1 and 2 of the _Testimonia_ implies that Quirinus was not a Christian of long standing.

1. _Test._ I.23. Among the pseudo-Cyprianic works included in Hartel's edition is the _Ad Vigilium episcopum de Judaica incredulitate_ and an _Adversus Judaeos_. For the _Ad Vigilium_, see Harnack, _GAL_, pp. 390 ff.

2. Tertullian, _Scorp._ 10.10.

But in Carthage the conflict of Church and synagogue was not a burning issue. Tertullian's treatise against the Jews is a document of discreditation rather than an expression of hatred.[1] Its purpose was to convert pagans rather than to defend Christians. The only Jew who appears as a trouble-maker in Tertullian is an apostate.[2] The Jewish community was not a fierce opponent at Carthage.[2]

For Cyprian the Jews were an even less pressing concern than for Tertullian. Aside from the first book of the Testimonia, they only appear in Biblical contexts for the bishop. No evidence is preserved in the correspondence of any Jewish actions against the Christians. They seem to have had no impact at all upon the Christian community at Carthage. Though Jews were active in the Decian Persecution at Smyrna no mention of them occurs during the trial and execution of Cyprian.[4] Though there was a Jewish

---

1. See Barnes, Tert., p. 92. W. Horbury, "Tertullian on Jews in the Light of De Spectaculis 30.5-6", JThS 23 (1972), pp. 455-8, has argued that Tertullian's De Spec. 30.5-6 reflects contemporary Jewish propaganda against Christ, proving Tertullian's having been influenced by that propaganda. However, this does not seem to affect the argument of Barnes.
2. Tertullian, Ad Nat. 14.2. On the relation of his notice to that of the same figure in Apol. 16.2, see Barnes, Tert., p. 92.
3. Ibid.
4. On the crowds that surrounded Cyprian when he was led to his execution, see Vita 15.4 where only Christians and pagans are mentioned.

145

community in Carthage, their existence seems to have been of no importance for Cyprian, except as a warning that disobedience to God would result in the loss of His favour.[1]

The second book of the Testimonia is on the divinity of Christ and the purpose of his mission. Particularly important is his position as an intermediary to God the Father.[2]

At a later time Cyprian was requested by Quirinus to add a third section to the work on the subject of Christian discipline and life.[3] Indicative of Cyprian's turn of mind, the book dealing with virtue and discipline is the longest and most comprehensive of the three. The bishop's mind ran to disciplinary and administrative questions rather than to the more abstruse questions of theology.

---

1. See Barnes, Tert., pp. 282-5, on the Jewish diaspora in the third century, and especially at Carthage.

2. Test. II, 26-8.

3. Test. III.101, praefatio. Doubts have been raised as to the authenticity of the third book of the Testimonia, especially because there is no mention of the first two books. But the work may have been directed (as a personal favour) to Quirinus. Alternatively, it may have been composed at two different periods; but through its value, it was included in the corpus. The best discussion is by Koch, CU, pp. 187-210. Koch's method establishes that the work is not foreign to Cyprian's style and method, and that the burden of proof is on those who would prove it not authentic. For a full bibliography, see Quasten, Pat., p. 363.

In compiling the Ad Quirinum, Cyprian compiled the first extant Biblical florilegium. Greek Christianity provides no parallel, though there are Jewish predecessors.[1] For one who had taught rhetoric, the compilation of central passages from the most important of all Christian texts would be a natural response. The use of anthologies in the schools provided an obvious example.[2]

Pontius paints a glorious picture of the virtues and appearance of the new bishop before the storms of persecution struck. He was a model of piety, rigour and severity. His discipline was moderated by an intense sense of pity and sanctity. Such brilliance emanated from his countenance that the minds of beholders were confounded by its radiance.[3] The bishop held to the middle road, mixing qualities that merited love and respect. Most of all he cared for the poor. Piety mixed with moderation marked him.[4] The picture may contain exaggeration, but the force of Cyprian's personality is displayed in the few extant documents that deal with the beginning of his episcopate.

Perhaps in the spring of 249, a council was held at Carthage with Cyprian presiding.

---

1. For an excellent study of both pagan and Christian florilegia, see the article of H. Chadwick, "Florilegium", RAC VII, 1131-60.

2. Chadwick, "Florilegium", 1131-43, and Marrou, Histoire de l'éducation, p.246.

3. Vita 6.1. The last point about confounding onlookers is reminiscent of Suetonius' remark on Augustus' pride in confounding onlookers with a glance, see Aug. 79.

4. Vita 6.4.

147

Already his commanding position among the bishops of North Africa is evident. The letters are either replies directed in his name or, if more than one bishop is listed, the name of Cyprian appears first.[1] Both Cyprian's secular background and the prestige of Carthage were responsible for the influence of the new bishop. His age may also have been a factor.[2]

One of the problems that the council was forced to handle was the appointment of clerics as tutores by testament.[3] Geminius Victor had, at his death, appointed a priest, Geminius Faustinus, as tutor. The post obviously grew out of some family relationship between the two men, but the degree of kinship cannot be determined.[4] As a letter was directed by Cyprian to the presbyteris et diaconibus et plebi Furnis, the see at Furni in Africa Proconsularis was apparently vacant. In 256 a bishop from Furni, called Geminius, attended the council of September 1.[5] The Geminii must have been an important family among the Christian population of the town. The bishop was most probably related to the two Geminii of Cyprian's epistle. Perhaps they

---

1. The letters are Hartel's, 1-4. For a discussion of their dates, see Appendix I.
2. His social standing was also an important factor.
3. Ep. 1.1/30.627. For a summary of the duties, see the discussion in J.A. Crook, Law and Life of Rome (London, 1967), p. 116.
4. A Geminius appears as bishop in the very city to which the letter was addressed. See SE 59.
5. SE 59.

148

believed that their preëminent position would enable them to circumvent the regulations. But citing the decisions of an unidentified council against such a practice Cyprian argues that the basis of the ruling is that such secular involvement distracts the priest from attending to the cares of his office.[1] But this infringement did not permanently injure the family. It may be that the bishop of 256 was this very priest, Faustinus. If not, he was certainly a relation.[2]

In another letter, probably a product of the same council in 249, Cyprian replies to a request by Rogatianus, a bishop having trouble controlling the activities of his deacon.[3] Rogatianus was unable to handle the deacon because the latter had found an ally.[4]

---

1. Ep. 1.1/30.627, citing the example of the Levites from the Old Testament, Ex. 6:16; Num. 3:14-20.
2. It is unfortunate that there is not enough prosopographical information available to ascertain important Christian families in the various sees in North Africa and their advancement in office. The same influence that permeated election to secular office must have played a part in election to clerical and episcopal office.
3. Monceaux, HAC, p. 210, identifies the bishop definitely as Rogatianus of Nova, SE 60. But the identification is not certain. Von Soden, "Prosop.", pp. 253, 269, identifies two bishops of that name and distinguishes the Rogatianus of 57 and 70. Nova is probably to be sought in Zeugitana rather than in Numidia.
4. Ep. 3.3/472.11, where the accomplice is called audiciae participem.

149

The reason for Rogatianus' difficulty may lie in the importance of the unnamed accomplice. Cyprian seems strangely reticent, withholding any mention of his name. Cyprian's reply already displays his high conception of the episcopal office.[1] The bishops are identified with the Apostles. It is God Himself who is directly responsible for the creation of bishops. The deacons were only created by the Apostles as aides after the ascension of Christ. The Church is with the bishops, and to rebel against it as this deacon has done is to lean towards heresy and schism.[2] For Biblical authority, Cyprian draws on the examples of rebellion against priests in the Old Testament, recalling as well the respect that Christ showed to priests.[3] Cyprian counsels caution. If the deacon continues his opposition, Rogatianus should proceed against him and his accomplice with deposition or excommunication. But patience and mercy are enjoined as the necessary preliminaries to a direct assertion of authority.[4]

This was to be Cyprian's first enunciation of his theory of the episcopate: the bishop is a direct successor of the Apostles. It is within the circle of bishops that the unity of the Church and its discipline are preserved. Any action against the bishops is a rebellion against the peace and discipline ordained by God. The seeds for the later conflict with Rome over the question of heretical baptism are already present within this early theory. For if

---

1. Further discussion infra pp.334 ff.
2. Ep. 3.3/471.16-472.5.
3. Ep. 3.1-2/469.17-470.15.
4. Ep. 3.3/472.5-6.

150

bishops have absolute power within the Church and are ordained by the Apostles, who can arbitrate their differences?[1]

A more general question confronted the council of 249. The bishop of Dionysiana, Pomponius, wrote to the council on the conduct of virgins who, after deciding to maintain their sexual abstinence, had been found sleeping with men, one of whom was a deacon. The question was complicated by the fact that although the women admitted their transgressions, they still insisted that they were virgins.[2]

As in his letter to Rogatianus, Cyprian

---

1. For a full discussion of Cyprian's theory of the episcopate, see _infra_ pp. 334 ff.

2. Benson, _Cyprian_, p. 46, rightly saw that Ep. 4 is to be connected with the treatise _De Habitu Virginum_. They are probably the result of the same incidents. The letter also provides us with the names of some of those at the council. The heading lists, along with Cyprian, the bishops Caecilius, Victor, Sedatus, and Tertullus. Caecilius came from Biltha in Proconsularis. Victor is more difficult to place. Four separate bishops can be distinguished by that name in Cyprian's correspondence. Von Soden, "Prosop.", p. 270, identifies the man mentioned in Ep. 4 with Victor from Gorduba, SE 40. But certain identification is not possible. Sedatus is probably the bishop of Thuburbo, SE 18, but whether from Minus or Maius, both in Proconsularis, is unknown. Tertullus' see is not identifiable, as he did not sit at the conference of 256, but it is most probable that it can be located in Proconsularis with the rest of the bishops listed.

151

states that his first concern is to stress the necessity of discipline and peace which have to be preserved within the Church.[1] He then reprimands the behaviour of the women. In order to maintain rigour the bishop must see that none of his brethren go astray. Because of their weakness and their dangerous effects, women should not be allowed to co-habit with men, for this only invites the devil.[2] These women have the means of destroying many souls. If they have no control and are unable to persevere in chastity, let them marry.[3]

Finally, Cyprian counsels that the self-styled virgins be examined by mid-wives to see whether they are still intact. If they are they may be re-admitted into the Church after receiving communion, on the condition that their penance would be more severe if they are caught again with men under the same roof. If on the other hand the mid-wives discover that a woman is no longer a virgin, she is to do penance equivalent to that of an adulterer. Perseverance in the practice will result in

---

1. Ep. 4.1/473.1-16. The short list of names in the headings may be the result of faulty manuscript tradition, or of the basic unimportance of the council. The large councils of Cyprian's latter years were concerned with questions basic to the Church's existence and function. The first council in his episcopate, however, would not have justified the same measure of concern, and therefore attendance may have been quite small.
2. Ep. 4/474.3-4, citing Eph. 4.27.
3. Ep. 4.2/474.15-20, recalling the famous "It is better to marry than to burn" of Paul.

permanent separation from the Church, for by continuing in their ways pseudo-virgins become models for the destruction of others.[1] Cyprian closes his reply with his opening thought on the absolute necessity of the congregation's obedience to the bishop. Outside the Church there is no salvation. The only means of preserving the Church is through discipline.[2] The whole of Cyprian's episcopal theory is here in germ.[3]

North Africa was not the only area troubled by this peculiar method of practicing virginity.[4] In a letter compiled by the synod sitting in judgment on Paul of Samosata, complaints are voiced on the possession by Paul and his clergy of virgines subintroductae.[5] The spread of the ascetic mode of life is first fully expressed in the literature of the third century. Sporadic references exist at an earlier date, but the first full-scale treatments of the purpose of such a life style are found in the third century.[6]

---

1. Ep. 4.4/475.20-477.9.
2. Ep. 4.5/477 and 13.4/478.1.
3. See infra pp. 310 ff.
4. For the whole question of virgines subintroductae, a translation of the Greek suneisaktoi gunaikes, see P. de Labriolle, "Le 'mariage spirituel' dans l'antiquité chrétienne", RH 137 (1921), pp. 204-25, correcting H. Achelis, Virgines subintroductae (Leipzig, 1902). See also Sister. Bernard Malone, "Christian Attitudes Towards Women in the Fourth Century: Background and New Directions" (Unpublished Ph.D. dis., University of Toronto, 1971).
5. Eusebius, HE 7.30.12.
6. For references and a good summary, see Baus, HCH, p. 295.

It is in this period that the first hint of large and influential groupings are presented, but no definite organization evolved.[1] The state seems to have acquired no set formula. All that was required was a more or less open oath to practice celibacy for the whole of one's life.[2] Though prompted in part by motivation specific to Christianity alone, it is part of the general turning away from the material world that marks much of the thought of the third century.[3] The rejection of the flesh and the world was, however, never complete. The history of the virgines subintroductae would indicate that though there may have been an intellectual rejection of the material world, many material activities were actively pursued.

Cyprian's magister, Tertullian, had betrayed an active concern for Christian women. His central view of them was that they are a potential snare, both for themselves and for their men, and they represent a pressing danger.[4] Even the angels of heaven had felt the power of female sexual attraction and had been seduced by the

1. Pseud. Clem. Ad Virg. 1.8.4, 1.2; Origen, Contra Celsum 5.49; Origen, In Ier. Hom. 20; Origen, In Iudic. Hom. 9.1; Tertullian, De Virg. Vel. 2.1, 9; Cyprian, De Hab. Virg. 7-12, 18-19; Ep. 4.
2. See Baus, HCH, p. 296.
3. See Dodds, Pagan and Christian, pp. 1 ff. The locus classicus is Porphyry's comment on Plotinus, that he was "ashamed to be in the body", Vita Plotini 1.
4. Tertullian, De Cult. Fem. 2.2. See A. D'Alès, La théologie de Tertullien (Paris, 1905), pp. 288 ff.; and Barnes, Tert., pp. 100-1.

154

daughters of men.[1] Therefore, it is not only vain but dangerous as well to improve one's physical beauty.[2]

Even if a woman vows virginity, there are still snares to catch her. In the state of continence, it is wise to block the path of all temptation and to veil the face. A woman will best guard herself and her virginity by denying her womanhood. Hence the practice of veiling the virgin is a necessity.[3] Most importantly, all luxury and vanity are bars to martyrdom. Since the end of the world is near and martyrdoms are being prepared for Christian men and women, such self-indulgence is wasteful.[4]

In the beginning of his episcopate, perhaps contemporaneously with his reply to Pomponius, Cyprian was moved by the actions of the virgins of Carthage to write and deliver a warning on the weakening of bonds of discipline among those who had pledged continence.[5] As the basis of his

---

1. Tertullian, De Virg. Vel. 7.
2. Tertullian, De Cult. Fem. 2.13.
3. Tertullian, De Virg. Vel. 15.
4. Tertullian, De Cult. Fem. 2.13.
5. The treatise has the traditional title of De Habitu Virginum. This is the title adopted by Hartel, based on manuscripts S (Parisinus 10592 = Suppl. Lat. 712) and W (Codex theolog. Würzeburgensis 145). Manuscript V (Codex Veronensis, saec. VII - ?) has De Disciplina et Habitu Virginum. Augustine, De Doctr. Christ. 4.21.48 has Liber de Habitu Virginum. But the Cheltenham List of 359-65 has Ad Virgines which, as Mommsen thought, may well have been the original title. For further discussion, see Schanz-Hosius, p. 342.

155

treatise, he turned to Tertullian's work on the subject.[1] He showed that he could use his sources with independence. His position as bishop placed him in another context from Tertullian. His standing demanded a less feverish, more fatherly approach. The harsh contours of Tertullian's diction and turns of thought were softened by the less angular rhetoric of Cyprian.[2] The works of Tertullian are utilized as a repertoire of thought and argument which Cyprian then polishes in his own way, while at the same time directing the thrust of the treatise towards his own goals, i.e., the maintenance of discipline and obedience to the bishop, neither of which were central in Tertullian's consideration of the subject.[3]

---

1. The De Cult. Fem. is the immediate source of the treatise. But there are also parallels with the De Virg. Vel.. See A.E. Keenan, De Habitu Virginum, Patristic Studies, 34 (Washington, 1932), pp. 13 ff., for a list of parallel passages. The parallels with Christian Greek literature, Tertullian's De Pudicitia and De Exhortatione Castitatis, Seneca and Apuleius, are not convincing. Rather, they are the repetition of commonplace.

2. cf. De Cult. Fem. 1.8 and De Hab. Virg. 11.2/195.3-24.

3. M.F. Wiles, "The Theological Legacy of St. Cyprian", JEH 14 (1963), p. 141, sees the problem rightly by stating that as a Christian Cyprian substituted Tertullian and the Bible for his pagan sources; but just as pagan writers did not slavishly copy Virgil or Horace, so Cyprian used Tertullian and the Bible as quarries for arguments and, in the case of the Bible, quotations to confirm his own ideas.

156

The basis for all religion and faith is obedience and fear. This is the guardian of hope, the path to salvation, the nourishment and kindling of one's natural gifts.[1] The Scriptures everywhere speak this truth.[2] God does not permit man to wander freely, especially the man who, having once obtained freedom from the ills of this world, voluntarily exposes himself again to their pernicious effects. We must be very careful that what has once been received from God is not again lost.[3] Cyprian speaks as a father warning virgins to persevere towards that goal which, though difficult, is of boundless limits and infinite reward.[4]

Special care is needed in the case of virgins who are "flos...ille ecclesiastici germinis, decus atque ornamentum gratiae spiritualis".[5] For they are a delight to the Church. The more they increase, the greater the enjoyment.[6]

Cyprian, like Tertullian, demands that anyone seeing a virgin should unmistakably recognize her as such; since she has no husband, any adornment would only be

---

1. De Hab. Virg. 2/188.6-8. On this view of discipline, see A. D'Alès, La théologie de S. Cyprien (Paris, 1922), p. 388.
2. Ibid. On the relation of some of the Scriptural passages of the De Hab. Virg. to the Testimonia, refer to supra p. 144, n. 1.
3. De Hab. Virg. 2/189.6-10.
4. De Hab. Virg. 3/189.11-22.
5. De Hab. Virg. 3/189.11-13
6. De Hab. Virg. 3/189.11-22. Notice Cyprian's stress on humility. Compare this with the tone of Ep. 4.

directed towards the lewd and concupiscent.[1]
The most difficult case of all is the woman
who, though a virgin, is possessed of wealth.
Cyprian devotes the majority of his treatise
to this problem.

The art of the rhetor is employed to
accentuate the impact of the bishop's
treatment. Four chapters open with the
formula locupletem te dicis et divitem.[2]
The information is essential for any
consideration of the wealth and social
standing of mid-third century African
Christians.

Wealthy women should avoid any display
of their riches. True riches are spiritual
and not of this world.[3] To appear in public
dressed elaborately is to belie the virgin's
state. It draws the glances and inflames
the desires of young men. Thus destruction
is set in motion for both the woman and the
men she entices.[4] Riches lead to pride, a
sin as deadly as lewdness. One should be
rich in Christ. Cyprian reacts violently
against the argument that all things made by
God were made for our use. Since riches were
made by God, they are therefore lawful for
use. Tertullian had already repudiated this
argument in the De Corona Militis.[5] Cyprian
apostrophizes: God did not make purple
sheep nor pearl necklaces. These are the
inventions of the devil. All such decora-
tions are the creations of fallen and sinful

---

1. De Hab. Virg. 5-6/190.17-191.16.
2. Chapters 8 to 11.
3. De Hab. Virg. 8/193.18-194.4.
4. De Hab. Virg. 9/194.5-17. The
almost obsessive fear of sex, and in
particular the tremendous effect of the
female body that appears in Christian
ascetic literature is yet to be treated
extensively.
5. Tertullian, De Cor. Mil. 2.4.

angels. It was they who gave to women the arts of cosmetics and self-decoration.[1] Should not these women who adorn themselves fear that on the Day of Judgment they will not be recognized by the Lord? They shall not even see Him, for the eyes that were a product of God's work have since been infected by creations of the devil. Married women have some excuse for the use of cosmetics, for they desire to please their husbands. But what exoneration is possible for a virgin?[2]

Women vowed to virginity must also be on guard as to what social functions they attend, and in what public places they are seen. Weddings are centres of unchaste discourse and drunkenness. There is nothing at such a celebration that is suitable for a virgin. The baths are also forbidden. To go to the baths is to expose what has been consecrated to God's use to eyes filled with carnal lust. Modesty and reserve are laid aside with clothing.[3]

Given all of this, the Church has

---

1. De Hab. Virg. 14. This passage goes back to Tertullian, De Cult. Fem. 2, which stresses the diabolical origin of cosmetics in the Book of Henoch. The authenticity of the work must have been in doubt for Tertullian devotes an entire section to its defense (chapter 3). Tertullian's influence may have resulted in Cyprian's own acceptance of this idea. See D'Alès, S. Cyprien, p. 225.

2. De Hab. Virg. 17/199.15 ff.; nunc seems better than Hartel's non, and is supported by Dv, at line 4.

3. De Hab. Virg. 18-19. See Porphyry, Vita Plotini, 1.

frequent cause to bewail her virgins, women who become adulteresses not to human husbands but to Christ.[1] Virgins who wish to remain pure should avoid all of these things. Though the toil is wearisome, the reward for self-discipline is great. Immortality and the Lord's kingdom are promised.[2] But bounty is also granted in this life. A .continent woman need not fear childbirth. The only master for such a woman is God and His Church. She need accept no mortal lord.[3]

The command that God had once given has now been overthrown. Now continence is enjoined rather than multiplication and fruitfulness.[4] This is not, however, a question of necessity imposed by God's command, though the higher sanctity is the possession of those who can deny the desires of the flesh. Let the virgins, old and young, stimulate one another to persevere, the old instructing the young, while the young provide incentive. Let rival proof of virtue lead on to a mutual glory.[5]

Cyprian's sermon contains little that is original on the subject of virginity. Most of it is culled from Tertullian and

---

1. De Hab. Virg. 20. On this type of adulterium, see H. Koch, "Virgines Christi", TU 31, hft. 2 (1907), p. 76, who comments also on its use in the writings of Tertullian.

2. De Hab. Virg. 20-21/201.15-202.24.

3. De Hab. Virg. 22/202.25-203.20.

4. For Tertullian's use of this argument, see Ad Ux. 1.3. See also the commentary on this, W.P. Le Saint, Tertullian: Treatises on Marriage and Remarriage, ACW 13 (Westminster, Md., 1951), pp. 6 ff.

5. De Hab. Virg. 24/204.23-205.5.

supported by Biblical quotation. But it gives us a glimpse into the process of continual disintegration and renewal that the Christian community was going through. Long peace had certainly taken its toll of the other-worldliness of the Christians of Carthage.[1]

Capellianus' attack had been on the primores among whom were few Christians. Thus the events of 238, while seriously affecting men of Cyprian's standing had little effect on the majority of the Christian community at Carthage. But even during the turmoil of Decius' reign, while the persecution was in progress, the phenomenon of the subintroductae remained a disturbing reality for Cyprian.[2] He seems himself to have found continence an easy yoke to bear. No record of wife or family before his entrance into the Church is extant.[3] Others had more difficulty, even in times of imminent peril.

The opening paragraphs of the De Habitu Virginum provide the key to Cyprian's problem. Discipline is necessary for salvation and the stability of the Church, but how is it to be enforced? This must have been particularly difficult for Cyprian at the start of his episcopate. The five presbyters who had opposed him never ceased being hostile towards the pagan parvenu.[4]

---

1. De Lapsis 5/213.13-214.15.
2. Ep. 13.5/508.1.
3. Note that the contention of E.W. Watson, "The De Habitu Virginum of St. Cyprian", JThS 22 (1921), p. 365, that Cyprian had a wife, is unfounded, as he misinterprets Vita 4.3 to mean that he acquired the widow of Caecilianus and his children.
4. Supra p. 139.

161

Religion could provide a safe outlet for the same forms of ostentation as secular life. Virginity offered an opportunity for "conspicuous consumption". Control without the sanction of physical force was always a problem. As Cyprian later discovered, moral sanctions are often not enough. While Tertullian defended a position, Cyprian's job was to control people. This constituted the essential difference in their handling of all questions about which they wrote.[1]

Cyprian's control of the virgins of Carthage seems to have been sufficiently established in 249. Only one reference to further trouble within the flock occurs.[2] But other more pressing problems appeared with the commencement of persecution, and the conduct of virgins must have assumed less importance. More significantly, Cyprian had early asserted his control as bishop. He was determined not to lose his office under any circumstances.[3]

A reply to Eucratius on the question of a converted actor throws further light on Cyprian's activities prior to the outbreak of the persecution.[4]

---

1. The usual judgment of Cyprian as a man of action rather than as an original thinker is correct. But action often involved him in formulating ideas to explain his actions. For this standard judgment, see D'Alès, S. Cyprien, p. 1, and Quasten, Pat., p. 373.
2. Ep. 13.5/507.20-508.16.
3. On the influence of the De Habitu Virginum, see Keenan, De Habitu Virginum, introduction, pp. 63 ff.; and R. Donna, "Note on St. Cyprian's De Habitu Virginum: Its Source and Influence", Traditio 4 (1946), pp. 399-407.
4. For date circa 249, see Appendix I.

162

Eucratius had asked Cyprian's advice with regard to an actor who had converted but who had persisted in his craft as a performer and instructor.[1] Cyprian's reply was uncompromising.

Tertullian had rigorously condemned any occupations dealing with idolatry or trafficking with paganism. His pupil faithfully applied his stand to the question of acting.[2] Acting was a profession which could only defile and debase the Church and destroy evangelical discipline.[3] As performance was forbidden, so also was the

---

4. (cont'd) This letter is not concerned with the council of 249. There is no reference to Cyprian acting in conjunction with other bishops, a feature of the letters which were a product of the council. It may in fact have been a result of the moral activities of the newly elected Carthaginian bishop at the council. Its concern with a disciplinary point may have been the cause of its inclusion in the collection with Ep. 1, 3 and 4.

1. Eucratius is probably from Thenae in Byzacena. See SE 29 and Von Soden, "Prosop.", p. 267. Von Soden rightly withholds certainty with respect to the accuracy of the identification.

2. Tertullian, De Idol. 28; Tertullian, De Spect., passim. The De Idol. has been dated to Tertullian's Montanist phase, circa 211, see Quasten, Pat., p. 310. But Barnes, Tert., pp. 53 ff. has shown that it should be dated to 196 or early in 197, thus falling into the Catholic phase of Tertullian's writings and more likely to have affected Cyprian.

3. Ep. 2.1/467.18-468.2, evangelicae disciplinae.

163

teaching of acting. For it means that though this one man may cease performing the devilish art, he substitutes others in his place. If the man were to plead poverty, Eucratius was to send him to Carthage where he might receive simple and frugal support from the superior resources of the Church.[1]

Cyprian had begun his episcopate well. Local opposition seemed at least for the present to have subsided. A council had been called at Carthage at which he had played a leading role, and he had played it well. Disciplinary problems had been successfully handled. But the test of the new bishop's ability was just beginning. Events taking place in Italy and on the Danube were to lead to severe internal dissension in the Christian community at Carthage. Cyprian's deepest crisis was yet to come.

---

1. Ep. 2.2/468.7-24. See Eusebius, HE 5.21.1, on the support offered by Rome in such a case as this.

164

Chapter IV: THE DECIAN PERSECUTION

The last year of the Emperor Philip's reign was marked by repeated political and military disturbances.[1] Probably in the late spring of 248 a rebellion broke out on the Danube setting up Ti. Claudius Marinus Pacatianus as candidate for the throne.[2] Rebellion flared up at about the same time in the East. The overly rigorous administration of the Emperor's brother, Priscus, who had been appointed Praefectus Praetorio Rectorque Orientis, resulted in a proclamation of Iotapianus as Emperor by the Syrian soldiers.[3] Syria provided another usurper, Uranius Antoninus, who survived until 253.[4] The number and seriousness of these revolts understandably disturbed Philip.

---

1. On Philip's reign, see CAH, pp. 87 ff. For the subsequent bibliography to 1959 see G. Walser and T. Pekáry, Die Krise des römischen Reiches (Berlin, 1962), p. 21.
2. For Pacatianus, see PIR[2] C 930. For date, see Wittig, RE XV.8, 1252. Also Zosimus, 1.20.2 and Zonaras, 12.19.
3. Aurel. Vict., 29.2. Polemius Silvius, Chron. Min. 1, 521, places the rebellion in Cappadocia. Zosimus, 1.20.1 synchronizes the revolt with that of Pacatianus. On Iotapianus' possible descent from a dynasty of Commagene, Syme, Emperors, p. 202.
4. PIR[2] I 195. Uranius styled himself an Antoninus, presumably to connect himself with the Severi. As he was of the sacerdotal dynasty of Emesa, he may have actually been a relative of Elagabalus.

Trouble in Moesia brought added misfortune to the State. The Goths, failing to receive tribute because of the troubled state of the Danubian provinces, invaded the area. The capital of the province of Lower Moesia, Marcianopolis, was besieged, but due to the efforts of Maximus, the city held out and the Goths were forced to end their siege.[1]

Distraught by the news, Philip turned to the Senate for support. Either the Senate would assist him, or he would offer to abdicate.[2] The question may have been a ploy to gauge his support among the senators. Had he abdicated the certainty of a short life expectancy would have been obvious to him. Decius, a Pannonian senator with local connections in the Danubian region and possibly the praefectus urbi, declared that the situation would right itself and that no intervention would be necessary.[3]

Decius had had a distinguished career. One of the few senators of Danubian extraction, he had probably been consul suffect sometime in the period from 223 to 233.[4] He had then assumed the consular governorship of Moesia Inferior in 234.[5]

---

1. For the invasion, see FGrHist IV, p. 466. Jordanes, Getica, pp. 91-2. For Maximus, PIR[1] M 309.
2. Zosimus, 1.21.1 and Zonaras, 12.19.
3. Zosimus, 1.21.1, Zonaras, 12.19. For his birth and patria at Budalia in Lower Pannonia, Eutropius, 9.4; Epit.de Caes.29.1.
4. For the consulate, see Wittig, RE XV, 1252.
5. This would have provided further connections in the area of Pacatianus' revolt.

In 238 he held Hispania Tarraconensis under Maximinus.[1] Sometime during the intervening years he may also have held the praefecture of the city.[2] This was an exceptional career for a man from an area which records few senators or consuls.[3] But Decius had married well. The nomenclature of his wife, Herennia Cupressenia Etruscilla, as well as the appearance of Perperna in the name of his second son, Hostilianus, betray connections with Etruria and with aristocratic ancestry.[4] This may have enabled Decius to speak for the Senate with authority. His advice proved accurate. By April or May of 249, Pacatianus was slain by his own troops. Iotapianus soon suffered the same fate. Only Uranius Antoninus lingered on in Syria, but

1. Much dispute has raged over the identification of the governor of Tarraconensis in 238 with the Emperor. But AEpigr. (1951), no. 9, made the identification reasonable beyond a doubt, despite the objections of G. Barbieri. For references see Syme, Emperors, p. 196. More interesting still is the pronounced loyalty shown by Decius to Maximinus.

2. John of Antioch, Müller, FHG, IV, p. 598, accepted by Wittig, RE XV, 1250. See the judicious remarks by Syme on this point, Emperors, p. 197.

3. On possible ancestors, see Syme, Emperors, p. 197. The first Danubian senator recorded is M. Valerius Maximianus. For his career, see AEpigr. (1956), 124.

4. For Henennia, see PIR^2 H 136. For a good discussion of the names, see Syme, Emperors, p. 197. On Hostilianus, see Wittig, RE XV, 1285.

his effect was purely local.[1]

Philip invited Decius to assume command and restore order in Pannonia and Moesia. It was dangerous, however, to send a man to govern his home province. The sources report that Decius refused the position of Dux Moesiae et Pannoniae, but Philip overrode his objections.[2] His protests may have been genuine, but the portrait of the reluctant usurper appears elsewhere in Roman history.[3] However, his dispatch to the Danube may have been an attempt to compromise with the local troops there. Priscus' handling of the situation in the East may have taught Philip that severity is not sufficient for success.

Zosimus reports that upon his arrival on the Danube, Decius tried to re-establish order.[4] A late and unreliable source states that his discipline was so exacting that a contingent of troops deserted to the Goths and made common cause with them against their fellow soldiers.[5] But his severity did not induce loyalty to Philip, and the troops proclaimed him Emperor.[6] Decius wrote to Philip protesting that he had no interest in empire, but was merely employing a delaying tactic until discipline could be

---

1. For the date of the end of Pacatianus' usurpation, see Wittig, RE XV, 1266. For the fall of Iotapianus, see Zosimus, 1.21.2; on this see also Zonaras, 12.19.
2. Zosimus, 1.21.2 and Zonaras, 12.19.
3. So Gordian I, see supra pp. 38 ff. For Claudius Gothicus, Syme, Emperors, p.162.
4. Zosimus, 1.21.2; also see ILS 249 and 822.
5. Jordanes, Getica 16.90.
6. Zosimus, 1.21.2 and Zonaras, 12.19.

restored. Philip was not convinced by his protestations and prepared his army to march against the new threat on the Danube.[1]

Decius had not had coinage struck in his own name. Perhaps he was trying to cover all possibilities. The armies on the Danube were prepared to move on Italy, but the reluctant usurper delayed the march of his troops.[2]

In September of 249 the armies of Philip and Decius met at Verona in northern Italy. The Emperor died in battle, after which his troops joined his successful adversary.[3] A fourth century tradition reports the consecration of Philip and his son, but its authenticity is questionable. Decius would have had little to gain from it. Unlike Septimius Severus, he could not claim to be avenging a predecessor.[4]

Avoiding the mistake of Maximinus, Decius made directly for Rome.[5] He was recognized by the Senate sometime in September 249.[6] A damnatio memoriae of the fallen Emperor was instituted.[7] To further

---

1. Zonaras, 12.19. There has been controversy as to whether this report by Zonaras is true. See A. Stein, RE X, 764, and Wittig, RE XV, 1266.
2. For the troops, see Wittig, RE XV, 1266. He is also probably right about the disputed coinage for Viminacium, bearing an 11th year for Philip. For another interpretation, see CAH, p. 93.
3. Zosimus, 1.22; Zonaras, 12.19; Epit. de Caes. 28.2; Aurel. Vict., 28.11.
4. Eutropius, 8.3. Also CAH, p. 94.
5. RIC IV, part 3, p. 109, with the legend Adventus Augusti.
6. See Wittig, RE XV, 1254.
7. Wittig, RE XV, 1267.

169

support his pretensions to rule, Decius adopted the cognomen Traianus, recalling the most military of Roman emperors who himself had been active on the Danubian frontier.[1] The populace was granted a congiarium, though less than the amount given by the two previous emperors.[2] After the initial modifications and celebrations and with the Empire generally at peace, Decius settled down to almost a year of residence at Rome.

The interim of peace did not distract the new ruler from military preparations for defense and if necessary for further hostilities.[3] Decius devoted his attention to strengthening the military highway that ran along the south bank of the Danube.[4] Construction and repair of roads was undertaken in Syria and in Galatia in the East, Africa, Spain and Britain in the West.[5]

The coinage proclaimed the slogans of the new reign:

"Pax aeterna; Felicitas saeculi;
Romae aeternae."

Securitas, Concordia and Pudicitia also

---

1. See acclamation preserved in Eutropius, 8.5.3. For his use of cognomen Traianus, Wittig, RE XV, 1246-7. On Trajan's subsequent fame, Syme, Emperors, pp.89-112.
2. Chron. of 354, 147. For relevant coinage, RIC IV, part 3, pp. 107 ff.
3. For supposed rebellion suppressed in Gaul by Decius (Eutropius 9.4) see Wittig, RE XV, 1268-9.
4. ILS 8922.
5. Spain: CIL II, 4809, 4812-3, 4833, 4835. Galatia: CIL III, 14184, 13644, 14155. Britain: CIL VII, 1163, 1171, 1174,

170

found their place on Decius' coin series.[1] But at the beginning of 250, the promised felicity and peace were broken. The Goths broke through the Moesian frontier in league with the Carpi, laying the province to waste.[2] Probably in March 250 Herennius, the elder son, was raised to the rank of Caesar and dispatched to the Danube with an army to deal with the Goths.[3] But before the intrusion of the Goths and the rupture of external peace, Decius was called upon to deal with internal dissension.

The historian Cassius Dio advances his own ideas on empire and government through the character of Maecenas. Part of his advice deals with the place of religion in the state and its relationship to the position of the emperor.[4] Dio counsels moderation as the guiding principle. The emperor is to allow no excessive honours to be voted to himself. Temples are not to be raised to the ruler, for they are wasteful of large sums of money. The emperor must gain honour and praise through the practice of virtue rather than by promoting flattery of his person and pressuring his subjects. No man can become a god by simple popular vote. Virtue is the only successful road to

---

5. (cont'd) 1180. For Africa, see Romanelli, Storia, p. 484.

1. RIC IV, part 3, pp. 110 ff.

2. Lactantius, De Mort. Persecut. 4.3.

3. Wittig, RE XV, 1261, on Herennius' elevation. For the troops, Aurel. Vict., 29.1.

4. F. Millar, A Study of Cassius Dio (Oxford, 1964), p. 104, argues that the speeches of Agrippa and Maecenas of Book 52 are aimed at Caracalla and not, as had been

171

immortality.[1]

Dio advises the conservative maintenance of tradition.[2] The emperor must foster the traditions of worship commended by the sanctions of hereditary practice. Those who attempt to innovate in religious questions or who attempt to distort tradition with strange rites are to be abhorred and punished. This is not merely for the sake of the gods but because the introduction of foreign practices arouses dissension; revolt and conspiracy spring up, and anarchy results.[3] No devotees are specifically named by Dio, but he singles out sorcerers and philosophers as types of would-be revolutionaries.[4]

Other proponents of the maintenance of pagan religion repeat Dio's sentiment. Caecilius, in the Octavius, essentially renounces his scepticism to make the plea that if knowledge concerning nature and chance is uncertain, the best course is for each nation to hold to its established rites. It is best to cease dogmatizing and to hold to gods who have the familiarity of companions from childhood.[5]

Celsus also had attacked the innovations of the Christians, feeling that the introduction of strange and alien ritual could only be destructive to the State. In fact,

---

4. (cont'd) thought, at Severus Alexander.
1. Dio, 52.35.1-6.
2. Millar, Cassius Dio, p. 179.
3. Dio, 52.36.
4. For collection of evidence on effect of these two groups, R. MacMullen, Enemies of the Roman Order. Treason, Unrest, and Alienation in the Empire (Cambridge, Mass.,1966), pp. 46-163.
5. Oct. 6.1.

172

the Christians were a band leagued together in a conjuration against the rest of the inhabitants of the Empire.[1] In the late fourth century, Q. Aurelius Symmachus was still pleading for the maintenance of the rites by which Rome had grown great in his petition for the restoration of the Altar of Victory to the Senate House.[2]

Rome had essentially acted in accordance with the terms laid down by Dio. It had been resistant to innovation but had proceeded sporadically and on a local level.[3] But the crises that continually racked the Empire both externally and internally demanded measures that were severe. Decius' coinage proclaims the standard legends of Pax aeterna and Securitas. The period of peace before the renewal of the Gothic advance on the Danube gave him the opportunity to promote this program within the Empire.[4]

Eusebius states that the Emperor Philip and his son were Christians. On the Paschal Day they had attempted to enter a church but the head of the congregation would not allow it until they had confessed their sins and agreed to do penance. Both readily agreed.[5] But the acceptance of Philip proved a heavy burden to the Christians. When Decius succeeded him, his enmity towards Philip caused him to persecute the Christians.[6]

---

1. Origen, Contra Celsum 1.10.
2. Sym., Relatio 3.19, 14, 17. For a sympathetic analysis, see S. Dill, Roman Society in the Last Century of the Western Empire. From the Fall of Paganism to the Advent of the Barbarians[2] (London, 1899) 30.
3. Barnes, Tert., pp. 143 ff.
4. Supra p. 170, n. 2.
5. Eusebius, HE 6.34.
6. Eusebius, HE 6.39.1.

Nothing other than the record of Eusebius, however, proclaims Philip's alleged Christianity. No deviation in coinage or titulature marks the event of his conversion. The celebration of Rome's first millennium by a series of games in 248 would suggest that he was not in fact a Christian. The Eusebian story bears all the marks of legend: the Emperor humbly confessing his sins to gain admittance to the Church - how different the actions of a later monarch, contemporary with Eusebius, when he chose to become Christian! No action was taken by Philip when Alexandria was suffering from persecution in the last year of his reign.[1] The Christianity of Philip should rather find its explanation in the actions of Decius: since Decius was a persecutor and had over-thrown Philip, the earlier Emperor must at least have been friendly towards his Christian subjects.[2] Certainly the motivation for the actions of Decius lay elsewhere.

Libelli found issued as certificates to those who had sacrificed in accordance with the edict issued by Decius in December 249 may throw some light on the question of his motivation.[3] The certificates preserved indicate that the edict was not directed specifically against the Christians, but was

1. Eusebius, HE 6.41.1.
2. There is also the remote possibility that Eusebius was influenced in his claim that Philip was a Christian by Licinius' alleged descent from Philip. But the only evidence for this is SHA Gord. 34.5, and this may just be another example of fiction in the SHA.
3. R.H. Knipfing, "The Libelli of the Decian Persecution", HThR 16 (1923) 345-90.

174

a general measure of sacrifice to be carried out by all inhabitants of the Empire.[1] Even a priestess of Petesouchos was forced to comply. There was no provision for a specific renunciation of Christianity. A century and a half earlier, when dealing with Christians, Pliny had added to the ceremony of libation and sacrifice the requirement that those who had renounced Christianity had to curse the name of Christ.[2] The Decian certificates, on the other hand, point to a sacrifice to the gods as a universal requirement, without singling out a particular group.[3] They stress that the recipient has always been a worshipper of the gods.

The libellus was couched in terms of a petition, according to its usual form. The petitioner asks the commission in charge of superintending the ceremony to certify that he has always sacrificed, poured libations, and shown piety to the gods. The petition then requests the commission to certify that the petitioner has poured a libation, sacrificed, and partaken of sacrificial

1. Knipfing, "Libelli", p. 345.
2. Pliny, Ep. 10.96.5.
3. The older view which is essentially that of Eusebius was that the act was a measure of persecution against the Christians specifically. This can be found in CAH, p. 202, and A. Alföldi, "Zu den Christenverfolgungen in der Mitte des 3. Jahrhunderts", Klio 31 (1938) pp. 323-48 = Studien zur Geschichte der Weltkrise des 3. Jahrunderts nach Christus (Darmstadt, 1967), pp. 285-311. For a view that this was a general measure, see J. Molthagen, Der römische Staat und die Christen im zweiten und dritten Jahrhundert, Hypomnemata 28 (Göttingen, 1970), pp. 70 ff.

meats in the presence of the commissioners.[1] All this is to be carried out in accordance with the edict's decree.

The form of the edict points to its being an act to ensure uniformity and loyalty towards the gods of the Empire. This affirmation of loyalty and reverence towards the gods who guarded the Empire's existence accords well with what is known of Decian policy. The Emperor ascended the throne after a period of severe external shocks from the Goths along the Danube. In the last years of Philip's rule, the pretenders who sprang up portended swift internal anarchy. In such a perilous position, military preparations were not sufficient in themselves. Decius came from an area that had few Christians.[2] He depended on an army in which Christians were rare. If divine power was to be solicited in time of crisis, he would be little disposed to allow for any dissidence. Jews were exempted because of their recognized status, but Christians had no such saving grace.[3]

Decius was not a free-thinker. There is no reason to suspect that his motives were only political. The legends that frame his coinage from the beginning of his reign are no doubt traditional, but stress can infuse new value into old traditions. Sentiments dormant in times of peace gain new life when stimulated by external threats. The sacrifice

---

1. Knipfing, "Libelli", pp. 346-7.
2. Baus, HCH, p. 379; RIC IV, part 3, pp. 166-89.
3. Molthagen, Der römische Staat, p. 64, rightly emphasizes that it is Church tradition which causes Christian writers to view the whole attack as an action directed solely against themselves.

seemed to have been an affirmation of unity and loyalty that sought the benefit of divine aid to help the Emperor preserve his domain. In some ways this is comparable to the Augustan religious revival of two and a half centuries earlier. After strife and bloodshed, Augustus sought to revitalize antique and obsolete ritual to bind Italy and to provide a deeper focus for her loyalties. It served at the same time to foment the unity of Italy and, through judicious manipulation, focus this unity on those outlets over which the State exercised control. One of the difficulties with the newer oriental cults was their lack of regulation and supervision. So Decius served both religion and politics.[1]

In a period of graver troubles, he reacted in a similar manner. When he reaffirmed the worship of the gods, he sought their help and pursued unity by suppressing the religious diversity that Dio had viewed as a source of threat and cabal.

In the case of the Christians, the threat was not idle. The Church of the third century had many of the markings of a state within a state. It possessed its own hierarchy, independent of government control. The ministers of the hierarchy dispensed monies and supported large numbers through charity, thus offering a livelihood and community independent of the Empire, and so in general conformed to Dio's notion of a cabal.[2] To argue that Decius was totally unaware of the Christians and the construction of their organization as a separate entity certainly would betray a lack of

---

1. R. Syme, The Roman Revolution (Oxford,1939),pp. 440 ff.
2. Dio, 52.36.

177

perspective.[1] In unifying the Empire, one of his objectives must surely have been the destruction of the hierarchical organization of the Christians, for they were potentially the most dangerous group of all and Decius must have known it.

The first evidence of active persecution is the death of the bishop of Rome, Fabianus, on the 20th or 21st of January 250.[2] Soon after the 24th of the same month Babylas, bishop of Antioch, was killed.[3] But the libelli thus far discovered in Egypt are all dated between June 12th and July 15th of that year. This has led some to posit a two-phased attack, the first in which only the clergy were involved, and the second in which general persecution

---

1. Molthagen, Der römische Staat, p. 70, argues that the measures of the Emperor were not directed specifically against the Christians, a judgment which should be accepted. But he underplays the motivation of the Emperor vis-à-vis the Christians. Surely Decius, resident in Rome and prefect of the city, was aware of them as a group of religious non-conformists who presented a potential danger. He may have had as at least one object of his measures their suppression as dissenters rather than specifically as Christians. After all, Dio's statement to which Molthagen refers (52.36) specifies that those who deviate from ancestral traditions in matters of religion should be punished for this offence.

2. Eusebius, HE 6.39.1. The date of January 20th is given by the Lib. Pont. I, pp. 148-9; and the Mart. Hiero. has January 21st. There is no way to decide between them.

3. Eusebius, HE 6.39.4 for the date.

ensued.[1] The evidence, however, does not warrant such a conclusion.

Dionysius, writing to the bishop of Antioch, mentions that the persecution in Alexandria did not begin with Decius' edict but had started a full year earlier. In Alexandria the persecution had arisen as a spontaneous expression of pagan hostility towards the Christians, and bore no relation to the imperial will.[2] Dionysius then continues to say that the persecution was followed by civil war, which diverted the population from further harassing the Christians. When the news arrived, bringing with it the imperial edict, it portended even worse disaster for the Church.[3] The account of Dionysius points to a single edict

---

1. This is Alföldi, "Zu den Christenverfolgungen", pp. 295-6, who connects it with the dies imperii of Decius. This unfortunately is not consistent with the evidence. The first indication we have of Decius in Egypt is a papyrus (P.Oxy. xii, 1636) which can be dated to 27 November 249. Thus Decius' first Egyptian regnal year dates from 29 August 249 to 28 August 250. So a date in December to coincide with the first recorded effects of the edict seems impossible. For the dies imperii, see A. Stein, "Zur Chronologie der römischen Kaiser von Decius bis Diocletianus", Archiv für Papyrusforschung 7 (1924), pp. 30-51.

2. Eusebius, HE 6.41.1-2. Some have taken the Greek to refer to a particular priest, i.e., Frend, M&P, p. 298. But the unusual vagueness of the expression used by Dionysius, i.e., hostis ekeinos ēn, perhaps points to the source of the persecution in the action of the devil.

3. Eusebius, HE 6.41.8-10.

179

of persecution which followed soon after the ascension of Decius. A date in December, or soon after, seems the most reasonable time for the arrival of the edict.[1] Thus Dionysius distinguishes only one edict in the period of persecution.

Further support comes from the list of those who suffered after the arrival of the edict. Included among these were four women, the young boy Dioscorus, and two Egyptians, Ater and Isidore.[2] Dionysius makes no distinction between clergy and other Christian victims. Since Babylas' death falls at the commencement of the persecution, there can be no argument that the authorities pursued different courses in different areas.

Cyprian's correspondence indicates that the lay-clerical distinction was not observed in Africa either. Epistle 5, which is one of the first of the series which deals with the Decian Persecution, is addressed to his clergy. He asks that various administrative functions of those who have been imprisoned be undertaken by the presbyters and deacons. No mention is made of any potential danger to the clergy themselves who remained in Carthage. So also Epistle 7, which probably opens the series; it implies that no danger awaits the clergy who remain in Carthage and quietly perform their tasks.[3] The De Lapsis also makes no distinction between clerical and lay when dealing with the effect of the persecution.

Though there is no evidence for any but the single edict preserved, the lateness of the dates of the libelli demands an

---

1. The papyrus is P.Oxy. xii, 1636.
2. Eusebius, HE 6.41.18, 20.
3. For the date, see Appendix I.

180

explanation.[1] Part of it may lie in the fact that the civil war and devastation in Alexandria took place prior to the arrival of the edict, hence disrupting its administration. Another possibility is that in the towns of the Fayûm from which the extant papyri derive, the commissions made circuits, and that these towns came later on their circuit. The provision for the administration of the edict which involved virtually every adult inhabitant in the Empire must have strained Roman resources severely. A bureaucracy which is essentially based on the utilization of city government at the lowest level would have had to expand itself to deal with a task of such magnitude. In no case is there evidence for more than one edict, or for the development of Decius' actions in several phases. The edict may have been proclaimed at Rome at the opening of the year 250 to coincide with the start of the new year.

The commission set up to enforce sacrificial edicts in Carthage consisted of five men. Cyprian compares the five presbyters who opposed his election to the commission of five notables who had been joined to the magistrates for the purpose of destroying the Christian faith.[2] The Martyrdom of Pionius does not specify the number on the commission, but mentions that men had been enjoined to act in conjunction with the local magistrate, Polemon, for the purpose of seeking out Christians and

---

1. For an attempted reconstruction of the edict based on the libelli, see Molthagen, Der römische Staat, pp. 60 ff.
2. Ep. 43.3/592.10-11.

inquiring into their faith.[1]

The magistrate was in charge of the actual proceedings.[2] He was apparently part of the imperial bureaucracy, as any action by a local magistrate would have been irregular.[3] The primores were probably employed to add local pressure to the more general pressure applied by the imperial government. They would also have been expected to be more familiar with the local inhabitants with whom the commission would have to deal. The procedure for the selection and compilation of the names is not made clear from the sources. Perhaps local tax registers were used, in conjunction

---

1. Some still do not accept the Passion of Pionius as being of Decian date; for example, J. Moreau, Die Christenverfolgung im römischen Reich[2], Aus der Welt der Religion, Forschungen und Berichte, N.F. 2 (Berlin, 1961) pp. 95 ff. For a decisive refutation of this, see T.D. Barnes, "Pre-Decian Acta Martyrum", JThS N.S. 19 (1968), pp. 527 ff., and Altaner-Stuiber, Pat., p. 92. For a discussion of the text, see H. Delehaye, Les passions, pp. 26-33.

2. Eusebius, HE 6.41.18, and Cyprian, Ep. 22/533.10-11. The interpretation of G.W. Clarke, "Some Observations on the Persecution of Decius", Antichthon 3 (1969), pp. 64-5, that the anguis of the letter refers to Decius himself, is questionable. The reference may more reasonably refer to the devil.

3. Pass. Pion. 15.6 and 19.1, where the local magistrates attempt to use their own power to destroy Pionius. It seems they were acting on their own initiative. The punishment does not take place until the arrival of the proconsul of Asia.

182

with the information supplied by the local
primores.

Some central area was chosen for the
sacrifice. At Carthage the Forum, centre
of city life, was selected.^{1} Altars were
set up so that sacrifices could be performed en masse.^{2} There were two parts to
the procedure. The first was a quaestio,
which involved the offer to sacrifice and the
questioning of the prisoner.^{3} If the
prisoner refused to be persuaded by the
magistrate and the commission, he would be
sent back to prison to reconsider the
errors of his ways.^{4} Celerinus, writing to
Lucianus in prison at Carthage, expresses
the hope that his letter will reach the
confessor before he has suffered for the
faith. The reference is not to illness but
to a second confrontation with the magistrate.^{5} Pionius is pressured to confess by
the local magistrates, and when he refuses
is sent back to prison to await the coming
of the proconsul.^{6}

The second presentation of the prisoner
appears to have been for sentence and
punishment, should he still be recalcitrant.^{7}

---

1. De Lapsis 8/242.11, ut ascenderent
forum.
2. Eusebius, HE 6.41.11; De Lapsis 8/
242.20 ff. For a discussion of the better-
known procedures of the Great Persecution,
see G.E.M. de Ste. Croix, "Aspects of the
'Great' Persecution", HThR 47 (1954), pp.
97 ff.
3. Ep. 38.1/580.10 ff.
4. See infra p. 184, n. 2, and Ep.
21.1/529.10 ff.
5. Ep. 21.1/529.10 ff.
6. Pass. Pion. 10.1.
7. Eusebius, HE, 6.41.18; Pass. Pion.

There is some indication, however, that while generally a two-stage procedure was followed, occasionally this formality was dispensed with and the prisoners were continually incarcerated.[1] This may indicate, however, that the penalties for such men actually involved detention in prison, and that their continued questioning was a further means of breaking them down after sentence had been passed.

The penalties inflicted were various in nature. Perhaps the edict had no statutory stipulation of particular penalties. The sentence would apparently devolve upon the discretion of the magistrate.[2] Obvious distinctions would be made with regard to the social standing of the individual within the community, and local pressures must have been a factor. The mode of execution for those who were Roman citizens was decapitation. Non-citizens were thrown to the beasts in the amphitheatre.[3] But at Lyons in 177/8, a Roman citizen, Attalus, was thrown to the beasts, although he was

---

7. (cont'd) 19. For this division, see article of C. Saumagne, "La persécution de Dèce en Afrique", Byzantion 32 (1962), pp. 1-29. Also Ep. 10.4/492.14 ff.
1. Ep. 37.2/576.4 ff.
2. The use of discretionary power in moves against Christians and other dissenters is amply evidenced. See de Ste. Croix, "'Great' Persecution", pp. 96 ff.
3. For the development of the new distinction between humiliores and honestiores and their differing status before the law, see P. Garnsey, Social Status and Legal Privilege in the Roman Empire (Oxford, 1970). For execution, see Garnsey, pp. 103 ff.

legally entitled to decapitation.[1] In a similar manner, Vibia Perpetua was executed in the amphitheatre with her slaves.[2] The legal status of those who perished or suffered under Decius is almost impossible to ascertain, but the wide variety of punishments exacted would indicate a great deal of discretion being allowed the magistrate.[3]

The sentences executed fell under three general headings: relegatio, confiscatio, and poena capitalis.[4] Cyprian makes frequent mention of banishment as a punishment for refusing to disavow one's faith. Deriding Florentius' claim to special sanctity, Cyprian lists as sufferers those who were in exilium relegati.[5] Elsewhere he mentions those whose goods were confiscated and who were then exiled.[6] Though it would be rash to hold that Cyprian's legal language is to be taken literally, the absence of any mention of a definite place of exile would certainly seem to point towards the penalty being one of relegation rather than of deportation. The penalty was widespread and references are frequent in Cyprian's

---

1. Eusebius, HE 5.1.47 ff.
2. Pass. Perpet. 18.1 ff.
3. Saumagne, "La persécution", pp. 1 ff. is far too schematic and formal in his statement of punishment.
4. Saumagne, Ibid, mistakes deportatio for relegatio. Deportatio involved confiscation and banishment to a specific place. It was generally not within the competetence of provincial governors. See Crook, Law and Life, pp. 272-3.
5. Ep. 66.7/731.21.
6. Ep. 19.2/526.10.

correspondence.[1]

Confiscation of goods appears generally linked to the other penalties, such as _relegatio_.[2] The addition was necessitated by the fact that _relegatio_ did not necessarily involve the loss of the exile's property.[3] This is a further argument against deportation as the legal form under which exile was imposed, as deportation normally required the automatic confiscation of goods.[4] Cyprian himself was awarded the penalty of confiscation, and in his letter of remonstrance to Florentius he records part of the edict: "Si quis tenet possidet de bonis Caecili Cypriani Episcopi Christianorum".[5] For a rich man, confiscation in itself could be a serious punishment; the poor have nothing to lose.[6]

Imprisonment was not a normal penalty under Roman law, but at times it was used as a means of temporary restraint until sentence could be passed.[7] Provincial governors did, however, strictly speaking, illegally use imprisonment as a punishment

---

1. Ep. 20.2/527.16 ff.; 24.1/536.11 ff.; 38.1/579.17; 42/590.1-8; 55.13/632.16 ff. Also _De Lapsis_ 2/237.14 ff.
2. _Supra_ p. 185, n. 4.
3. Dig. 48.22.4, and F. Cabrol and H. LeClercq, _Dictionnaire d'archéologie chrétienne et de liturgie_ (15 vols. Paris, 1903-53), Vol. X: _s.v._ Martyr, 29, 2426.
4. Crook, _Law and Life_, p. 273.
5. Ep. 66.4/729.15-16.
6. See _infra_ p. 192.
7. Crook, _Law and Life_, p. 274; Garnsey, _Social Status_, p. 149: "It was not recognized as a penalty but as a coercive measure".

and a corrective measure.[1] Decurions could be placed under less stringent forms of custody but, particularly with the Christians, little account was taken of status. Often the prison was employed in its normal function as a place of detention until a sentence of banishment could be passed.[2] Clear evidence of the use of prison as punishment in itself is less available. But the extreme length of Maximus' stay, as well as that of other members of the Christian community at Rome, would indicate that it was being used as the punishment itself.[3]

The infliction of capital penalties in the West appears to have been somewhat restricted. Decius' actions were aimed at destroying the structure and the power of the Church rather than at the extermination of its members.[4] Cyprian's correspondence provides few specific examples of the infliction of a death penalty, though it is filled with exhortations of perseverance unto death as the most desirable path for the true believer.[5] Some examples of the death

---

1. Dig. 48.19.8.13.
2. Ep. 24.1/536.11. Celerinus may have been released because he was banished, but the case is far from clear.
3. Ep. 37.2/577.5. Notice Cyprian's reference to their being led out of prison confessing and being reincarcerated (37.1/ 576.4 ff.). This displays the fine line between detention and prison as a form of punishment in its own right. Saumagne, "La persécution", p. 6 is wrong in denying its absence as a punishment.
4. For Africa, infra p. 192.
5. Ep. 10.2/491.3 ff.; also 12.1/ 502.6 ff.

penalty are given however. He recommends the presbyter, Numidicus, because he encouraged martyrs for the faith during the persecution and because he himself was stoned and half-burned. Left for dead, he was found and revived by his daughter.[1] The circumstances of his ordeal, however are unclear. The occasion of the incident would point to a spontaneous action by the crowd, agitated by Numidicus' exhortations, rather than to a planned execution.

Another of those who died as a result of the actions of the authorities was Mappalicus. The exact cause of death is again not clear. Cyprian mentions his courage in the face of the African proconsul's torments, but he omits the precise circumstances leading to his death. Lucianus, a Carthaginian confessor, names him as one of those who died in quaestione.[2] The most complete list of those who died in the persecution is preserved in Lucianus' reply to a letter of Celerinus from Rome. None of the qualifications added to the list definitely point to a legal condemnation of the persons who died. One met his death in the mines, another in prison from unspecified causes.[3] A third perished presumably from the torture suffered at the hearings, and a great majority died from hunger while in prison.[4] Lucianus states that the deaths of

---

1. Ep. 40.
2. Ep. 10.4/491.3 ff.; 22.2/534.18.
3. Damnatio ad metallum plays a far larger part in the Cyprianic corpus during the Valerianic Persecution, infra pp. 343 f.
4. Ep. 22.1/534.3 ff. Lucianus mentions that others are perishing as he writes. The case of Paul is presumably a death of hunger and thirst.

those who perished from hunger and thirst were the results of imperial command.[1] The presumed reference is to the actual imprisonment, rather than to the deliberate killing of prisoners by starvation. There were quicker and more economical means of arranging for death. Lack of food and drink may have been an inducement to recant, but not a formal death sentence.[2]

In Africa no deaths recorded can be attributed beyond a doubt to actual execution. They are rather a by-product of haste and perhaps anger over Christian resistance.[3] Elsewhere Roman officials and the local populace were less hesitant about ending the lives of recalcitrant Christians. Eusebius lists the deaths of fourteen persons as a result of the persecution of the prefect of Egypt.[4] Ten died by fire, and four were executed by the sword.[5]

---

1. Ep. 22.2/534.3 ff.
2. The cases of starvation recorded by Tacitus are those of important individuals whom the Emperor wished to remove "unsensationally", e.g., Annales 6.25.1. Christians generally would not fall into such a category.
3. The case of the Christians who were with Numidicus is the only reasonable counter-example. See supra p. 188, n. 1.
4. The prefect was Sabinus, PIR[2] A 1455. A. Stein, Die Praefekten von Aegypten in der römischen Kaiserzeit, Diss. Bernenses, series 1, fasc. 1 (Bern, 1950), pp. 140 ff.
5. Eusebius, HE 6.41.14-23. Note that the executed male was a soldier and possibly entitled as a citizen to beheading. Nothing is specified as to the status of the women. Except for those males who are specified as Egyptians, perhaps non-citizen

189

Elsewhere in the East, Eusebius records the death of Alexander, a bishop of Jerusalem, as a result of imprisonment.[1] Origen suffered torture but not death in the same persecution. Pionius suffered death by fire.[2] Little else is preserved of Christian sufferings in the East where death was the intention. Numerous late and fictitious martyrdoms were attracted by the fame and magnitude of Decius' reputation as a foe of the Christians. Commodian saw him as the Anti-Christ.[3] But the majority of such compilations are worthless as well as late.[4]

There is virtually no evidence that death was a prescribed punishment for Christians in the West. The information available records that deaths resulted from accidental or intentional over-zealousness in the questioning of believers. Even if the result was intended by the authorities, there is no record of it as an actual sentence.

In the East, however, the activities of the Egyptian prefect, as recorded by Eusebius and the officials of Smyrna in the

5. (cont'd) inhabitants of the chora, no distinctions are drawn.

1. Eusebius, HE 6.39.2-3.
2. Pass. Pion. 19.
3. Commodian, Carmen Apol. 1-5. Also see J.P. Brisson, Autonomisme et christianisme dans l'Afrique romaine de Septime Sévère à l'invasion vandale (Paris, 1958), pp. 33-121, who rightly dates Commodian to the mid-third century. The reference in the Apol. is certainly to Decius, Herennius Etruscus and Hostilianus. In general, see Altaner-Stuiber, Pat., pp. 181 ff.
4. See Delehaye, Les passions, pp.239ff

Passion of Pionius, would indicate the existence of death sentences, although examples of these are few. A total of fifteen persons are actually known to have been executed. The remaining two would seem to have perished as those in the West, that is, from the ordeal of torture and prison rather than by execution. The conclusion that Decius' primary purpose was at least outward conformity and not extermination is thus established for both East and West.

The proclamation of the edict in Africa found a community totally unprepared for its onslaught. The general absence of restrictions on Christians had led to an ostensible _modus vivendi_ with their neighbors.[1] Apostolic severity in life and manners decreased with the increase in the size and the broadening of the composition of Christian society. Mixed marriages had taken place between Christians and pagans, pressuring the Christian partners to be more accommodating to the surrounding pagan environment.[2]

The general standards of behaviour among Christians had tended to be assimilated to those of the surrounding pagan community. The hierarchy, particularly the bishops, had neglected their congregations in search of material gain.[3] Christians were

---

1. _De Lapsis_ 5. On _longa pax_, see _supra_ p. 63.
2. _De Lapsis_ 6/240.21.
3. _De Lapsis_ 6. There must be a change in the text here. _Procuratores regum saecularium_ would not seem possible. _Rerum_ is more plausible, and attested in Rv and in W. See F. Millar, "Paul of Samosata, Zenobia and Aurelian. The Church, Local Culture and Political Allegiance in Third-Century Syria", _JRS_ 61 (1971), p. 12.

191

totally unprepared when the Emperor's edict arrived in January 250.

Generally in Africa Christian resistance was weak in the face of the government's measures, and for the most part it collapsed; a great proportion of the community came forward voluntarily to comply with the provisions of the edict.[1] Some exaggeration may be allowed. The same reaction occurred in Alexandria. Dionysius reports that many members of his flock came forward voluntarily to sacrifice. The bishop stresses that the more important members of his church had the additional pressure of their private businesses to urge them to comply with the authorities.[2] The heroic days of the Christian community had ended with its expansion.[3] Dionysius fled the officers of the prefect. In Carthage Cyprian fled the soldiers of the proconsul and went into exile.[4]

Cyprian's flight created problems for him as did Dionysius'. His motives were questioned. Some said that fear was the reason for his flight, and not concern for his flock.[5] After his death in the Valerianic Persecution, the old charges of cowardice reappeared. His death at the hands

---

1. De Lapsis 7/241.11-242.9.
2. Eusebius, HE 6.41.11-13.
3. See the comments of Baus, HCH, p. 223.
4. Ep. 7 is the first letter written from exile. For its dating, Appendix I should be consulted.
5. Ep. 8, from the bishopless clergy in Rome, is an indictment of Cyprian's desertion of his flock. See Dionysius, apud Eusebius, HE 6.40 ff. for a similar problem of justification.

192

of the authorities had not stilled the doubts caused by his earlier flight. Pontius was moved to defend his hero's action.

According to Pontius, Cyprian had fled the persecution not for himself but for the welfare of his congregation. God purposely spared him, that his eloquence might supply the needs of his flock. All orders of the Christian community were recalled to faith and duty by his wonderful eloquence. There was fear, but the fear that Cyprian felt was not of secular might but of God's command.[1] His life was necessary for the welfare of his fellow Christians. The flight was a precaution of the deity; through his safety the strength and cohesion of God's people was assured. All was the result of divine consilium.[2] Dionysius also called on God to justify his flight to the Egyptian country-side. For him too it was God's judgment that made him flee, not his own.[3]

Cyprian's own justification is less clear. In defending his conduct to the Roman clergy, he states that at first he stood his ground in accordance with the instructions of the Lord, to fulfill his pastoral responsibilities (sicut Domini mandata instruunt). Then he went into hiding not for his own safety but for the general peace of the brethren.[4]

The majority of references in the correspondence concern Cyprian's reasons for

1. In Vita 7.13 there is an obvious reference to the motive presented by the bishop's opponents.
2. Vita 7-8.
3. Eusebius, HE 6.40.1.
4. Ep. 20.1/527.3-15.

193

remaining in exile, however, rather than those for taking flight. Writing to the Carthaginian Church soon after his departure, he claims that his return would provoke pagan reaction and violence.[1] Again, writing to Rogatianus and the confessors, the same reason is invoked to explain his prolonged absence.[2] The continued reiteration of this explanation would indicate the pressure that must have been on him to return from exile.[3]

Even after conditions had improved, Cyprian did not return.[4] What motivated his continued exile at this point is not at all clear. Perhaps he felt his return might still spark action against his flock. Certainly the divine motives that Pontius stresses generally seem to have been outweighed by more practical considerations. In discussing his return Cyprian remains concerned that his presence will create further problems for the Church.

We cannot recover what made Cyprian join his Alexandrian counterpart in flight. Comparison and justification based on his experience in the Valerianic period will not do.[5] Part of the explanation may

---

1. Ep. 5.1/478.11-479.5.
2. Ep. 6.1/480.4-481.3.
3. Ep. 5.1/478.11 ff. is less clear, referring only to indefinite reasons: "Et quoniam mihi interesse nunc non permittit loci condicio". See also Ep. 14.1/509.6-510.11.
4. Ep. 17.1/521.3-522.2; 18.1/523.13-524.8; 19.
5. Saumagne, "La persécution", pp. 25 ff., bases the main thrust of his argument on Cyprian's later conduct. But this is to ignore Cyprian's internal development.

194

be in the bishop's conviction that his life would be of service to his congregation. His constant correspondence and support played an important part in keeping the Christians together as a unified community. One key factor, on a more practical level, was the ease of his flight. Cyprian's contacts among the leading pagans who did not desert him were probably useful in ensuring that he could still function in his office even at a distance.[1] They may have been unable to assure him protection unless he could withdraw from Carthage. The clergy remaining in the city still seemed to have been able to function, though their ranks were depleted.[2] Cyprian's copious correspondence points to his place of exile being within easy reach of the capital.[3] The constant coming and going of messengers probably points to an open exile. Such activity would have been impossible to conceal. The exiled bishop must surely have acted in concert with his pagan friends who allowed him his life and function if he would withdraw from Carthage. Their interest was a destruction of faith, not of individuals. Cyprian's motivation seems to

---

1. For these friends at a later period, see *Vita* 14.3.
2. Ep. 5, 7 and 10 prove that the persecution was sporadic and that the clergy could still function even when some were imprisoned.
3. The correspondence deals with minor points of discipline, as well as appointments of new clergy later on in the persecution. Only a residence close to Carthage could have put Cyprian in a position to exercise his office in such matters of detail.

have been more complex than has been allowed. In this case self-interest and community good pointed to the same course. Other bishops provided support for his action. His goods were confiscated by order of the proconsul.[1] He must have been allowed to take some of his property into exile with him, as one of his first concerns was to see to the welfare of the indigent, and part of their need was to be supplied from his own resources.[2] His exile was not to include severe poverty among its hardships.

The control of a community under attack must have tried the administrative talents of a man even with Cyprian's expertise. The chain of command had to be reestablished so that he could exercise his control without his actual physical presence. A network of messengers and local representatives was established to convey and execute his instructions.

Members of the lower clergy acted as Cyprian's messengers and conveyers of news. Naricus the acolyte, would convey monies from Cyprian and deposit them with Rogatianus, the priest; the latter would distribute various amounts for the care of the poor.[3] A more important function was assigned to the presbyter Tertullus. Cyprian says that it was he who was responsible for his own retreat from the city. It was also Tertullus whom Cyprian assigned to defend his action before the members of the Cartha-

---

1. Ep. 66.4/729.15-16.
2. Ep. 7: de quantitate mea propria.
3. Ep. 7. See also Ep. 41, heading. Ep. 41 shows that Rogatianus had been acting in an administrative capacity, and there is no hint at all of his imprisonment.

196

ginian Church.[1] Tertullus functioned as a source of intelligence for the exiled bishop, relaying information about the dates of death of those who perished in the persecution and performing other less specified tasks.[2]

In letter 41 Cyprian names the bishops Caldonius and Herculanus and two others, Rogatianus and Numidicus, to act as his vicarii.[3] How long this organization had been functioning cannot be ascertained. Certainly this Rogatianus was identical with the Rogatianus in the letters marking Cyprian's initial exile who had been functioning as Cyprian's deputy from the beginnings of the persecution.[4] Numidicus may be a more recent addition, identical with the man promoted by Cyprian later on in the persecution.[5] Caldonius was, for a while, imprisoned, but he presumably remained at Carthage and may have been active on Cyprian's behalf throughout most of the tribulations of the Carthaginian Church. Herculanus first appears in this letter, and nothing can be deduced as to the length of his residence at Carthage. Attrition may have played a part in changing the personnel available for Cyprian's use. Caldonius was imprisoned, but he escaped. Tertullus, the faithful aide, disappears from the correspondence without a trace.[6]

---

1. Ep. 14.1/509.5 ff.
2. Ep. 12.2/503.14 ff.; 14.1/509.5 ff.
3. Ep. 41.1/587.13.
4. Ep. 7.
5. Ep. 40.
6. Caldonius imprisoned, Ep. 24. Tertullus is, as Hartel saw, not identical with the bishop mentioned in the headings of Ep. 57 and Ep. 70.

197

To add to Cyprian's difficulties, his flight was censured by the Roman clergy, whose own bishop had died at the commencement of the persecution. The clergy of Rome ironically excused Cyprian's attitude because of his importance - almost a direct mockery of Cyprian's own reason for flight.[1] They proclaimed the duty they felt not to flee, but to remain with their people to guide and support them through the crisis. The clergy are the shepherds of the Lord's flock, and as good shepherds are obliged to lay down their lives for the sake of the sheep.[2] Their fear was not of the actions of the rulers of this world, but rather of God. Their Church stands firmly. Though important persons have given way, the clergy must remain to strengthen their faith and prepare the people for a second combat which will extinguish the defeat of the first.[3] The ironical reference to the weakness of important people must surely have been aimed at Cyprian.

Roman influence could be disruptive of the control that Cyprian had retained over his congregation, and he therefore felt obliged to reply to the veiled accusations. His reply skillfully invoked the glorious death of Fabianus, pointing out that though it provided an illustrious testimony to the faith, it left the congregation of Rome bereft of leadership and opened it to dis-integration.[4] Cyprian goes as far as to question the genuineness of the letter as a product of the Roman clergy and asks for proof, hinting that it shows the corruption

---

1. Ep. 8.1/485.19 ff., 14.2/510.12 ff.
2. Ep. 8.1/485.19 ff., quoting John 21:16.
3. Ep. 8.2/486.20.
4. Ep. 9.1/488.20 ff.

198

of error and perhaps fraud.[1]

Cyprian needed all the authority he could exercise over his flock. Carthage had responded poorly to the effects of the edict. The faith of many had collapsed at the first onslaught, although initially the efforts of the authorities were surprisingly lax.[2] Though Cyprian fled into exile, many of his clergy had remained in the city performing their normal duties.[3] While masses of Christians had capitulated, the administrative machinery appears to have worked in a fitful manner. Some who refused to give way remained in custody, while others were released and continued to function.[4] A large part of the community may have given way, but the impetus seems to have spent itself in the first assault.[5]

---

1. Ep. 9.2/489.13. Colombo, "S. Cipriano", p. 27 calls the writers of these letters rigorists, but the appellation is doubtful. Cyprian obviously felt called upon to defend his conduct rather than to attack their position. Benson, Cyprian, p. 87, calls it mere interference, but in later issues such as rebaptism, Cyprian felt no compunction to refrain from interfering elsewhere.

2. For effects, see supra p. 192.

3. As the correspondence attests through the first section, 1-43, dealing with the Decian Persecution.

4. So Caldonius, Ep. 27, was imprisoned and then released. Tertullus, not mentioned as arrested, functioned along with Rogatianus as deputy for Cyprian.

5. Ep. 11.1/495.10 ff. laments the loss of so many, but this must be taken as relating to the mass sacrifices at De Lapsis 8, at the beginning of the persecution.

The authorities wanted apostates not martyrs.[1] Cyprian discovered that his main task lay in preserving the discipline of the Christians who had not apostasized, and in supporting those who had undergone various punishments and had continued in their faith despite them. They were to serve as models and form the nucleus of the Church, once the wave of the government's attack had subsided. The situation created a complicated structure of degrees of complicity among the members of the bishop's community.

Those who had in some way succumbed to the efforts of the government were divided into three categories. The sacrificati were those who had complied with the full requirements of the edict, while the turificati had burned incense to the gods but had not partaken of the meat which had been sacrificed.[2] The second category consisted of the libellatici, those who had purchased certificates without formally giving sacrifice and thereby obtained immunity from the actions of the authorities.[3] The last group followed Christ's injunction to flee from the city of persecution and they left Carthage, remaining in hiding to emerge later at the end of the troubled period. Later they came to be regarded on a level with the stantes, those who had stood firm in the Church's trial. Tertullian

---

1. Mongelli, "La chiesa", p. 118.
2. Ep. 30.3/520.21 ff.; also 55.2/ 624.14-22.
3. Ep. 55.13/633.2; De Lapsis 26-28/ 255.25-258.16. Benson, Cyprian, pp. 80-1, is wrong, but he was writing before the discovery of papyri of libelli, see Monceaux, HAC, p. 216.

200

had a lower opinion of such conduct.[1]

Cyprian found his efforts dispersed in dealing with the myriad categories resulting from the opening turmoil of the persecution of Decius. Part of his correspondence was directed towards supporting the faith of those who were actually in prison in Carthage. Their stand might be the cement to bind his Church together after the effects of the persecution had ceased and, if an effort was made to upset his own position they might serve as his most important supporters.

Early in his exile he addressed a letter to Rogatianus and others who were in prison with him in the capital.[2] Cyprian urged them to think not of earthly death and pain, but rather of heavenly reward and the divine gift of immortality. The sufferings of the present are small in comparison with the rewards that the future holds.[3] The letter also tells us that the authorities had imprisoned those who refused to sacrifice, without regard to age or sex.[4] Women and young men received special notice. They had transcended the limitations of age and sex.

---

1. Tertullian, De Fuga 12, 13; stantes, De Lapsis 3/238.22-239.8; 22/253.16-254.5; 25/255.1-24; 27/256.22-257.19.

2. Ep. 6. This man cannot be the same as the Rogatianus who acted as Cyprian's agent in Carthage. Cyprian points to the confessor's infirm condition, which would hardly have been appropriate for the activities demanded of Cyprian's vicarius.

3. Ep. 6.2/481.4.

4. Ep. 6.3/482.21 ff. See Eusebius, HE 6.41.12 ff. for the treatment of these groups in Alexandria.

In the same letter Cyprian admonished other martyrs and confessors to persevere. Their blood may yet extinguish the flames of persecution. They are the divine army of the Lord. Their death buys immortality as its reward.[1]

Cyprian had frequent recourse to various descriptions of the militia Christi. No doubt Tertullian had exerted his influence.[2] But the frequent use of the phrase in Cyprian betrays a connection with some basic concept in his own sense of Christianity.[3] Cyprian viewed the Church as a divine camp, constantly under the menace of the devil's attacks. The martyrs were the shock troops. Their steadfast repulsion of the efforts of the adversary to break the camp open and destroy the faith and morale of its inhabitants was central. They were the line which had to face and break the attack of the world upon the camp of God.[4]

Cyprian felt called upon by the Divine Commander himself to counsel and guide these troops. The martyrs and confessors were granted power and prerogatives, but the central authority of the bishop must remain as a check and guide on their activities.[5] Part of the authority was claimed by the

---

1. Ep. 10.2/491.3 ff.
2. Tertullian, Ad Mart. 1, 3.3-4. Also see H.A.M. Hoppenbrouwers, Recherches sur la terminologie du martyre de Tertullien à Lactance, Latinitas Christianorum Primaeva 15 (Nijmegen, 1961), pp. 146 ff.
3. Ep. 48.2/657.24; 15.1/513.6; 28.1/ 545.3. Novatianus also uses the term, Ep. 30.2/549.17; 37.3/578.6; Ad Fort. 1.
4. Ep. 38.2/547.
5. De Lapsis 20-21/252.22-253 ff.

bishop on the basis of his office.[1] Another part, however, was the product of his direct relationship with God.[2] To hearten the faithful, one of his most common approaches was to claim that the persecution had not only been devised as a chastisement of the sins of the Christians themselves, but had long been prophesied.[3] Christians had revolted from the discipline of the Lord and now had to pay the price.[4]

As further evidence that the persecution was a result of the neglect of discipline, Cyprian cites a vision.[5] The vision is stated to have taken place before the persecution, but it is not clear who actually experienced it. Cyprian adds that the present letter was also motivated by a divine vision warning of the falling away of Christians from the path of virtue.[6]

Cyprian was prepared to acknowledge the validity of dreams of others. Under the stress of the persecution, night visions were supplemented by visions that occurred in the daylight among young children.[7]

---

1. Infra pp. 328 ff.
2. On the subject, see A. von Harnack, "Cyprian als Enthusiast", ZNT 3 (1902), pp. 177-91.
3. Infra p. 279.
4. Ep. 11.3-4/497.8-498.9. On its chronological place, see Appendix I.
5. Ep. 11.4/498.9 ff.
6. Ep. 11.5/498.23. The visionary here is probably Cyprian.
7. Ep. 16.4/520.5. Harnack, "Cyprian als Enthusiast", pp. 190-1, shows that Cyprian differentiated between visions of the daytime and those at night, the latter being visiones, while those during the day were ecstases. Ecstases possibly indicated

203

Visions were an enduring part of Cyprian's character and are a regular feature of contemporary Christianity. Cyprian's fellow bishops were susceptible to visionary experiences.[1] Their visions lent supernatural support to the community in times of crisis.[2] Visions helped to sanction actions such as the appointment of new clergy.[3] They could be used to bolster authority.[4] That they had political and practical uses, particularly in bad times, did not make their authenticity suspect. They were facts of psychic life which were recognized by the whole community. They could be used, as other facts, to support or attack practices and institutions. To infer fictitiousness or conscious calculation would be to yield too much to modern scepticism.[5]

---

7. (cont'd) sudden possession. A further problem of classification is introduced by Harnack, p. 180, by assigning some dreams to the category of urtypus, that is, dreams based on some standardized pattern. Harnack questions their veracity by contrasting them with real visions. But as E.R. Dodds has convincingly shown, in The Greeks and the Irrational (Berkeley and Los Angeles, 1951), pp. 108 ff., cultural patterns induce dreams of different structures. That the culture provides the pattern, however, does not invalidate the truth of the vision. Most dreams incorporate cultural patterns in one form or another.

1. De Mort. 19/308.25-309.15.
2. Ep. 11.1/495.10 ff.
3. Celerinus, Ep. 39.1/582.5.
4. Ep.66.10/734.3 ff.
5. Harnack, "Cyprian als Enthusiast", p. 177, seems to be inclined to assign too much credit to calculation.

204

Cyprian constantly tried to maintain control over his own clergy from his place of exile. The actions of the bishopless Roman clergy in casting doubt on his flight had undoubtedly added to his problems.[1] Much of his correspondence is aimed at controlling those clergy who remained behind. Some of them were eliminated by the persecution, but it can be inferred from the tenor of Cyprian's correspondence that the organization remained intact.[2] The admonitions and exhortations were directed to sustaining as well as controlling. Cyprian concerned himself with regulating the attendance of the remaining Christians upon martyrs who had been imprisoned.[3] They dispensed monies for the care of those imprisoned and the poor who were deprived of sustenance.[4] He found it increasingly difficult to maintain his control.

With the provisions of the edict fulfilled, by the spring of 250 the force of the persecution seemed to wane. The continuing devastation of the Goths on the Danube caused Decius to follow his son, Herennius, in an expedition against them. Decius probably arrived in mid-summer; his son had reached the area in April or May.[5] Decius became involved in a long and

---

1. Ep. 8.
2. Ep. 5 implies the continued functioning of the clergy, even at the beginning of the persecution. Ep. 11.1/ 495.10 and 14.1/509.6 ff. point to heavy casualties, presumably also among the clergy.
3. Ep. 5.2/479.6.
4. Ep. 5.1/478.11 and Ep. 7.
5. For the time of arrival, see Wittig, RE XV, 1270, and his references.

205

intricate campaign.[1] Naturally his attention was diverted from the internal problems that had occupied him at the beginning of his administration. The constant diversion of resources must also have diminished the effectiveness of his internal policy. The task of enforcing the edict was one of unprecedented magnitude, straining the Empire's administrative resources to the fullest extent. The imperial bureaucracy had always been spread thinly over its area of jurisdiction, and constant attention to the edict's provisions further weakened its effectiveness in performing its customary tasks, even with the aid of local officials. Cyprian's correspondence alone is sufficient indication of the general failure to enforce the provisions of the edict. Even at the height of governmental activity, the clergy functioned.[2] Decius may have decided that the internal enemies of the Roman order could wait, diverting the major portion of his resources to deal with the invading Germans.

But the lessening of the government's activities against the Christians brought fresh problems for Cyprian. The initial success of the edict had created great numbers of Christians who had lapsed from the faith.[3] They now attempted to regain admission to the Church, for it was no longer dangerous to be a Christian. With the

---

5. (cont'd) For later bibliography, see Walser-Pekáry, Die Krise, p. 24. For the gradual subsiding of the persecution, Ep. 20.2/527.16.
1. Wittig, Ibid.
2. Supra p. 195.
3. Supra p. 199.

206

diminution of earthly troubles, heavenly rewards again appeared desirable. Coupled with this pressure, the martyrs and confessors who had survived the worst days of the persecution provided a new menace and acted as a counterweight to Cyprian's authority.[1]

Tertullian had placed a high value on martyrdom.[2] He violently attacked those among the Christians who believed that martyrdom was to be avoided if possible, and Gnostics who believed that conversion in this world was of no consequence.[3] Persecution was a gift of God sent to test His followers. The Biblical injunction to flee no longer applied; it had been historically conditioned for the time of the Apostles. Christians now had the duty to remain and die.[4] So high a value on martyrdom was a common notion among African

---

1. The words "martyr" and "confessor" seem to be synonymous, as seen by E.R. Watson, "The Style and Language of St. Cyprian", _Studia biblica et ecclesiastica_ 4 (1896), p. 290. E.L. Hummel, _The Concept of Martyrdom According to St. Cyprian of Carthage_, _Studies in Christian Antiquity_ 9 (Wash., 1946), p. 3 points out that though Tertullian usually reserved the appellation of "martyr" for those who actually died for the faith, he sometimes extended it to those who had confessed and were preparing for death. See _Ad Mart._ 1.1, _martyres designati_. Cyprian extends the term to include those who would logically be called "confessors", e.g., Ep. 66 and 38.2/580.20.

2. Tertullian, _Scorp._ 15 and _Ad Mart._, _passim_.

3. Tertullian, _Scorp._ 15.6.

4. Tertullian, _De Fuga_ 6.

207

Christians.[1] Part of Cyprian's exhortation, therefore, was concerned with maintaining the confessors within the paths of normal ecclesiastical discipline.[2] Already before the cessation of the persecution, dissension had crept in to disrupt the community of martyrs and confessors in their confinement. Some of them had been puffed up with pride at their new status.[3] Others had had sexual intercourse with women.[4] Their dissension was dangerous for the bishop. The prestige he lost in flight could only be compensated by the full support of those who had undergone trials that he himself had avoided.[5]

Cyprian's conception of the origin of the persecution made his dealings with those who had not fled more complex. He saw the persecution as the fulfillment of God's plan for His people, long expected and predicted by the Prophets and the Scriptures.[6] Its direct cause lay in the want of faith and discipline of the Christians.[7] Long

---

1. Ep. 15.1/513.5 ff. Cyprian regarded the petitions of the martyrs as inherently legal. He reserved the right to interfere, but did not question the martyrs' sending of libelli on behalf of those who had given way during the persecution.
2. Ep. 13.4/506.21.
3. Ep. 13.4/506.21.
4. Ep. 13.5/507.11 ff.
5. The extreme apologetic of the Vita points to this as an enduring weak spot in Cyprian's position. More than just the Roman clergy were upset by the action of the bishop.
6. De Lapsis 7/241.11.
7. Ep. 11.1/495.11; 15.3/515.5; 16.4/ 520.5; De Lapsis 5-6.

peace had corrupted their obedience to God.[1] Men had devoted themselves to the search for profit and the fulfillment of their boundless greed.[2] Even the bishops of the Church shared in this infamy. Envy raged unchecked among the Carthaginian Church.[3] Many were behaving viciously. Men and women used cosmetics to deface the handicraft of God. Marriage was prostituted by Christians who joined with pagan spouses.[4] Thus Cyprian viewed the persecution as both punishment and testing.[5] Given this view, his attitude towards the actions of the martyrs and confessors could not but be favourable.

His view of martyrdom was not, however, in the rigorous tradition of Tertullian who felt that for a Christian to flee and not confront his persecutors was to disobey God.[6] Cyprian's attitude was not as rigid; though he valued martyrdom highly, it was not to be sought voluntarily. If it comes, it is God's will and should be met.[7] God alone is the judge of the hour of martyrdom.[8] Flight must be in accordance with His will.[9]

The glory of those who stand firm is, of course, greater, for Cyprian envisages them as doing spiritual warfare with the

---

1. De Lapsis 5/240.3.
2. De Lapsis 5/240.3.
3. Ep. 11.1/495.11; De Lapsis 5/240.3.
4. De Lapsis 6/240.13.
5. Hummel, Concept of Martyrdom, p.39.
6. Tertullian, De Fuga 6.
7. "gift of God", De Lapsis 10, and De Mort. 16; "not to be sought", Ep. 19.2/525.12.
8. Flight is allowed by Cyprian, in contrast to Tertullian. See De Lapsis 10, and Benson, Cyprian, p. 75.
9. De Lapsis 10/243.19.

adversary of God.[1] Christ is the spiritual imperator of the divine army.[2] Christians are bound to serve by accepting baptism, their equivalent of the sacramentum of the soldier.[3] The Church is the divine camp from which the martyrs issue forth to do battle with the adversary. The commandments of the Lord are the weapons of the Christians.[4] Those who become heretics are deserters and rebels.[5] The contest is for Cyprian an agon, a certamen.[6] The martyr in his victory carries off the palm.[7] In undergoing suffering and torture in the divine contest, he is imitating Christ and obtaining union with him.[8] He becomes another Christ.[9] Martyrdom grants a total remission of sins to the spiritual warrior.[10] The second baptism, which is of blood, contrasts to the first which is of water.[11] It leads directly to heaven where the martyrs

1. Ep. 10.1/490.5.
2. Ep. 15.1/513.5 ff.; dux, Ep. 6.1/480.3; protector, Ep. 10.3/492.5.
3. Ep. 10.2/491.3 ff. See D'Alès, S. Cyprien, pp. 227 ff.
4. Ad Fort., praefatio 4.
5. Ep. 58.10/665.24.
6. Ep. 8.1/485.18 ff.; 19.2/526.15. The Roman clergy also use the expression, Ep. 8.2/491.17. For Cyprian's use of Greek words, see Watson, "Style and Language", p. 213.
7. Ep. 39.3/583.3. See De Dom. Or. 26 with special reference to note of Reveillard, ad loc..
8. Ep. 6.2/482.3-4 and 57.2/651.
9. Ep. 76.2/829.3-830.13.
10. Ad Fort., praefatio 4.
11. Ep. 73.22; Ad Fort., praefatio 4.

210

sit and judge with God.[1]

Such a valuation of the martyr and confessor placed Cyprian in a difficult position. Sharing with his contemporaries this exalted concept, he was faced with a dilemma. The persecution of Decius had resulted in apostasy on a previously unknown scale. Cyprian's own conduct was suspect. His diminished prestige was a weak spot in his relationship with the martyrs. If they were influenced in any way by the large numbers of those who had fallen away but sought re-admission to the Church, it was possible that his authority might be seriously challenged.[2]

The pressure of the lapsed upon the martyrs and confessors was great. They pressed the soldiers of Christ to grant them

---

1. Ep. 6.2/481.21-2; 6.3/483.7.
2. Brisson, Autonomisme, pp. 59 ff., argues that this was also a period marked by strong social tensions, as evidenced by the writings of Commodian. There is little evidence of widespread social disorder. The Cyprianic corpus makes it fairly plain that the split on various issues in the North African Church was on doctrinal rather than social lines, though Cyprian's previous social position may have caused part of the enmity towards him felt within the clergy. Brisson's view of Christianity, particularly at p. 285, is far too biased towards perceiving it as inherently hostile to the Roman State. Persecution bred hatred, but the change in State policy under Constantine led to a rapid accommodation which would surely not have been possible had the State and Church been as antithetical as Brisson conceived them to be. He reads back developments of the 4th century, esp. Donatism.

211

a _libellus_ which would either grant recon- ciliation with the Church or at least offer the hope of it.[1] They pressured the confessors to accede to their demands for a petition for reconciliation.[2] Some confessors, proud of their new position, responded to the petitions as a means of exercising their new status and power.[3] They began to issue _libelli_ in general terms granting peace.[4] Cyprian protested that such a general pardon had never before been granted by any of the martyrs.[5] Another problem was added to Cyprian's load by priests acting in conjunction with the confessors who were slipping from his control.

The faction of presbyters that opposed Cyprian's election seems never to have been satisfied with the bishop's performance.[6] Nothing is heard of them in Cyprian's correspondence in the first years of his episcopate. No sharp issues seem to have divided the Carthaginian Church which would provide an opening for them to apply pressure.[7] The commencement of the perse- cution and the great numbers of lapsed could bring about the overthrow of Cyprian and the victory of the faction of the

---

1. Ep. 18.1/523.19-524.
2. Ep. 15.3/515.8; 19.2/525.13.
3. Ep. 13.3/505.24; 14.3/512.
4. Ep. 15.4/516.5, _communicet ille cum suis_.
5. Ep. 15.4/516.1.
6. Ep. 43.1/590.10 ff.
7. Freppel, _Saint Cyprien_, p. 193, questions the motives of those who opposed Cyprian, but his extreme bias vitiates his conclusions, including the one contained herein.

212

presbyters.[1] They first appear to have worked with the bishop rather than against him. Four of them wrote to him asking that easier terms be granted to the lapsed in the reception of the petitions from the confessors. But Cyprian, perhaps unsure of himself and under tremendous pressure, took the path of greatest safety and deferred any final decision until the persecution ceased and a common council could be held which could deal with the issue.[2] The deferral of action seems to have incited his antagonists. They began to align themselves with those confessors who were willing to grant a general peace in opposition to the bishop's injunctions.[3] Cyprian's attempt to

---

1. Unfortunately, except for the letter of Lucianus, nothing remains of the literature of Cyprian's opponents in the controversy, and he represents them as totally self-interested. But it would be rash to conclude that the reality was as Cyprian portrays it. Their own genuine concern, seconded by their opposition to Cyprian, may have led them to enter upon the course of action which they followed. The evidence is not available to decide the relative weight of the various factors which impelled them to adopt this course. In fact, the entire situation of mass defection was a new and startling development for all concerned.
2. Ep. 14.4/512.15 ff. Cyprian unfortunately does not preserve the content of the letter to the four priests. Given their later behaviour, it probably corresponded with the inferences reached by Cyprian. His position that a council should be called as the final arbiter is a constant refrain, Ep. 14.2/510.12 ff.; 17.3/522.20 ff.; 20.3/ 528.14 ff.
3. Ep. 16.3/519.8, where they are named

avoid open opposition was futile. The priests continued to encourage the martyrs to grant immediate restoration to the lapsed and began to admit them to communion and offer the Eucharist in their name.[1] In a letter to his clergy, Cyprian compared the heinousness of the sin committed by the lapsed with the gravity of far smaller infractions. He pointed out that even in cases of smaller infractions a period of penance is imposed, after which the guilty are re-admitted to confession and then communion when they receive forgiveness from the bishop with the laying on of hands.[2] But again the cautions of Cyprian had no effect on his flock, and he appears to have fallen back on the claim that nothing could be settled until the persecution ceased and a general council would be called.[3]

The priests who allied themselves against their bishop ignored his instructions and continued to grant peace to the lapsed on

---

3. (cont'd) in a circuitous manner. Cyprian was trying to avoid an open break.

1. Ep. 16.2/518.

2. Ep. 16.2/519.1 ff. On the question of penance for sins other than idolatry, the bibliography is long and controversial, particularly on the edict of Callistus. See K. Adam, Das sogenannte Bussedikt des Papstes Kallistus, Veröffentl. aus dem Kirchenhistor. Seminar München, 4, 5 (Munich, 1917); B. Poschmann, "Die altchristliche Busse", Hdb. der DG 4, 3 (Freiburg i.Br., 1951), pp. 18-41. On the identification of the bishop of the De Pudicitia with Callistus, see Barnes, Tert., p. 247; see also Appendix 7.

3. Supra p. 213, n. 2.

their own conditions.[1] At the beginning of the summer the rebellion seemed to have spread, and at least for a time Cyprian could not communicate with his clergy who presumably were under the influence of his opponents.[2] Though the force of the persecution had spent itself, danger arrived from another quarter. Summer was the time of sickness and ill health in North Africa.[3] This presented an immediate problem for the bishop, opening up the possibility that many of the lapsed might die without reconciliation and thus open a split in his Church. He decided to relent and allow those who held certificates of peace from the martyrs to obtain that peace if they were injured or ill. They must confess before a priest or, if none were available, before a deacon. If the cleric lays on his hands, they will obtain peace.[4] This action did not, however, allay the disturbances which had begun to rack the Carthaginian community over the reception of the lapsed back into the Church.[5]

The prestige and easy access of Rome complicated matters for Cyprian. The priests in control during the interregnum of

1. Ep. 17.2/522.4.
2. Ep. 18.1/523.13.
3. Ep. 18.1/523.18-19. See D.D. Sullivan, The Life of the North Africans as Revealed in the Works of St. Cyprian, Patristic Studies, 37 (Wash., 1933) p. 37.
4. Ep. 18.1/523.13; 19.2/525.13. Dionysius in Egypt relates an interesting case of a lapsed individual receiving communion on his death bed, apud Eusebius, HE 6.44.2 ff.
5. Ep. 18.2/524.9.

215

the Roman bishopric had initially been cool to Cyprian's conduct.[1] The flow of refugees between the two cities contributed to the need for the head of the Carthaginian Church to placate them, or at least come to some modus vivendi. To ignore Rome was to provide an opening for his opponents to use its prestige for their own purposes.[2] Cyprian attempted, through his correspondence, to assert the correctness of his own position and to win the alliance of the Roman clergy. He forwarded to them a dossier of his correspondence containing his defense.[3]

The crux of his defense was that he had performed the tasks that belonged to him as bishop of his flock.[4] More importantly, the Romans had pressed for aid to be given to the lapsed who were ill and desired communion. Cyprian had moved towards their position by

---

1. Ep. 8.
2. The easy access of Rome is well illustrated by the correspondence of Celerinus with Lucianus, Ep. 21.4/532.3 ff., on refugees from Carthage. Benson, Cyprian, pp. 87 ff., characterizes the action of the Romans as interference, but the close connection between the two communities demands more than such an off-hand dismissal. For the close economic relationship, see Haywood, Roman Africa, p. 62.
3. Ep. 20.2/527.16. The exact letters are a matter of some dispute, but most probably the thirteen mentioned by Cyprian were letters 5-7 and 10-19. See Appendix I. This may have been the initial beginning of the collection that we now possess. See Von Soden, "Die Cyprianische Briefsammlung: Geschichte ihrer Entstehung und Überlieferung" TU N.F. 25, hft. 3 (Leipzig, 1904), pp.19 ff.
4. Ep. 20.2-3/527.16-529.9.

216

allowing those with certificates to obtain peace when in mortal danger.[1] Deferring all action until a council could be called had proved unsatisfactory. It would have alienated everyone.

The question of penance and re-admission formed the central difficulty of Cyprian's administration. The previous state of the question is far from clear, as was Cyprian's own stand.[2] In his collection of Biblical quotations, he had included the heading: "Non posse in ecclesia remitti ei qui in Deum deliquerit."[3] This would imply that idolatry was not a sin that could be forgiven by the Church on earth. The point is reaffirmed in the De Lapsis, where Cyprian castigates those who pretend to grant remission of sins against God. The Lord alone can grant such forgiveness.[4]

---

1. Infra p. 224.
2. There are essentially two conflicting views. The first is held by B. Poschmann, "Zur Bussfrage in der cyprianischen Zeit", ZKT 37 (1913), pp. 25-54 and 244-65; and Poschmann, Penance and the Anointing of the Sick (Montreal, 1964), trans. and revised by F. Courtney, pp. 54ff. who holds that penance for sins in general antedated the crisis of the Decian Persecution. The opposing view is most forcefully put by Koch, "Die Bussfrage bei Cyprian", in CU, pp. 211-85, and Harnack, HD, II, pp. 108 ff. See also M. Bévenot, "The Sacrament of Penance and St. Cyprian's De Lapsis", ThSt 16 (1955), pp. 175-213, which supports the position of Poschmann.
3. Test. III.28/142.6-7.
4. De Lapsis 17/249.17-250.2. This seems decisive to me as to Koch, CU, p. 216. Poschmann's argument, in "Zur Bussfrage",

Such a position might have been accepted under ordinary circumstances, but the great numbers of lapsed provided an unparalleled situation. At first Cyprian held firm against even those who sought peace through an intercession of the martyrs, deferring any decision until the end of the persecution.[1] But the combined strain caused by his own clergy and the influence of Rome prompted his gradual recession from that stance.[2] Further pressure was to cause him to retreat more.[3] Cyprian looked to a second trial to wipe out the sins of the fallen as the most appropriate method for the lapsed to redeem themselves during the persecution.[4] But such principles were no longer consistent with the broad scope of the Christian community. Its boundaries had been too far extended for him to expect extreme virtue from all its members. To maintain his position, Cyprian found that compromise was the only useful approach.

The main opposition among the martyrs and confessors came from the circle of Lucianus and his fellow prisoners. The

---

4. (cont'd) that the lapsed expected to be received back and that therefore the contrary proposition holds, is weak. The basic flaw in his argument is the assumption of universal similarity in practice. Cyprian's position was not necessarily the customary position of all bishops on the question. Cyprian, his colleagues, and the lapsed all had different conceptions.

1. Ep. 20.2/533.
2. Ep. 20.3/528.14. Also Ep. 18.2/ 524.9.
3. Ep. 55.17/635.22 ff. See Koch, CU, pp. 257 ff.
4. Ep. 25.

original impulse for granting unrestricted peace to the lapsed came from an older associate of Lucianus, Paul, who probably died in the spring or summer of 250.[1] Paul apparently provided the impetus for the general granting of petitions by these martyrs. He then won over Lucianus who pursued the same general policy after Paul's death, and claimed the latter's sanction for his actions.[2]

Perhaps Cyprian's social position was a source of friction. The confessors had discovered a means of quick advancement with their new prestige.[3] They must have sensed the power of the bishop and attempted reconciliation by sending Cyprian notice that the peace they had granted was extended only to those who conducted themselves in a manner agreeable to Cyprian. But the bishop was not appeased.[4] In opposition to them and to the priests who opposed him, he began to rally support for his position.[5]

---

1. Ep. 22; 27.1/540.11 ff.; 35.
2. Ep. 27.1/540.11 ff.; 22.3/535.10 ff. Certificates were also issued in the name of the confessor, Aurelius, who seems to have been unable to write, Ep. 27.1/540.11.
3. Frend, M&P, p. 306, stresses the low social status of the martyrs in general. The basic reason may be that they, unlike men of Cyprian's standing, could not gain the requisite protection of influencial friends. But that can only be a secondary consideration. The split was essentially religious rather than social.
4. Ep. 23, written by Lucianus in the name of all.
5. Ep. 26. Benson, Cyprian, p. 92, is wrong about the priests using confessors. Ep. 22 makes it evident that

219

To strengthen his stance, he dispatched another missive to the Roman clergy to explain his opposition to Lucianus and his fellow martyrs.[1] The letter is a reaffirmation of the position taken in his earlier letter to them. But the situation seems to have deteriorated further outside Carthage. Other bishops evidently did not have Cyprian's prestige or education. The pressure of the lapsed for re-admittance grew so great that riots ensued outside Carthage.[2] Cyprian drew specific attention to Lucianus' action which would probably be known of at Rome through his friend Celerinus. His approach had been to study closely the merits of individual cases, but the time-consuming process bred very little satisfaction.[3]

The power of the confessors had already diminished through a split in their ranks. Celerinus had already joined Cyprian and was later to be promoted to the clergy as a reward for his sufferings and his agreement in doctrine with the bishop.[5] The confessors Moyses, Maximus and Nicostratus in Rome also supported his position, lending their prestige to his campaign

---

5. (cont'd) the impetus for reconciliation came from among the confessors, though later on community of interest brought the two groups closer together.

1. Ep. 27.1/540.10, referring to Ep.20.

2. Ep. 27.3/542.13, located in provincia nostra, which probably refers to Africa Proconsularis. Ep. 48.3/607.10-11 shows that Cyprian considered Numidia and Mauretania as attached to his province rather than as a specific part of it.

3. Ep. 27.2/541.16.

4. Ep. 27.3/542.13, and 39.

220

against the easy granting of peace. Cyprian was quick to thank them.[1] In addition, he had begun to replace clergy who had succumbed during the persecution with his own candidates, one of whom was a confessor.[2] Though this action conflicted with his own determination to wait for the end of the persecution and a council for reorganization, the appointments were essential to extend and consolidate his control.

The reply to Cyprian's letter was in a tone different from that of the Roman clergy early in the persecution. In elegant Latin, it was the work of the presbyter, Novatianus, who must have replaced the drafter of the first letter to Cyprian.[3] Later church

---

1. Ep. 27.4/543; 28. Also Eusebius, HE 6.43.20.
2. Ep. 29. One confessor was Optatus; the other, a former reader.
3. For Novatianus' authorship of Ep. 30, see Melin, Studia, pp. 4 ff. The background of this extraordinary man is unfortunately veiled in obscurity. The only source of any importance is Eusebius, who depends on a hostile account (HE 6.43.13), a letter of Cornelius, his opponent at Rome, to Fabius, bishop of Antioch. It is to be noted that Eusebius uses the incorrect form of the name, i.e., Novatus. This may simply be a result of his attempt at standardizing the spelling of the name. But surely Cornelius had the right spelling, and this may indicate some intermediate source or translation in Greek that had already confused the Roman with the Carthaginian presbyter. See P. Nautin, Lettres et écrivains chrétiens des IIe et IIIe siècles, Patristica, 2 (Paris, 1961), pp. 143 ff., on the correspondence of Cornelius with

221

writers record that Novatianus was born in Phrygia, but they offer no evidence to support this.[1] A birth date around 200 may not be far from wrong.[2] From the style of his writings, Novatianus seems to have received good rhetorical training, though nothing is known of his employment previous to his duties as a cleric. His early training may have included some Stoicism since his extant works indicate a leaning towards that philosophical persuasion.[3] The time of his conversion is unknown, but

---

3. (cont'd) Fabius. On Novatianus' conception of the Church, see H.J. Vogt, Coetus Sanctorum. Der Kirchenbegriff des Novatian und die Geschichte seiner Sonder- kirche (Bonn, 1968).

1. For the name, see RE XVII.1, 1139. On place of birth, Philostorgius, HE 8.15; Pacatianus, Ad Sympron.. Ep. 1.3, PL 13, 1054. There is no contemporary evidence for the subject, and one would think that Phrygian birth might have been based on that of the arch-heretic Montanus. H. Weyer (ed. and trans.), Novatianus: De Trinitate. Uber den dreifaltigen Gott, Testimonia, 2 (Dusseldorf, 1962), p. 5 thinks that Latin was Novatianus' native tongue, but expertise is no proof of linguistic origin.

2. No positive evidence can be established, but for what it is worth, Cornelius represents Novatianus as seeking the episcopal office for a long time before the break during the Decian Persecution, Eusebius, HE 6.43.5.

3. Harnack, HD, II, p. 283; M. Spanneut, Le stoicisme des pères de l'église de Clément de Rome à Clément d'Alexandrie, Patristica Sorbonensia, 1 (Paris, 1957), pp. 340-1 and 374-5.

222

Cornelius states that it resulted from some physical or emotional illness which led to the use of exorcists after whose ministrations, close to death, he received baptism by effusion.[1] Raised to the presbyterate by Fabianus, Novatianus may already have gathered prestige from his treatise on the Trinity.[2] Cornelius' report that he refused to hold office during the persecution has no other support. But Cyprian's correspondence with Rome prior to the 30th epistle indicates that Novatianus was not in control of the sentiments of his fellow presbyters. By the summer of 250, however, he gained control of at least a faction of the Roman clergy and could reply in their names.[3]

---

1. Eusebius, HE 6.43.14. The source is hostile, but there is no reason to doubt that Cornelius, writing while Novatianus was alive would invent the charges against him. Cyprian too was a late convert.
2. Eusebius, HE 6.43.16-17 states that according to Cornelius, Novatianus denied his presbyterate before the authorities in the Decian Persecution. Therefore, he must already have received it from Fabianus. The date of the De Trinitate is obscure; for plausible argument dating it to the period 235-40, see Weyer, Novatianus, p. 14. The most recent text of the works of Novatianus will be found in G.F. Diercks (ed.), Opera Novatiani, Corpus Christianorum, Series Latina 4 (Turnholti, 1972). For bibliography see Quasten, Pat., p. 219, and Altaner-Stuiber, Pat., pp. 170-2.
3. Ep. 30 by Novatianus, and 55.8/ 629.1 ff. This fact alone would tend to discredit the testimony of Cornelius about Novatianus' cowardly behaviour during the persecution. His rise to power in its last phase would seem impossible had he so

Novatianus' reply complied with Cyprian's most ardent wishes and granted him full support. Cyprian's policy of granting peace only to those who had certificates and were in danger of death was accepted by Novatianus and the Roman clergy, as well as the Roman confessors whom Cyprian had contacted through his correspondence.[1] Hints were dropped that in Rome also there was pressure on the part of the lapsed.[2] Cyprian's desire to withhold action until a council could be assembled was also approved in Rome.[3] But stress was still laid upon the need to wait for the election of a Roman bishop, which was impossible for the present due to the continuing actions of the authorities.[4]

---

3. (cont'd) thoroughly discredited himself at its beginning. His rise to power must have been earlier, as he refers to letters sent to Cyprian prior to Ep. 30 (30.3/550.21).

1. Ep. 30.8/555.23, for support of peace to the ill. See 30.4/552 for the confessors who were in the group headed by Moyses.

2. Ep. 30.3/550.21; 30.8/555.23 also lends support to the view of penance adopted by Koch, see supra p. 217, n. 4.

3. Ep. 30.5/552.15.

4. Ep. 30.5/552.15. A. D'Alès, Novatien: Étude sur la théologie romaine au milieu du troisième siècle (Paris, 1924), p. 156, insists that this reference betrays self-interest. But it is simply a wise reminder to Cyprian that nothing final can be done by the Roman clergy until a new bishop is elected. Notice the reference to letters appended to that preserved in Cyprian's correspondence by Novatianus,

Cyprian began to use the weight of his new ally to counter those who opposed him among his own people. His clergy was quickly informed of the support he had received from Rome.[1] More importantly, Cyprian put forward what would be the key to his position in the entire controversy and in his future theological disputation - the unique grandeur of the office of the bishop.[2]

In confronting the claims of heretics to possess the true doctrine of Christ, Irenaeus and Tertullian had asserted that the orthodox churches could guarantee the truth of their doctrine by the succession of their elders. This succession was identical with the unbroken succession of the bishops which guaranteed the continuity of the tradition back to Christ and the Apostles.[3] These successors of the Apostles had received a heritage of truth with their office.[4] Cyprian had begun to assert this idea in its strictest interpretation.[5] The

---

4. (cont'd) indicating that he had also sent letters to Sicily - a further indication that the dislocations of the mid-third century were not so severe as portrayed by the Epitomators and Chroniclers of the fourth century. See Clarke, "Barbarian Disturbances", pp. 74-87.

1. Ep. 32.

2. On his conception of his relationship to Rome, infra pp. 328 ff.

3. Tertullian, De Praescr. Haeret. 32; Irenaeus, Adv. Haer. 3.3.1.

4. See Harnack, HD, II, pp. 69 ff.

5. Harnack, HD, II, p. 85, n. 1 draws a distinction between Cyprian's earlier views that the Church was constituted in episcopo et clero et in omnibus creden-

225

position of the bishop was a direct result of divine law. The Apostle Peter was established as the rock upon which the Church had been built. From his institution there had been an orderly succession of bishops. The Church was stabilized upon these officers, with every action being under their ordinance and guidance.[1] The reasons for the development of Cyprian's view of the power of the bishops is obvious: under the pressures of opposition, the bishop was forced to acknowledge his own position as Scripturally supreme, in order to guarantee himself against the attacks of other members of the community.

Cyprian had now formed two pillars with which to support himself against those of his clergy who had adopted a lenient position towards the lapsed: the support of Rome, and his own conception of the role of the bishop. These were to become central concepts for the remainder of his tenure as bishop. He had begun successfully to mobilize his wavering clergy, whereas at the beginning of the summer he had even had difficulty communicating with them. His constant supervision even from exile and the establishment of his representatives in Carthage began to have effect.

Cyprian's earlier reaction to leniency towards the lapsed had been confined to terms of general remonstrance, but his

---

5. (cont'd) tibus, from which Cyprian narrowed his view to an aristocratic idea that the Church was ruled by bishops alone, as a result of the Novatianist crisis. But Ep. 33 indicates that this conception existed prior to the crisis at Rome.

1. Ep. 33.1/567.8. Bévenot, "Sacrament of Penance", p. 178.

226

careful construction of a power base had proven effective. The earlier coldness of his clergy had been dissipated, and they now began to act according to his instructions, even to the extent of excommunicating a lapsist priest and his deacon.[1] Their further compliance is indicated by the fact that they required Cyprian's judgment about individuals who had fled during the persecution and subsequently returned. The bishop prudently delayed his reply, referring the question of their status to a council after the persecution.[2]

The thinning of the ranks of his clergy allowed Cyprian to nominate his own candidates in order to strengthen his hand now and during the contest which would surely erupt at the end of the present troubles. Moreover, the candidates selected were all from the group which had suffered in the persecution and could thereby claim the prestige of being martyrs and confessors in addition to the prestige of their office. On another level, they had deserved well of both the bishop and the community, and this was a propitious time to reward them for their adherence to the faith.[3] Celerinus would prove an

---

1. Ep. 34.1/568.10 ff. The presbyter was Gaius from Dida. The location of Dida is unknown, but it was probably in the vicinity of Carthage. Bayard, "Notes sur la Vita", p. 85 hypothesizes that it may have been at the site of the present town of Djedeida, about 25 km. from Tunis. See Mesnage, L'Afrique chrétienne, p. 193.
2. Ep. 34.4/570.14.
3. Ep. 38, Aurelius; Ep. 39, Celerinus; Ep. 40, Numidicus.

exceptionally worthwhile choice. Closely linked to the prestigious group of confessors in Rome headed by Moyses and Maximus, he could further bind this group to favour Cyprian's view of the lapsed.[1] He was closely tied originally to the group of confessors at Carthage led by Lucianus who had opposed Cyprian and could therefore be an effective example to those still in opposition to the bishop.[2]

Cyprian was forced to tread warily. He realized the irregularity of his appointments.[3] To give further support to his actions, he again addressed Novatianus in Rome, asking for support of his earlier candidates.[4] Novatianus again seconded Cyprian's judgment, and he came out strongly in favour of the bishop's relatively rigorist position on the restoration of the lapsed.[5] In addition, he supported Cyprian's position to exclude Privatus, former bishop of Lambaesis, refusing to recognize his representative.[6]

Opposition to Cyprian's policy on the lapsed continued into the year 251.[7] It began to assume shape and structure. Originally his major opponents were the five

---

1. Ep. 37. Eusebius, HE 6.43.6.
2. Supra p. 218 f.
3. Ep. 38.1/579.15-580.19.
4. Ep. 35. Here Cyprian asks support for the candidates who had already been nominated by him, Saturus and Optatus, see Ep. 29.1/547.10.
5. For Novatianus' authorship of Ep. 36, see Melin, Studia, pp. 16 ff.
6. On Privatus, supra p. 2, and Ep. 36.4/575.18.
7. Ep. 37.2/577.5 marks the beginning of 251.

priests who had opposed his election to the bishopric.[1] But a new and energetic figure took the place of leader among them, the deacon Felicissimus.[2] The machinations of the priests had singularly failed, but the energetic intervention of Felicissimus reanimated Cyprian's enemies.[3] Rather than simply administering peace to the lapsed against the bishop's command, he directly confronted Cyprian.[4] He stated that those who remained in communion with Cyprian would be excluded from his own. The tactic was an inevitable prelude to the establishment of a counter-church at Carthage. The opposition was now to be direct and total rather than sporadic. Felicissimus had brilliantly discovered the best means of controverting the re-established authority of the Carthaginian bishop.

The presbyter Novatus' appointment of Felicissimus as deacon had been a master stroke.[5] Cyprian replied to this new assault on his authority in a strongly worded letter to his congregation and clergy. Stressing the continued treachery of the priests, he compares them to the council of five that accompanied the magistrates during the persecution.[6] His opponents are

---

1. For them, supra p. 139.
2. He first occurs in letter 41, which is linked to 43, probably in January or February 251.
3. Cyprian recognizes him as a new factor, Ep. 41.2/588.8.
4. Ep. 41.2/588.8.
5. Ep. 52.2/617.18 ff. The recital of crimes here, and in Epit. de Caes. 41.2, cannot be adequately judged because of the one-sided nature of the evidence.
6. Ep. 43.3/592.7.

229

compared to the false prophets whom the Lord warned his disciples to expect.[1] He accuses them of spurning the tradition of God. They are a snare to the lapsed for whom one fall should have been sufficient.[2] He stresses the extraordinary position of the bishop, comparing him to the priest and judge of the Old Testament. To disobey him would be to expect death from God.[3] Most important, Cyprian was at last able to fix a date for a council to resolve the problems that had beset his community. The council was to convene after Easter 251.[4]

Cyprian's protest caused his friends and deputies at Carthage to take action. Caldonius, with two other bishops, and the priests Rogatianus and Numidicus, excommunicated Felicissimus and certain of his followers. But no action was taken against the priests who had been their supporters and presumably the central basis of their party.[5]

---

1. Ep. 43.5/593.25.
2. Ep. 43.6/595.5.
3. Ep. 43.7/596.10.
4. Ep. 43.7/596.10. On the date of this council, see Monceaux, HAC, pp. 43 ff., who rightly dates it to the spring of 251, and hypothesizes another council, perhaps in the autumn, which dealt with the business of Novatianus. But there is no need to do this, nor does the correspondence of Cyprian give evidence for more than one council, which had an extended session.
5. Ep. 42. For its relationship to Ep. 43, see Appendix I. The persons named in the letter give no real indication of the composition of the party in opposition to Cyprian. Obviously the clergy, presumably the strongest portion of the faction, are

After a stay of approximately fifteen months, Cyprian's self-imposed exile was at an end. He returned to his congregation sometime after Easter 251.1 The persecution had effectively ended before the death of Decius. In June 251 the Emperor perished in a battle against the Goths in the Dobrudja.2 The treachery of the Dux of Lower Moesia, C. Vibius Trebonianus Gallus, appears to have been responsible for the disaster which destroyed both the Emperor and his elder son.3 Questions of the succession and the immediate lack of political stability shook the Empire. For the time being, the Christians were safe. The campaign for internal uniformity that had marked the home policy of Decius had to be abandoned in the confusion that marked his death.

The first task that greeted the bishop after his return to Carthage was the calling of a council in the late summer of 251, to resolve the question of the lapsed and reunite the shattered body of the African Church. Probably in the last months of his exile, Cyprian had written two speeches dealing with these problems. They were to be ready before the assembled bishops as the definitive statement of his views. All his powers and rhetorical training were to be utilized in order to make them

---

5. (cont'd) excluded. All of those selected are of low standing, except for Augendus who appears with Felicissimus.

1. For the length of exile, see Harnack, GAL, p. 308.

2. On the date of Decius' death, see Wittig, RE XV, 1252.

3. For Gallus, see PIR1 V 403, and infra pp. 267 ff.

convincing.[1]
Cyprian opened his statement on the
lapsed with a paean to the end of the

1. Ep. 54.4/623.16, where the use of
legeram undoubtedly points to the reading of
the De Lapsis and the De Unitate at the
council. Therefore, the treatises were
composed before the council, which appears
from the correspondence to have been held
shortly after Cyprian's return to Carthage.
Thus the arguments of Koch, CU, pp. 79-82,
are correct, despite the objections most
recently of M. Bévenot, St. Cyprian's
'De Unitate'. Chapter 4 in the Light of the
Manuscripts, Bellarmine Series, 4 (London,
1939), pp. 58 ff. Bévenot dismisses the
argument from legeram without justification.
Furthermore, he seeks to show that the
treatise does not specifically refer to
bishops. Certainly chapter 5 refers to part
of his audience as being composed of bishops,
as does chapter 7. But Bévenot neglects to
consider that the councils of the third
century included more than bishops among
their personnel. The other reasons against
the early composition of the De Unitate
advanced by him are equally fallacious. He
points to the fact that before the
announcement of the Novatianist schism,
there was no split among the bishops at the
council. But given the sparse information
available, the assertion is gratuitous.
Further, the problems that had racked
Carthage would more than justify such a
position on Cyprian's part. With Felicissimus' new policy, his adversaries had gone
over openly to the attack, refusing
communion with those who remained in
communion with Cyprian. It would be under-
estimating the skill of the bishop to deny

232

devastation of the Church and the return of peace.[1] The Lord had restored faith to the world.[2] In this recital of praise, Cyprian puts the valiant stand of the confessors after the martyrs. In a passage full of military metaphor, he recites the deeds of the confessors and martyrs who had so delighted their mother the Church with their actions.[3] They afforded a glorious spectacle in the eyes of God, rejecting the sacrilegious contacts and the sacrificial meat of the idols. With these male heroes are joined women of similar resolution, triumphing over the world and the weakness of their sex at the same time.[4]

1. (cont'd) that he could foresee troubles that might break out in Carthage, should his opponents be successful and take more extreme measures. Koch's dating of the treatise to March 251 needs modification. In chapter 1 of the De Lapsis, Cyprian refers to the death of Decius, indicating that this chapter was not written earlier than late June or early July, 251. Either the entire treatise was composed after that period, or the first chapter was altered. The latter seems more reasonable, given Cornelius' election in March 251 and the absence of any indication that there was a 3 or 4 month delay after Easter in the calling of the council. The most recent text of the De Lapsis will be found in M. Bévenot (ed.), Opera Cypriani, Corpus Christianorum, Series Latina 3, Pars 1 (Turnholti, 1972).

1. De Lapsis 1/237.1-13.
2. De Lapsis 1/237.1-13.
3. For the development of the metaphor of Church as mother, see J.C. Plumpe, "Ecclesia mater", TAPA 70 (1939), pp. 535-55.
4. De Lapsis 2/237.14-238.22; Ep. 13.

The prestige they had won in the course of the persecution made them a central factor at the council. Cyprian needed their support if he was to impose his own views.

The *stantes* deserved an almost equal glory. They clung to the unshaken foundation of the heavenly precepts, maintaining the divine tradition, braving the loss of property, the destined punishments and the bodily discomforts.[1]

Some thought less highly of those who had fled.[2] But the havoc wrought by the government needed the support of the whole remaining body of the Church, and Cyprian knew this. Tertullian had allowed no flight in time of persecution.[3] Cyprian, however, was confronted with an extraordinary situation in which flight seemed a well-chosen course. So many had simply given in to the persecutors. In any case, such reasoning allowed him to justify his own behaviour. For a Christian, not to deny his faith was equal to an affirmation of faith. Withdrawal provided the second grade of glory and was a private affirmation. Confession would have occurred had the exile been apprehended.[4]

Even with the disaster that had befallen the Christian community, continued Cyprian, self-pity was not the answer. The cause of this grief lay with the Christians themselves. Their sloth and lack of faith induced God to send the

---

1. De Lapsis, Ibid. Benson, Cyprian, 75.
2. De Lapsis 3/238.23.
3. Tertullian, De Fuga 6.
4. De Lapsis 3; cf. canonical letter of Peter of Alexandria.

persecution as a reproof and a test.[1] Weakness and lack of discipline was made manifest by the large number who betrayed the faith of their own free will, and not through the threat of violence. They knew that service of Christ entailed danger, and they failed in that service. In their weakness they ascended the Capitol jostling one another to be first in betrayal.[2] Encouraging one another, they mutually destroyed each other. Even children were presented to perform the sacrifice and thus corrupted by their parents.[3]

For such crime there is no excuse. Flight was a possibility, but greed and the attachment to worldly goods prevented it. He who professes himself a Christian has a far greater patrimony to guard, that of the promise of heaven. In guarding their earthly wealth, they have relinquished their heavenly patrimony.[4]

Had the lapsed suffered torture, had the pain of the body overcome the strength of the spirit, this could be forgiven. But the fallen have no excuse. Thus the bishop has the duty to provide remedies for this

---

1. On Cyprian's theories of the origin of the persecution, supra p. 208.
2. De Lapsis 7-8/241.11-243.6. In St. Cyprian: The Lapsed. The Unity of the Catholic Church, ACW, 25 (Westminster, Md., 1957), p. 81, n. 34, Bévenot takes "Capitolium" to refer to Rome. Surely the reference is local and is a synonym for Byrsa. Nothing in the treatise points outside of Carthage.
3. De Lapsis 8-9/242.10-243.18. See the illustrative story chapters 24-5.
4. De Lapsis 10-12/243.19-245.8.

spiritual illness. A timid doctor who stays his hand can be the cause of more harm than good. So the bishop as doctor of souls should take care that all necessary treatment is afforded, even if this treatment results in pain and anguish. The patient will later appreciate his service and render thanks to the strict physician.[1]

Now a new disaster is added to persecution.[2] Contrary to the Gospels and the laws of God, a deceptive admission to communion is being presumptuously given.[3] In their urgency, the lapsed no longer tread the slow and painful road to true recovery. Without any expiation of their sins or confession, before sacrifice offered by the priests or the imposition of hands, before they have appeased the menacing anger of the Lord, they rush to the sacrament and thereby defile it.[4] Those who offer this fraudulent

---

1. De Lapsis 13-14/246.8-247.23.
2. Cf. Ep. 43.3/592.7, written at about the same time.
3. De Lapsis 15/247.24. The use of quorundam is an obvious reference to Felicissimus and his followers. But notice that throughout the De Lapsis, no named reference is made to Cyprian's opponents. They are always mentioned in general terms, presumably a diplomatic gesture which would make the ultimate reconciliation easier and give less offense to those bishops present who might support them. Bévenot, "Sacrament of Penance", pp. 175-213, tries to show that these references and those in chapters 17-20 make better sense if interpreted as referring to actual individuals. But aside from Felicissimus and Novatus, so little is known that identifications are problematic.
4. De Lapsis 15-16. For the ritual of

peace to the lapsed are like a pestilence to them. This is not an admission to communion but a bar from it. It is a new persecution and temptation.

Only the Lord can grant forgiveness. Man cannot be above God who alone controls forgiveness.[1] This does not contradict the power or merit of the martyrs. But it is rashness on the part of anyone to think he can break the divine discipline. God concedes. Man can only plead, even if he should die in God's cause.[2]

With a brilliant piece of exegesis of

---

4. (cont'd) penance in the third century, see Baus, HCH, p. 333, and Bévenot, "Sacrament of Penance", p. 200.

1. Chapter 17 and the text of Test. III.28 appear to favour Koch's interpretation (supra p. 217, n. 2) that the penance and reconciliation granted were conceived as given by the Church, with final judgment reserved to God. Those such as Bévenot and Poschmann who have argued against this, have no grounds in Cyprian's writings. But the question has been needlessly debated because of the false dichotomy and rigidity of thinking involved. Everyone is ready to repeat the statement that Cyprian was a man of affairs and not a theological expert, but all have refused to follow this to its logical conclusion, that as the doctrine of penance developed, the dividing line between the forgiveness of man and God, always narrow, became gradually fused. Since the only demonstrative forgiveness was that of the Church, the sign was assimilated to the act.

2. De Lapsis 18-19/250.4 ff. Cyprian's examples are from the Old Testament: Moses, Jeremiah, and Daniel.

237

Matthew 10:32, Cyprian establishes that the merit of the martyrs is dependent solely on the law of God: "He that shall confess me before man, I will also confess him before my Father who is in heaven; but he that shall deny me, I will deny him also." If God does not deny the individual who died for Him, neither can He excuse the man who has rejected Him on earth. Martyrs and confessors destroy their own merit by granting hasty reconciliation to the lapsed against the command of God.[1]

Thus Cyprian draws the logical conclusion of his argument: if the Gospel fails, the martyrs fail. The martyrs cannot act against the Gospel, for this will destroy them.[2] The persecution should have been a warning against arrogance. Warnings have been given, but the day of punishment is yet to come.[3]

As numerous incidents have shown, God's displeasure with those who sacrificed has been great.[4] So also with those who received the libellus without sacrifice. Cyprian points out that these individuals had also served an earthly master, bending the knee to a human decree. God can see into the heart. He can discern our secret thoughts in our words and actions.[5] Even those whose thoughts are impure should show a salutary humility, manifest their guilty conscience, and lay bare its burden. They must seek treatment for their souls. God cannot be

---

1. De Lapsis 20/250.6. This is the central and telling argument of the bishop against his opponents.
2. De Lapsis 20/252.7.
3. De Lapsis 23/254.6-15.
4. De Lapsis 24-26/254.16-256.22.
5. De Lapsis 27/256.23 ff.

238

denied. Cyprian even here recommends repentance, even though there was no overt act or crime against divine law.[1]

Since other alternatives only grant a false and damaging peace, the bishop counsels that the lapsed should seek satisfaction and forgiveness through the right channels while these are still available. In true contriteness, let God be implored. But the sinners' conduct must show sincere intentions. The old moral persuasions must be abandoned. To win God's forgiveness, one must join oneself with those of good counsel. Full penance is required, penance displayed in the countenance of the sinner. Those who do not recognize their sins must be avoided, for they are blinded and cannot perceive them. Those struck with the blindness of the fool remain self-contented and do not follow the divine precepts. They have no real reconciliation, but merely presume it for themselves. Joining themselves to apostates and unbelievers, they take error for truth and put their faith in man rather than in God.[2] Such men must be avoided at all cost. They are a destructive and treacherous pestilence. They beguile their prey with a false promise of salvation that destroys all hope for salvation.[3]

There is hope for the fallen, but only in a measured and genuine repentance. Serious wounds require long and extensive treatment for an effective recovery to take place. The patient must pray assiduously and spend his time in tears and lamentations. He must undertake good deeds. He must avoid

---

1. _De Lapsis_ 28/257.20 ff.
2. _De Lapsis_ 31-33/260.3-262.2.
3. _De Lapsis_ 34/262.3-10.

the ties of the world, especially those of property. To those who follow such a regime, God will show mercy. By such a procedure, the lapsed will win new courage and ardor in the faith, and God will grant them their arms once more. Genuine repentance prepares the way for the renewed man to go forth into the fray, and may result not only in forgiveness from past transgressions but in the hope of a future crown.[1]

Cyprian's presentation of his case was brilliant. It cut the ground from under his opponents. He had established his position on penance as the only stand in accord with Biblical injunctions. With the support of his newly regrouped clergy and the name of the Carthaginian see, he stood in a strong and almost unassailable position. The meeting of the council in his own territory assured that he could bring the maximum amount of pressure to bear on those bishops or clergy who might have been reluctant to oppose the demand of the lapsed for immediate re-admittance to the Church. But the struggle had assumed a deeper and more threatening aspect. Felicissimus' actions involved a questioning of Cyprian's whole role in the Church.[2] The very position of the bishop was challenged. Even before his return he realized that this was the thrust

---

1. De Lapsis 35-36. This may be the result of the unstable internal situation of the Empire. Decius' death did in fact grant only temporary respite to the Christians. Cyprian could well have seen that the State's present retreat was merely a change for tactical regrouping rather than a genuine change in its internal policy.
2. Supra p. 229.

240

of Felicissimus' attack.[1] Cyprian met it at the council with his statement on the foundation and function of the episcopate, the De Catholicae Ecclesiae Unitate.[2]

He opens the treatise warning his congregation of the devil. The persecution had failed, so now the adversary would attack with wiles and tricks. To be on one's guard against obvious danger is an easy matter, but to maintain vigilance against guile is more difficult. Yet if care is taken, the enemy can be unmasked and defeated.[3] The only way to assure victory is to carry out God's command and adhere to the teachings of Christ, for it is by these commands that eternal life is assured. There security is founded upon a rock; nothing can overcome it.[4]

---

1. Ep. 43.5/593.25.: "Qui contra episcopos rebellarunt".
2. On the title, see Ep. 54.4/623.16 ff.; Fulgentius, De Remiss. Pecc. 1.21; and Hartel, app. crit., p. 209. The most recent text of the De Unitate will be found in M. Bévenot (ed.), Opera Cypriani, Corpus Christianorum, Series Latina 3, Pars 1 (Turnholti, 1972). See also Bévenot, The Tradition of Manuscripts: A Study in the Transmission of St. Cyprian's Treatises (Oxford, 1961).
3. De Unit. 1/209.
4. De Unit. 2. Controversy has arisen over the object of the De Unitate. The first to generally assert that it was addressed to the schism of Carthage and not to the situation at Rome was J. Chapman, "Les interpolations dans le traité de S. Cyprien sur l'unité de l'église", RevBén 19 (1902), pp. 246-54 and 357-73; 20 (1903), pp. 26-51; also Chapman, "The Order of the Treatises and Letters in the Manuscripts of St. Cyprian"

Cyprian goes on to warn his audience of the machinations of the devil. His cunning and guile are endless. Having seen his temples deserted and his idols torn down, the adversary decided that the best attack upon the truth was to assume its guise in order to conquer it. How else could a message as clear as the message of Christ meet such opposition among the pagans?[1] But

---

4. (cont'd) JThS 4 (1902), pp. 103-23. He argues that the object was Felicissimus and has been supported and reinforced by Koch, CU, pp. 83 ff. Bévenot, St. Cyprian's 'De Unitate', p. 66, has tried to controvert their arguments, but without success. See infra p. 245, n. 2. If the early date of the treatise's composition is accepted, the possibility that it was directed against Novatianus is remote. In Ep. 45.1 Cyprian writes to Cornelius that he was directing his letter to the bishop, indicating that this was the stage when Cornelius received recognition from Cyprian and not before. This letter was written during the conference. Thus if the treatise was composed prior to the conference, it would have had to have been directed against Felicissimus and not against Novatianus who was still an unknown quantity to Cyprian and, moreover, had earlier given his support to Cyprian against the lapsed elements at Carthage. Cyprian's hesitation in recognizing Cornelius is also evident from Ep. 43.3 which is essentially an apology. In fact Cyprian may have communicated with Novatianus also before he was certain of the conditions prevailing in Rome. The correspondence may have been removed when the decision to support Cornelius had been made.

1. De Unit. 3/211; cf. Oct. 27.8.

242

those whom the devil fails to blind completely he leads into new paths of falsehood. He invented heresy and schism to destroy the unity of the faithful.[1] Those who submit to these inventions believe they are truly Christians, but they have fallen into a new realm of darkness. Satan became the anti-Christ under the name of Christ, and with lies that have the outward appearance of truth he deceives the heretics. The explanation is that men have failed to go back to the true basis of all Christian reality, the teachings of the Divine Master.[2]

Cyprian chooses as his support the text of Matthew 16:18, in order to stress the original oneness of the Church's power on earth. Though all the Apostles had been given a similar power, the primatus had been assigned to Peter alone.[3] The primatus was not an indication of Peter's singular power with respect to the other Apostles, as Cyprian himself makes clear.

---

1. De Unit. 3/211; unitatem: see Bévenot's note to his translation, The Lapsed, p. 101, n. 17.

2. De Unit. 3/211. See Appendix VI on the status of chapter 4.

3. Controversy has raged over the precise meaning of primatus here. H. Koch, Cathedra Petri, Beihefte zur Zeitschrift für die neutestamentliche Wissenschaft, 11 (Giessen, 1930), p. 52, sees this as implying a temporal seniority. He certainly established the case that Peter is, for Cyprian, an Urtypus of the bishop. But as Bévenot has stressed, "Primatus Petro Datur: St. Cyprian on the Papacy", JThS N.S. 5 (1954), pp. 19-35, the meaning of primatus is more variable. It

243

But Peter, through the express command of the Lord, becomes the foundation of the unity of the Church.[1] Though there are many bishops, the congregation they serve has a unified origin, and the bishops themselves as the recipients of Peter's power share in this basic oneness.[2] Though shared by many, the episcopate is a single institution with a single foundation built on the unity of the Church.[3] While the power of the episcopate is divided among the many bishops, all share the same source of authority.

Cyprian continues his reiteration of the unity of all believers by appealing to Scriptural _topoi_.[4] But the unity of the

---

3. (cont'd) can be taken in the sense of primogeniture, De Bono Pat. 19. But it can also mean primacy in the sense of political superiority, Pliny, NH 24.17.102. The term here would seem best to refer not to mere temporal priority but to a special singling out of Peter by this Scriptural passage as the bearer of an honorary primacy. As Cyprian points out, it was not a primacy of power: "Quamvis apostolis omnibus parem tribuat potestatem". Peter is a symbol for Cyprian, as Koch, Cathedra Petri, p. 59.

1. De Unit. 4/212, app. crit., 1. 14: "una ecclesia et cathedra una monstretur, et pastores sunt omnes, sed grex unus ostenditur".

2. Ibid.

3. De Unit. 5/213 ff. See M. Bévenot, "In solidum and St. Cyprian: A Correction", JThS N.S. 6 (1955), pp. 244-8, who rightly sees no reference here to the position of Rome.

4. De Unit. 6-9/214.15-218.13, esp. part 7, on the garment of Christ.

Church, founded on the unity of its bishops, is continually threatened. Heresies and factions continually arise to shake its foundation. The Lord permits them, leaving man's will free to test his faith.[1] The proof of the faithful results in the unmasking of the faithless. Though Cyprian refuses to name his opponents, Felicissimus is the obvious target of his wrath. He has seized authority without divine sanctions and has disregarded the authority of the bishop.[2] Such conduct cannot be justified. Cyprian characterizes his adversaries as plagues and viruses which can fatally infect and destroy the body of the faithful.[3]

The party of Felicissimus was prepared with its own arsenal of Scriptural authority to contest Cyprian. Their choice was Matthew 18:20 where Christ says: "Wherever two or three are gathered together in My Name, I am with them." Attacking their use of this verse, Cyprian interprets the passage as a call to peace and concord, not

---

1. De Unit. 10/218.14. There is an obvious connection with Cyprian's reasons for persecution. All these events present problems for an omnipotent God, who is also incapable of evil.

2. De Unit. 10/218.14. Bévenot, The Lapsed, p. 113, n. 87a, assumes that the reference of "qui nemine episcopatum dante episcopi sibi nomen adsumunt" is to Novatianus. But there need have been no actual connection with Rome. After all, Felicissimus had established his own communion. The point here is his assumption of power. Cyprian had by this time not yet decided on the legitimacy of Cornelius' election. Supra p. 241, n. 4.

3. De Unit. 10/218.14.

as license for the establishment of a separate Church. The text applies only to those who heed the basic commandments of the Lord, which Cyprian's opponents (according to Cyprian) obviously fail to do.[1]

Salvation and the sacraments are only valid within the Church, he continues. Baptism given outside the Church is no baptism at all.[2] So martyrdom ceases to be martyrdom if performed outside the Church.[3] Revolt against the body of the Church, founded upon the bishops, only leads to damnation and destruction. The Old Testament provided the Carthaginian bishop with examples of the disasters that had befallen other opponents of religious authority.[4]

But Felicissimus had managed to find support for his opposition among the confessors, and Cyprian had to deal further with a difficult subject. His own conduct and the prestige of the martyrs and confessors necessitated a delicate balance of praise and blame. His task was to sort the sheep from the goats, by preserving the value of the confessors' action while limiting its efficacy for the individual. Confession does not make an individual invulnerable to sin. Take note of the adulteries, rapes and dishonesties that mar the lives of some of the confessors.[5] Confession in itself has its limitations. It is a first step to glory but not its consummation. Martyrdom is the final perfection.[6]

---

1. De Unit. 12/220.3 ff.
2. De Unit. 11/219.5 ff.
3. De Unit. 14/222.5 ff.
4. De Unit. 16-19/224.13-227.22.
5. Supra p. 208.
6. De Unit. 21/228.15-229.22.

If confessors are to reap the full benefits of their actions, they must show their sinlessness by humility. Let them imitate Christ who preaches that to humble oneself is to exalt oneself.[1] If the confessors oppose the bishops, and through them the Church of Christ, they can no longer keep their status.[2] Judas is a salutary example for all those who would oppose the divine rules upheld by Cyprian and his supporters.[3]

Following up his shrewd statement of the Scriptural basis of ecclesiastical unity and his attack on his opponents, Cyprian reiterates a call for the regrouping of the Carthaginian Church. Those who would seduce and destroy must be ignored. A true Christian must refrain from dissension. In the time of the Apostles, unanimity prevailed. This was the reason for the efficacy of their prayers. This guaranteed that they would be the recipients of God's mercy.[4]

But, as Cyprian reminds those assembled, this unity has now disappeared. As charity and generosity fade, so dissension increases. With the increase in wealth, each man begins to look to his own affairs, neglecting the welfare of his neighbor. All thoughts are now directed towards present gain. No time is taken to contemplate the future and the wrath that the Lord has in store for those who neglect to follow His commands.[5]

Christians must once again return to apostolic unanimity. The past inertia must

---

1. De Unit. 21/228.15-229.22.
2. De Unit. 21/228.15-229.22.
3. De Unit. 22/229.23 ff.
4. De Unit. 25/232.3-11.
5. De Unit. 26/232.12-26.

be cast aside. Good works must brighten the path that leads out of the abyss of darkness and error. Given that the Lord's commands are obeyed, it becomes impossible that the faithful should be tricked and perverted by the devil even while they sleep. Under Christ, the true Christian shall come at last into his rightful dominion.[1]

Thus Cyprian established a firm basis for authority in the face of his enemies.[2] The authority of the Church is buttressed by the authority of its bishops. But the position of the bishop was to complicate the situation further.

Since the death of Fabianus over a year earlier, the Roman Church had functioned without a bishop. Various presbyters performed the tasks of guiding the Church and of representing it to other Christian churches. With the decrease in the level of the persecution, an opportunity finally presented itself for the election of a successor to the martyred Fabianus.

In the early days of the persecution, the Roman community was governed by one or more unknown presbyters; but at least by August 250, the correspondence between Rome and Carthage was in the hands of Novatianus.[3] To what extent this reflected his control of the community is not ascertainable. But he was also in correspondence with Sicily, and the tone of the letter received by Cyprian indicates his position was strong among the Roman

1. De Unit. 27/232.27-233.15.
2. On the changing concepts, see Harnack, HD, II, pp. 210 ff.
3. For the date, see Appendix I, and Harnack, GAL, p. 347.

priests.[1]

Novatianus' views on the lapsed had, at least until September 250, coincided with those of Cyprian. But the lessening of the persecution opened the question of the succession in Rome, and this threw a new light on the status to be given those who had lapsed during the persecution.

The leading role of Novatianus in the period before the election of a new bishop, in addition to his close relationship and agreement with the Carthaginian see, made his own election likely. But another candidate, Cornelius, became the new bishop of the Roman see, elected and ordained by sixteen bishops.[2] A previously unknown figure, the manoeuvrings that led to his election are lost to us.[3] His election probably fell near the end of March 251.[4]

The attraction of Cornelius remains a mystery. His career was probably regular,

---

1. Ep. 30.5/552.15 ff.
2. Ep. 55.24/642.3 ff.
3. The Lib. Pont., 150, records that Cornelius was of Roman origin: "natione Romanus pater Castinus".
4. The Lib. Pont., 150, gives Cornelius two years, two months and three days in office. The Liberian Catalogue gives the same figure plus eight days. The end of his reign fell around June 25, 253. Counting back two years, two months and eleven days gives a period around the middle of March 251. Allowing a few days interval between Lucius and Cornelius, the election should have fallen sometime in the second half of March 251. See Harnack, GAL, p. 351, who cites Ep. 43 as evidence when it contains no information whatsoever on the development of the schism at Rome.

249

unlike that of Novatianus.[1] But it appears that the advantage enjoyed by Cornelius was due to his lack of rigidity on the question of the lapsed. Like Cyprian he was willing to bend to face the situation at hand.[2]

Novatianus lacked the flexibility of his opponents. During the persecution he had taken the stand that those who had lapsed should do a long and protracted penance, and that only at the moment of mortal danger should they be re-admitted into the Church.[3] But he had allowed for modifications in these conditions at the end of the persecution when there would be an opportunity to call a council of bishops to decide the matter.[4] His position received support from the most important group of confessors among the Roman Christians. Moyses, Maximus and their fellow prisoners supported the decision of their priest.[5] Perhaps the election of Cornelius was a blow to Novatianus' ambition. In any case, he remained inactive for some time after the election.

The spark that set the situation aflame at Rome came from Carthage. Novatus, one of the leaders of the faction which opposed Cyprian, journeyed to Rome, perhaps to obtain support for his group. Newly installed and anxious for recognition, Cornelius must have seemed an unlikely supporter. Novatianus offered better material for the purposes of Novatus. His defeat made him more vulnerable

---

1. Ep. 55.8/629 ff. But the information is definitely prejudiced in favour of Cornelius.
2. Ep. 55.3/625.1-18.
3. Ep. 30.
4. Ep. 30.
5. Ep. 49; Eusebius, HE 6.43.6.

to suggestion, and Novatus took advantage of it. Though his own position on the lapsed was diametrically opposed to that of the Roman presbyter, the Carthaginian realized that if he could win the support of Novatianus and help him obtain the bishopric against Cornelius, this would place him in a stronger position to deal with Cyprian's resistance in Africa. He proceeded to encourage Novatianus to elect himself in opposition to Cornelius. At the very least, this would embarrass Cyprian who had been in close contact with and received support from Novatianus against Novatus' own faction; it would provide the prestige and support which might swing matters against Cyprian at the spring council on the question of the lapsed. Doctrinal differences could for the time be submerged or left to one side.[1]

Novatus held a lenient position towards those who had lapsed during the persecution, whereas Novatianus was rigorist in his interpretation of penance. But limited gains must have outweighed such distinctions. Novatus needed an ally, and Cornelius needed

---

1. The sources are fairly unanimous in their appraisal of Novatus' role as the instigator of Novatianus' election against Cornelius: Jerome, Vir. Ill. 70; Lib. Pont., 151; Ep. 52.2/617.18 ff.; Eusebius, HE 6.45.1, from a letter of Dionysius of Alexandria to Novatianus, which reports that Novatianus disclaimed responsibility for the schism, and that he had been goaded into his election. Such disclaimers are difficult to accept, and Novatianus' later conduct would give little indication that he was reluctant to press his claims to the Roman see.

251

support too much himself to risk aligning himself with the enemy of the powerful and influential bishop of Carthage. Events proved Novatus right. Cornelius undertook an extensive campaign to attract recognition at Carthage. Novatianus, however, was perhaps nursing thwarted ambition and upset at what he might have considered his unjust neglect by the clergy of Rome.[1] Moreover, he possessed the added attraction of holding the support of the powerful group of confessors whom Cyprian himself had done his best to woo. He was also an educated man and could add eloquence and learning to his onslaught against Cyprian.

Novatus had far less to offer Novatianus He could, however, claim a strong base at Carthage. Novatianus, however, had enjoyed friendly relations with Cyprian and might offer himself as an arbitrator for the troubles at Carthage. The steady traffic between Rome and Carthage and the large resident African population in Rome may have had appeal if Novatianus should move to make a test of strength with Cornelius, and Novatus may have promised more than he could deliver.[2] Both men may have acted from genuine motives, each using the other for what they considered to be the divinely approved manner of dealing with the pressing problem of the fallen.[3]

---

1. Eusebius, HE 6.43.8.
2. On Africans resident in Rome, see Oct. 1 and Haywood, Roman Africa, p. 54; Ep. 21 of Celerinus.
3. Mongelli, "La chiesa", p. 126, thinks that Novatus was moved by personal ambition. The case is far from obvious, as the foregoing reconstruction has made clear. Often basic differences are submerged for

Novatianus moved against Cornelius and sent out representatives to obtain Italian bishops for his own consecration.[1] Three bishops were found and consecrated Novatianus bishop of Rome.[2] The event probably occurred at the end of March or the beginning of April 251.[3]

Relying on his old relationship with Cyprian, and in need of consolidating his position, Novatianus sent representatives to the African council to gain recognition

---

3. (cont'd) immediate advantage, a case in point being the conduct of the late Byzantine emperors with respect to the papacy.

1. Eusebius, HE 6.43.9. The exact time of Novatus' trip to Rome is unknown. Benson, Cyprian, p. 138, hypothesizes early March 251. Little evidence for this is available however. Cyprian mentions that after appointing Felicissimus as his deacon, Novatus sailed to Rome, Ep. 52.2/622.4-14. Felicissimus first appears in the correspondence in Ep. 41.1/587.4-588.7. If Cyprian is correct, then the early March date for his mission to Rome would be acceptable.

2. Eusebius, HE 6.43.9-10. The account of Cornelius must be taken as strongly biased against his opponent, and the details of drunkenness and guile may be an exaggeration. The exact course of events is lost.

3. The date is a conjecture. It must have been fairly soon after Cornelius' election, since the embassy to the council of Carthage arrived soon after the news of the election. No closer approximation of the date is possible.

by Cyprian and his fellows.[1] Their arrival must have seriously disturbed Cyprian. His relations with Novatianus had been good, and his support had been useful. On the other hand, Cornelius was eagerly soliciting recognition. Cyprian had time to act with caution. To Cornelius' demand for immediate recognition, he replied that Cornelius was no doubt the legitimate bishop, but he would await the results of the inquiry of the two bishops sent to Rome to investigate the matter.[2]

At almost the same time as the arrival of Novatianus' emissaries at the council, the return of Pompeius and Stephanus, two African bishops who had been present at Cornelius' ordination, decided the situation.[3] Cyprian was still hesitant, perhaps not clear on how the situation was developing in Rome after the departure of the bishops. He refused to put anything in writing and promised to convey his sentiments to Cornelius only by word of mouth.[4]

Cyprian approached the matter from the most logical standpoint. The most advantageous outcome of the schism for the Church and for himself was reconciliation. Thus while supporting Cornelius, he pledged himself to work for reconciliation.[5] Cornelius was far from reassured and sent a

---

1. cf. Ep. 44.1/597.9-598.8, with the names of those sent.
2. Ep. 44.1/597.9-598.8. The importance of the matter is attested by the sending of Caldonius, on whom Cyprian had often relied.
3. Ep. 44.1/597.9-598.8.
4. Ep. 44.2/598.9-18.
5. Ep. 44.3/598.19-599.9.

further letter to Cyprian chiding him on his hesitation.[1] Cyprian attempted to mollify him by proclaiming that he had publicly read Cornelius' letter to the council while he had withheld that of Novatianus.[2] Cyprian reminded Cornelius of his own troubles. The proceedings against Felicissimus were sent to Cornelius.[3]

Cyprian must have been satisfied with Cornelius' attitude and the canonicity of his election. When certain priests in Hadrumetum had, on what appeared to be Cyprian's orders, directed their correspondence to the clergy at Rome instead of to Cornelius, Cyprian quickly corrected the error.[4] He assured Cornelius that he now recognized him as sole bishop and disowned Novatianus.[5] Cyprian went a step further. The main support for Novatianus among the confessors at Rome had been the group surrounding Moyses, who died before the end of the persecution.[6] The prestige of that

---

1. The letter is not preserved, but its general tenor can be inferred from Ep. 43.3/ 592.7-27.
2. Ep. 45.2/600.15-602.3.
3. Ep. 45.4/603.4-16.
4. Ep. 48.1-2/606.5-11.
5. Ep. 48.3/607.5-19.
6. The Lib. Pont., 151, states that Moyses died after eleven months and eleven days in prison. This would probably put his death in December 250, meaning that Cornelius (Eusebius, HE 6.43.20) was lying when he reported that Moyses became a Novatianist and then returned to the Church. Cyprian's correspondence seems to fit this dating. The last letter to contain Moyses' name is Ep. 31. The group at this time was composed at least of Maximus and

255

group was an important accretion of strength to the party of Novatianus and Novatus. Though his correspondence, Cyprian attempted to draw these men away from the opposing faction, recalling the pernicious effect of division in the Church and stating that they were breaking divine law by supporting an unlawful bishop.[1] Celerinus, who had been associated with the group, may have been active in Cyprian's cause, but there is no specific evidence to support this.[2]

The pressures on the confessors and perhaps their own recognition of their dislike for the Novatianist position on penance led to their desertion of that cause. An embassy was sent, consisting of Urban and Sidonius, affirming the willingness of the group to go over to Cornelius.[3] Cornelius decided to exhibit

---

6. (cont'd) Nicostratus. Again Cornelius (HE 6.43.6) mentions Urban, Sidonius, Maximus and Celerinus, with the addition of Moyses. But Celerinus must have already been back in Carthage and a member of the clergy there (Ep. 37). The dating of the return of the confessors was soon after the first embassy (Ep. 44.1/ 597.1-2). Ep. 52.1 is rather uncertain. Cyprian talks of the coming of the "haereticæ pravitatis nocens factio ipsa" to Carthage. This is further borne out by Ep. 52.2/617.18-619.7 which speaks of Novatus as leaving Rome.
1. Ep. 46.
2. Given Celerinus' close association with the group at Rome, one would expect Cyprian to utilize this relationship.
3. Ep. 49.1/608.15-610.6. Benson's theory, Cyprian, p. 122, that the polemic against the Jews by Novatianus alienated

256

his prize publicly. The confessors were examined by priests because of the numerous letters which had been sent to various churches in their name.[1] Cornelius gathered the clergy to hear their repentance, even assembling five bishops who happened to be present in the city. The confessors then made their obeisance to Cornelius in front of the clergy and the congregation of Rome, declaring that they had been led astray by the imposture of Novatianus, but that they

---

3. (cont'd) Moyses, and that this was the reason for the desertion of him by the confessors, rests on insecure foundations. The single and obvious fallacy is that the confessors returned after the death of Moyses, Ep. 47. There is no definite information on the ultimate origin of Moyses. A Jewish name does not necessarily imply a Jewish Christian, nor is the issue brought up in any of the extant evidence. The dating of the De Cibis Judaicis is a separate problem. Harnack, GAL, p. 398, dates it from the address to the period when Novatianus was already a bishop, and he seems right in doing so. The other possible anti-Jewish work not canvassed by Benson is the Adversus Judaeos, the latest text of which is D. van Damme, Pseudo-Cyprian Adversus Judaeos, gegen die Judenchristen: die älteste lateinische Predigt, Paradosis, 22 (Freiburg, Switz., 1969). This was already included among Cyprian's work in the Cheltenham List of 359-65, but controversy has raged over its authorship, see Harnack, GAL, p. 400. The balance of the evidence is against Benson's theory.
    1. Refer to Ep. 49.1/608.15-610.6 of Cornelius.

257

now realized there must be one bishop and that Cornelius was to be he.[1]

Cyprian must have been overjoyed at the reception of the confessors back into the party of Cornelius. With their desertion, Novatianus had lost one of the strongest bases of his support. Cyprian replied to Cornelius' report of the matter with extensive and genuine sentiment.[2] The confessors also hastened to inform the Carthaginian bishop of their change of heart.[3] Cyprian answered with praise of their actions and a defense of his own stand on the question of penance.

The Church, according to Cyprian, must include base vessels as well as those of precious metal. It is the duty of the clergy to make those of base metal precious, for in this they will receive their reward from the Lord. To throw out those who have sinned is a presumption more than human. Severity must be tempered by justice.[4]

The desertion of the confessors who had supported Novatianus opened the way for Cornelius to move once and for all against his opponent. A council was called at Rome of sixty bishops and a number of presbyters and deacons, and Novatianus and his supporters were excommunicated.[5]

---

1. Ep. 49.2/610.7-612.5.
2. Ep. 51, 52.
3. Ep. 53.
4. Ep. 54.2/622.4-14.
5. Eusebius, HE 6.43.2. The dating of this council presents a difficulty. Cyprian mentions a synod of Cornelius, which some have accepted as dated by the reference in Ep. 55.6/627.13 as contemporaneous with Cyprian's council at Carthage. But the synod at Carthage was of long duration, probably

Novatianus had managed to extend his influence far beyond the confines of Rome. He had entered into correspondence with Fabius of Antioch, Dionysius of Alexandria, Helenus of Tarsus, and Theoctistus of Caesarea.[1] Fabius and some of the others had been leaning towards Novatianus' approach to the problem of penance, and Dionysius employed his pen to try to dissuade them.

The appeal of Novatianus is understandable. His position conformed to the early ideas of Cyprian on the subject and the general concept of penance in the early Church. The Church cannot forgive sins; only God has that ability.[2] Novatianus viewed the visible Church as a group of the elect, the true believers who had demonstrated their faith and had not fallen away. Cyprian allowed that the wheat must be mixed with the tares in this world, even if God were to be the final judge of a man's guilt.[3] Novatianus completely excluded those

---

5. (cont'd) from March through the summer of 251, and this gives little indication of the exact period for the Roman council. Also, Cyprian refers to the council at Rome as deciding and agreeing with his own position on the lapsed, not with a decision on Novatianus which is the only question Eusebius reports the council as considering. It may well be that both the excommunication of Novatianus and the question of the lapsed were decided at the same time, but it is far from definite. See Lawlor and Oulton on this problem, Eusebius, p. 231.

1. Eusebius, HE 6.46.
2. Ep. 30.1/549.4-16.
3. Ep. 55.25/643.14-644.2.

who came under the heading of idolater or sacrificer.[1] Whether sins such as adultery or fornication were included among those crimes leading to loss of communion was a moot point.[2]

The persecution brought about a change in the concept of the nature of the Church. The sporadic harassment on the part of the Roman government prior to the Decian Persecution must have resulted at times in apostasy. This apostasy could be handled by more rigid means of penance. But the action of Decius provoked a situation in which the older methods could be maintained only at great cost. If rigorism was to be allowed, the tremendous numbers who had fallen during the persecution would be driven away from the Church forever.[3]

Novatianus had been willing to accept the consequences of such action. It coincided with his view of what the Church should be. Others were less ready to sacrifice the fruits of Christian expansion for purity.[4]

---

1. Harnack, HD, II, pp. 109-10, seems to take too much for granted in his picture of the anti-episcopal structure of the Church of Novatianus, though he makes the worthwhile point that the position of the bishop seems far more important in Cyprian.
2. Ep. 55.27/644.20-646.7, states that Novatianus allowed communion to these categories. But the charges are so standard that doubt may be entertained on that point.
3. Ep. 55.17/635.22-636.12. Cyprian realized the danger of such a position to the organization of the Church.
4. The oath reported by Cornelius, apud Eusebius, HE 6.43.18, is dubious at best. For Novatianus' theology in general,

The combined efforts of Cyprian and Cornelius impaired the success of Novatianus bid, but he remained a potentially disruptive force. Other bishops, as well as those in the East, were drawn to the austerity of his position.[1]

Among the works of Cyprian has been included a treatise directed against Novatianus by an unknown author.[2] The vituperation it contains far surpasses Cyprian's own outbursts against him. The author presents Novatianus as a perfidious heretic, unclean and defiled by sacrilege.[3] He is a man who strives against the ordinances of God. Central to his character is a mad rush for the episcopate, a striving for power rather than a true pastoral care for the Christian people. The orthodox display the righteousness of their case by their refusal to seek power; the heretics reveal their iniquity by their insane quest for it.[4]

The major attack on Novatianus' doctrines centres on a series of Scriptural interpretations of archetypical figures. The raven and the dove loosed from the ark represent the pure and the impure.[5] The ark symbolizes the Church tossed upon troubled waters.[6] The heretics are ravenous

---

4. (cont'd) see D'Alès, Novatien, and Harnack, HD, II, pp. 108 ff. On the vexed question of which works are actually by Novatianus, see Harnack, GAL, pp. 398 ff. and Quasten, Pat., pp. 212 ff.
1. Infra pp. 264 f.
2. See Appendix VIII.
3. Ad Nov. 1/52.9-53.18.
4. Ad Nov. 2/53.19-55.17.
5. Ad Nov. 2-6/53.19-58.3.
6. Ad Nov. 5/56.11-57.8.

261

wolves in sheep's clothing.[1] Scriptural authority is also adduced. The Scripture exhorts sinners to repent through conversion, mourning, fasting and weeping. God is merciful.[2] The Old Testament Prophets exhort to repentance. Thus Isaiah proclaims, "I will not be angry with you forever, nor will I abstain from defending you always".[3] Though the Bible proclaims forgiveness and that Christ redeemed us at the cost of His blood, the followers of Novatianus have neglected this message.[4] They have therefore ceased to be Christian and have become Novatianists.[5]

Lacking Cyprian's eloquence, the author directs all the force of his opposition to excluding the lapsed, and the disasters that must ensue if the doctrine of Novatianus was to prevail.[6] These factors must have strongly influenced the vote of the spring council. The crisis over Novatianus helped to give shape and substance to the position that Cyprian had assumed. Under the guidance of Cyprian's eloquence and political acumen, the council must have realized that the unity preached in the treatise could only be cemented by a relaxation of the rigours to be imposed on the lapsed. Some, however, remained uncertain, and Cyprian was forced to clarify his position at least once, admitting that he had changed from his first stand on the question.[7]

---

1. Ad Nov. 14/64.1-28.
2. Ad Nov. 9/59.9-17.
3. Ad Nov. 10/59.18-60.29.
4. Ad Nov. 13/62.20-63.26.
5. Ad Nov. 8/58.14-59.7.
6. Ad Nov. 9/59.8-17.
7. Ep. 55 to Antonianus, probably

The final resolution of the council turned in Cyprian's direction. It provided that the _libellatici_, after an examination of the individual cases, should be admitted back into the Church, while the _sacrificati_ should only be given communion in the event of danger of death.[1] The council of Carthage received support from Cornelius, mindful of his debt to Cyprian, and Rome passed a similar resolution in

---

7. (cont'd) Numidian, see Von Soden, "Prosop.", p. 261. The change of Cyprian's position is registered at Ep. 55.3/625.1-18.

1. Ep. 55.17/635.22-636.13. See Poschmann, "Zur Bussfrage", p. 52. Monceaux, _HAC_, p. 47 and 222. Koch, _CU_, p. 264, argues that _interim_ here means first in relation to the _sacrificati_ and is not to be taken to mean that the _libellatici_ were immediately received back after the council. But his interpretation seems strained. Firstly, the proviso of the examination of individual cases points towards immediate reception back into the Church, Ep. 56.2/648.19-649.22. Where Cyprian again refers to the council, he mentions that only those doing penance will receive absolution in case of _timor mortis_, which would refer to category two, the _sacrificati_. So Ep. 57.1/650.16-651.16 again supports the acceptance of the _libellatici_ immediately back into the Church. M.-C. Chartier, "La discipline pénitentielle d'après les écrits de Saint Cyprien", _Antonianum_ 14 (1959), pp. 142-3, infers from Ep. 55.22/639.8-640.23, that there were two types of rigorists, those who refused penance and those who refused absolution but allowed penance. The distinction is not a genuine one, as the end was damnation in any case.

263

council.[1]

The solution had been one of compromise for the bishop of Carthage, who had moved towards a more lax view of the role of the Church in the world. Unity and preservation had proved more important than rigorism in theology.[2] Cyprian valued the demands of organization and the maintenance of episcopal power as the most essential ingredients for salvation. He had managed a manoeuvre common to men of power and faith, that is, the reconciliation of seemingly incompatible claims. He had reconciled the maintenance of his own power with the demands of Christ and salvation. There seems no doubt that his convictions were genuine, if not a little opportunistic. More importantly, he had successfully intervened in Rome, maintaining his prestige at the most important of his neighboring sees. The lapsists at home faded into obscurity since the bishop had undermined their position by conceding to their demands. The later appointment by the lapsed of the priest Fortunatus, one of the five who opposed Cyprian from the onset, was a measure of desperation and a failure.[3]

Felicissimus did not give up, even journeying to Rome to try to upset the arrangements there. But his movement had spent itself and was no longer a threat to Cyprian.[4] The Novatianists, at the other end of the spectrum, had also attempted to challenge the structure of the Church by setting up their own organization of bishops

---

1. Ep. 55.6/627.14-628.8.
2. Ep. 55.22/639.8-640.23.
3. Ep. 59.9/676.1-677.13.
4. Ep. 59.1/666.10-667.4, dated to the summer of 252. See Appendix I.

264

and they were more successful in their attempts.[1] The Novatianist Church was to have a more enduring future than that of the lapsed, but it was never again to be a serious challenge to the Catholic position.[2]

No sooner had the effects of the storm been weathered than further clouds appeared on the horizon. The Emperor Gallus was bent on renewing the policy of Decius, and a new threat was thus directed at a still distracted Church.

---

1. Ep. 55.24/642.3-643.13.
2. Baus, HCH, p. 338, n. 104, for references to the later Novatianist Church.

265

Chapter V: INTERIM

Following the death of Decius and his son in June 251, Gallus was proclaimed Emperor by the troops of the Danubian legions.1 The defeat of his predecessor left the new Emperor in a dangerous position. His troops were in no condition to confront the Goths after the previous Roman disaster, and in Rome C. Valens Hostilianus Messius Quintus, younger son of Decius, was still alive and potentially menacing. Hostilianus was proclaimed Augustus on the news of his father's death and provided a rallying point for disaffection against the new Emperor.2 Gallus' obvious move was to secure peace as quickly as possible on the Danube and head for Rome to eradicate the threat to his regime. A treaty was made with the Goths allowing them to keep the booty they had taken. They were further granted an unmolested withdrawal into their own territory, the retention of the captives they had taken, particularly at

---

1. Eutropius, 9.5. The responsibility of Gallus for the death of Decius is debatable, but his later animousity seems established by J.F. Gilliam, "Trebonianus Gallus and the Decii: III et I cos", Studi in Onore di Aristide Calderini e Roberto Paribeni, 1 (Milan, 1956), pp. 305-11. See RE VIII A 1986, for bibliography. The later reputation of Decius may have necessitated a scapegoat, but the question remains open.
2. See RE XXV 1 1273 ff. for his age, and compare Hanslik, RE VII A 1186-7. For a more youthful Hostilianus, see CAH, p. 167.

267

the sack of Philippopolis, and an annual subsidy to remain at peace.[1] Gallus' son Volusianus was made Caesar.[2] Together they set out for Rome.

At first Hostilianus was only recognized as Caesar by Gallus, but soon after the arrival of father and son at Rome, Decius' son was recognized as Augustus.[3] To further cement his relationship to the line of the previous Emperor, Gallus adopted the new Augustus, perhaps at the same time as he was recognized as Augustus.[4] Etruscilla, wife of Decius, though forced into retirement retained her title of Augusta, which the wife of the new Emperor did not assume.[5] Gallus may have been uneasy about the question of the legitimacy of his own claim to Empire. The adoption of Hostilianus and the retention of the title of Augusta by the widow of Decius were calculated to placate and draw closer the supporters of Decius.

Whatever plans Gallus might have had

---

1. Zosimus, 1.24.2; Zonaras, 12.21; Jordanes, Getica 106. The extremely negative view of Zosimus towards Gallus may have led him to exaggerate the shamefulness of the peace. Under the circumstances, another course for Gallus is not obvious.
2. On the proclamation of his son as Caesar, see Aurel. Vict., 30, who, with Eutropius, using the KG as a source, made Gallus and Hostilianus one person. Zosimus, 1.24.2 and Eutropius, 9.5 report that Volusianus was made Augustus at the same time as his father, but the proclamation of him as Caesar is borne out by the coinage, see RIC IV.3, pp. 153 ff.
3. RE VIII A 1986-7.
4. CAH, p. 167.
5. RIC IV.3, p. 153.

were seriously affected by the arrival of a deadly plague from the East. It had started in Ethiopia and moved as far west as Rome by 250.[1] Cyprian is the only contemporary author to describe its symptoms, though the tendency among ancient authors to imitate the descriptions of their predecessors introduces some doubt as to his accuracy.[2]

The plague was characterized by diarrhoea, accompanied by the growth of sores about the jaws, vomiting, and redness of the eyes. In some cases,, the loss of limbs was involved, an impairment of hearing, or the inability to walk.[3] Whatever the nature of the plague, its effects were widespread.[4] Hostilianus died a few months after his elevation to Augustus.[5] Around

---

1. Deduced from the coins with the legend: APOLL(INI) SALUTARI. See RE VIII A 1988. The plague seems to have lasted intermittently for twenty years, and to have caused the death of the Emperor Claudius Gothicus, according to the Greek tradition, Zosimus, 1.47. Zosimus, 1.26, mentions the plague as breaking out under Gallienus, but this must surely have been a recurrence. For a similar situation, see P. Ziegler, The Black Death (Harmondsworth, 1969), p.242 where outbreaks of the plague are recorded for 1348, 1361, 1368-9, 1371, 1375, 1390 and 1405.

2. So the description of the plague in Procopius is taken from Thucydides, 2.49.

3. De Mort. 14/305.14 ff.

4. Zosimus, 1.26.

5. Probably by November 251, RE VIII A 1988. Zosimus, 1.25 reports that Hostilianus' death was caused by Gallus, and was not the result of the plague. But his bias against Gallus might account for this.

this period, Gallus' son Volusianus was raised to the rank of Augustus.[1]

The plague struck Carthage with great force.[2] The normal social rites and ceremonies that had characterized life for both Christian and pagan inhabitants broke down. The bonds of family and kin were destroyed. Men fled from their own kin in fear of contagion. The streets of the city were littered with corpses. Men turned toward immediate gain, ceasing to respect customary duties. In short, the death toll was high enough temporarily to upset the entire fabric of the community.[3] This additional blow, coming after the disasters of the persecution and the blows aimed at Church unity, severely affected the Christian community, and Cyprian was forced to rally his congregation in the face of new anguish.

The Lord, according to Cyprian, had already predicted that mankind would suffer plague, famine and war.[4] But a new and apocalyptic element is added: these disasters are portents that the Final Judgment and the coming of the Kingdom of

---

1. RE VIII A 1989.
2. Vita 9.1.
3. Though made difficult by the frequency of names and the lack of identifiable characteristics, a study of those names disappearing after 252-3 might at least give some idea as to the percentage of clergy carried away by the plague. For similar reactions during medieval plagues, see Ziegler, The Black Death, passim, and for the best semi-fictional and psychological treatment, see D. Defoe, The Journal of the Plague Year, Penguin Books (1966), first published in 1722.
4. De Mort. 2/297.15 ff.

God are at hand. They should be met not with fear and weakness, but with joy that the final reckoning is approaching.[1] The theme becomes characteristic of Cyprian's thought in this period.[2] For a man seeking to explain the horrors that had descended upon the community, the predicted end of all things in Revelation seems appropriate.[3] Other periods of stress produced like expectations.[4] Cyprian remained convinced that the end of the world was at hand, and from this conviction he developed an apologia.[5]

The Scripture says that the just live by faith. If one is secure and truly follows this precept, the plague is no longer anything to fear. The Lord's promise nullifies all such fears.[6] The world is nothing else than constant warfare against the devil. The soul suffers persecution from lust, avarice, gluttony, and ambition daily. Death offers peace and a complete withdrawal from the fray.[7] The true basis for his congregation's fear is lack of faith. They take the promises of mortal men on trust, but they refuse to trust in God.[8]

The plague makes no distinction between Christian and pagan, but rains destruction

---

1. De Mort. 2/297.15 ff.
2. Infra pp. 277 and 279.
3. If we assign Commodian to this period (i.e., the 250's) then others shared Cyprian's view.
4. See Ziegler, The Black Death, p.242.
5. Infra pp.277 and 279.
6. De Mort. 3/298.16 ff.
7. De Mort. 4-5/299.10-300.9; 7/320 ff; 15-16/306.9-307.17.
8. De Mort. 6/300.10 ff.

down upon both.[1] Cyprian had shown his concern for pagans as well as for Christians during the plague, advising that charity be given to all. Others felt less happy that God had made no special dispensation for His people.[2] Cyprian counters the complaint: since we are still in the flesh, as are our pagan neighbors, we are heir to all the evils that attack the flesh.[3] Moreover, Christians are marked not only for eternal life but for more suffering than others, as it is they who must bear the brunt of the devil's onslaught. Cyprian completes this equation of freedom from sin and righteousness by adducing examples such as Job, the Apostles, and Abraham, all of whom had suffered, and indeed suffered more extremely, because of their very righteousness.[4]

Those who say that death by plague robs men of the glory of martyrdom are mistaken. Martyrdom is a dispensation of God, not a choice made by man.[5] Besides, the Lord can see into the hearts of men; if virtue is present, even if it has no worldly sign, it will be rewarded.[6] A vision of a dying bishop is adduced to show that death is a command of God and must not be avoided

---

1. De Mort. 8/301.7 ff.
2. Vita 9.7. The fragment at 9.8 should be accepted as Cyprian's own composition, though not included in the extant corpus. The condition of the corpus makes this no argument against authenticity, see Pellegrino, Vita, ad loc., p. 132.
3. De Mort. 8/301.7 ff.
4. De Mort. 9-13/302.9-18 - 308.24.
5. De Mort. 17/307.18-308.11. For earlier development of this idea, supra p.246.
6. De Mort. 17-18/307.18-308.24.

or delayed.[1] Cyprian also had visions and commandments directly from God, urging him to declare publicly the necessity and fruitfulness of the plague for Christians.[2]

Cyprian strove to renew the faith and hope of his community, but this was not sufficient. With the breakdown of all bonds, what was required was a reaffirmation of virtue towards one's fellow man, and a return to God through faith.[3] These needs resulted in the treatise, De Opere et Eleemosynis, delivered as a sermon probably some time during the plague.[4] The close of the persecution shut off the normal route to Christian perfection through martyrdom. As the De Mortalitate indicated, this presented a grave problem for those who felt that the indiscriminate deaths caused by the plague had robbed them of the possibility of perfection and the martyr's crown.[5] Cyprian pointed out that there were other ways to purge sin besides martyrdom, less heroic perhaps but effective.[6] The remission of sins granted once and for all at baptism still requires charity and good works.[7] No one should flatter himself that he is possessed of a pure and immaculate heart; all need spiritual medicine.[8]

Scripture continuously admonishes a Christian to do good deeds and give alms for

---

1. De Mort. 19/308.25-309.15.
2. De Mort. 20/309.16-310.3. On visions, supra p. 203.
3. See Monceaux, HAC, p. 304.
4. For date, Appendix III, pp. 296 f.
5. De Mort. 18/308.13-24.
6. De Op. et El. 2/374.3-24.
7. Ibid.
8. De Op. et El. 3/375.1-15.

the poor.[1] Almsgiving does not exhaust the patrimony, but contributes to a divine treasure that the government cannot touch or take away.[2] What can be bought in this world? Even the offices of state are mere vanities and shadows.[3]

Christ has provided the example for all Christians in his life of self-denial and sacrifice.[4] So too the Christians of apostolic times, warmed by the sparks of the new faith, did not stint with their worldly possessions, but sold all their goods and in so doing became sons of God by a spiritual parenthood.[5]

God provides all for our common use. The earth and sky are for all men. In selling all earthly possessions, we imitate His charity and claim the glorious palm of salvation. Thus we satisfy Christ the Judge and God his Creditor. Charity is a divine and illustrious quality which opens paradise to us and the Kingdom of Heaven. Whatever disaster ensues, the Lord will remember these acts on the Day of Judgment.[6]

Cyprian's admonishment to his congregation may have served more than one purpose. Pontius states that Cyprian was a man of charity and goodness, not only aiding his fellow Christians but exhorting his congregation to look after pagans as well. No doubt a multitude of motives entered into the enjoinment of this command: natural human decency, the influence of

---

1. De Op. et El. 5-8/376.16-380.7.
2. De Op. et El. 9-11/380.8-382.19.
3. De Op. et El. 13-24/383.9-393.8.
4. De Op. et El. 1/373.1-374.2.
5. De Op. et El. 25/393.9-394.2, and Tertullian, Apol. 41.3.
6. De Op. et El. 26/394.3 ad fin..

Scriptural commendation, the simple necessities of health in a city that was mainly populated by pagans. But Cyprian's late entry into the Church and his pagan friends built ties which would further obligate him to help. Some of his flock may have opposed such charity to unbelievers. Part of the purpose of the De Opere et Eleemosynis may have been to meet this challenge.[1]

Along with the apocalyptic hopes and fears that mark the De Mortalitate, another trend of Cyprian's thought is marked. The world appeared to be in a state of senile decay, changing and passing away. Since shipwreck was imminent, Christians should have no reason to regret their departure.[2] The trials of his episcopate had fused millennial expectation with all he had undergone, and this was to bear fruit in the Ad Demetrianum, in confrontation with charges of pagans against the Christians.

Natural disasters had often raised the level of pagan hatred for their Christian neighbors. The pagans felt that it was the lack of attention paid to the gods which resulted in their wreaking vengeance on mankind. It had occasioned persecution and martyrdom in the past.[3] The year 252 witnessed the great plague, and the old

---

1. For a contrary view, see E.W. Watson, "The De Opere et Eleemosynis of St. Cyprian", JThS 2 (1901), pp. 433-8.
2. De Mort. 2/297.15 ff. This is an old pagan topos most fully expressed in Lucretius, Book 5. See W.M. Green, "The Dying World of Lucretius", AJP 63 (1942), p. 128.
3. Apol. 40.1 ff.; Firmilian, apud Cyp., Ep. 75.10/816.16-818.7.

reproaches and threats reappeared.[1]

In his continued dealings with the pagan community, Cyprian occasionally encountered effective opposition. One of his opponents was a certain Demetrianus, who frequently attended Christian meetings and had some success through heckling and raising doubts among the faithful of Cyprian's congregation.[2] The exact status of Demetrianus is unknown, but Cyprian refers to him as "qui alios iudicas aliquando". It may be that Cyprian is referring to his being employed in some judicial capacity, perhaps the proconsul's court or some local magistracy.[3] Perhaps they met when, before his conversion, Cyprian was involved in rhetoric and possibly in the courts at Carthage. The relationship ended with Demetrianus' trying to destroy the foundations of his friend's faith.

Demetrianus advanced the time-honoured theory that the recurrent disasters - plagues, droughts, famines - were the result

1. Ad Dem. 2/352.5 ff.
2. Ad Dem. 1/351: "Oblatrantem te et adversus Deum...nam cum ad me saepe studio magis contradicendi quam voto discendi venires..."
3. Ad Dem. 10/357.23-358.19. This phrase has occasionally given rise to far-fetched interpretations. The translator of ANF 8, 423, deduces from it that Demetrianus was the proconsul of Africa. More reasonably, Monceaux, HAC, p. 274, argues that he was perhaps one of the five primores attached to the magistrates during the Decian Persecution. But the phrase points rather to a present occupation. There is no evidence that the five judged at all. Their actions in the Pass. Pion. 3 and elsewhere

276

of the refusal of Christians to pay homage to the old gods.[1] Cyprian's argument is that the world's problems result from other causes. One factor was the ageing of the world. In essence, Cyprian applies a biological model to account for the loss of the powers of nature.[2] Thus the sun when it sets gives off light and becomes weaker at each setting. The moon too wanes. Even men themselves are produced inferior to their ancestors. Once the life of a man could reach eight or nine hundred years, but now one can hardly reach the century mark.[3] This is the law that God ordained for all His creations, that in time they must perish. In the process, the great become small and the strong become weak.[4]

His second refutation of Demetrianus is centered upon a purely apocalyptic explanation of the end of the world. The "last times" which he had felt approaching during the persecution again appear to Cyprian and this time support the Scriptures' announcement of the end of the world. The world itself is displaying the predictions of Scripture, and verifying the account given in Christian writings.

Cyprian's third and major argument is reminiscent of a favourite device of Tertullian. By a retorsio, the very grievance that excited Demetrianus against

---

3. (cont'd) appear to be irregular. They probably operated simply as a consilium. Monceaux's deduction that Demetrianus was a large slave owner, from chapter 8, is ludicrous. Only one slave is mentioned, and then only as an example.
1. Ad Dem. 2-3/352.6-353.19.
2. Ad Dem. 3/352.19-353.19.
3. Ad Dem. 4/353.20-353.54.
4. Ibid.

277

the Christians is turned upon him.[1] It is not neglect of pagan gods that has caused disaster, retorts Cyprian, but the neglect of the one true God by the pagan that lies at the root of present troubles.[2] God is angry and threatens because pagans refuse to turn to Him. All woes - the lack of rain, the sparse growth of plants, the pestilent breezes - are a chastisement and discipline from the Lord.[3] If service is refused to God, is it any wonder that fountains dry up and that the earth is less fertile? The plague is God's punishment for disobedience. All is the result of the sins of the pagans. Their wickedness is rampant. Unchastity, greed, avarice and rapine are committed by them.[4] And the servants of the true God are attacked. True religion is overturned by false superstitions. Demetrianus' followers are not content with failing to worship the Lord, but redouble the outrage by persecuting those who do.[5]

After this wholesale indictment of his opponent's arguments and morality, Cyprian returns to the legal justification of the persecution of the Christians. He redeploys Tertullian's argument in the Apologeticum about the contrary procedure used against the Christians.[6] Cyprian challenges Demetrianus: to be a Christian is either a crime or it is not! If a man confesses, why do you not put him to death, granted that it is a crime? If it is no

---

1. For the use of retorsio in Tertullian, see Apol. 43.1.
2. Ad Dem. 5/354.8-24.
3. Ad Dem. 7/355.20-356.10.
4. Ad Dem. 8-11/356.11-358.10.
5. Ad Dem. 12/359.16-360.14.
6. Apol. 1 ff. and Oct. 28.4.

278

crime, why do you then persecute the defendant? It is a senseless procedure.[1]

Christians have no need of revenge. That is why when they are approached and tortured, no attempt is made to extract vengeance. God has repeatedly granted it on behalf of his worshippers.[2]

Cyprian again warns them that the end of the world is near, and that they should turn their minds towards eternal salvation. When the Day of Judgment comes, then shall the persecutors experience the endless wrath of God and burn in the fires of hell. Their tortures will be infinite.[3] In the description, and in his delight at the fate of unbelievers, the bishop vividly recalls Tertullian gloating over the horrors that await the pagans at the Last Judgment.[4]

Cyprian exhorts Demetrianus to give up his evil persecution of the Christians and share with them the gift of eternal life. The gift of immortality will yield eternal happiness.[5]

Cyprian's apology manifests a weakness which Lactantius later cited as the single reason for denying him the status of an ideal apologist for the faith. The basis of Cyprian's exposition is the Christian Scripture.[6] Since Cyprian, with his training and background, was well aware of the frame of mind of an educated pagan, his apology would seem to have been directed at his own people rather than as a defense of

---

1. Ad Dem. 13/360.15-361.8.
2. Ad Dem. 18-19/363.20-365.2.
3. Ad Dem. 23-24/367.21-369.19.
4. Apol. 23.15-16.
5. Ad Dem. 25/369.20-370.14.
6. Lactantius, Div. Inst. 5.1.

279

Christianity against the pagans.[1]
Demetrianus' attitude was soon to find more
than verbal expression.

After a period of quiet that marked the
early part of Gallus' reign, information
began to reach Cyprian that the government
was contemplating another attack upon the
Church.[2] The rumours had so disturbed the
people of Thibari that Cyprian was forced
to send them a letter to try to cement
their faith.[3] The rumours further confirmed
Cyprian in his belief in the imminent
destruction of the world.[4] He fortified the
people by recalling the exploits of the
Maccabees when faced with a similar
situation.[5] A tone of resolute resistance

---

1. Pellegrino, Studi, p. 132, believes
that Cyprian's style and manner were so full
of Biblical quotations and allusions that
this would have been his normal apologetic
style, regardless of his audience. But
surely this is to ignore his pagan background
and the differences of the other treatises in
subject matter (except the Ad Donatum, which
is based on the moral excellence of the
Christian). Monceaux, HAC, p. 277, overrates
the originality of the work which is based
upon Scripture and commonplaces.
2. Ep. 57.1/650.16-651.15; 58.1/
656.5-657.11; 59.2/667.5-668-20.
3. Ep. 58. Thibaris was located in
the proconsular province at modern Thibar,
near Teboursouck in Tunisia. See Mesnage,
L'Afrique chrétienne, p. 159.
4. Ep. 58.2/657.12-658.24.
5. Ep. 58.6/661.14 ff. For a
good discussion of the use of the Maccabees
by Christian writers, refer to Frend,
M&P, pp. 19-21.

pervades his letter. But the bishop felt that more was needed to fortify the faithful after the disasters under Decius. At the council held in the spring of 252 under the threatening shadow of government action, further measures were taken to strengthen the Christian community.[1]

In a letter to Cornelius, Cyprian informs him that the assembled bishops had decided that a general peace should be granted to all the lapsed, because of the threat that a new persecution introduced to the Church.[2] Forty-two bishops attended the council of May 252.[3] But Cyprian and those assembled felt called upon to defend their new policy against those who might view it as simply a tactical move which violated Church discipline.[4] The council claimed that their action would fortify both those who remained - even if they received the crown, they would still need the arms of the Church - and also those who fled for the Lord's name, lest they perish without communion.[5] The letters give rise to no suspicion that Cornelius disagreed.[6]

The difficulties of the plague and the impending government action mobilized the faction of Felicissimus. Cornelius must have been encouraged in his policy of "flexibility" by the behaviour of Novatus during his stay in Rome and the latter's support of Novatianus. The action of the

1. For the date, Monceaux, HAC, p. 47.
2. Ep. 57.1/650.16-651.16.
3. Ep. 59.10/677.14-678.10.
4. Ep. 57.4-5/653.12-656.4.
5. Ep. 57.4/653.12-655.4.
6. See C. Favez, "La fuite de S. Cyprien lors de la persécution de Décius", REL 19 (1941), p. 191.

council of May 252 undermined further the position of those lenient towards the lapsed, since in effect Cyprian had out-manoeuvred them by giving communion to all who did penance. In one move he had removed the majority of their followers. The fact that he possessed constituted and recognized authority in perilous times must have been an added difficulty for Felicissimus. The earlier attempt of Novatus to influence the Roman see in favour of the lapsed had failed with the establishment of Cornelius as bishop of Rome. And perhaps Novatus was lost to their cause and joined Novatianus' faction at the other end of the spectrum. Nothing more is heard of him in the letters of Cyprian, and Felicissimus holds the unchallenged primacy among Cyprian's lapsist opponents.[1] With the lack of success at Carthage, the party of Felicissimus was pushed into a more radical position to maintain itself. Felicissimus had enlarged the faction to embrace the deposed bishop Privatus of Lambaesis.[2] Rejected by Cyprian and his council, Privatus joined the faction of Felicissimus and took part in the consecration of Fortunatus as anti-bishop of Carthage.[3]

---

1. Ep. 52.3/619.8-16 is the last mention of Novatus.
2. Supra p. 2.
3. Privatus at council, Ep. 59.10/ 677.14-678.9. The consecration of Fortunatus, 59.9/676.1-677.13 and 59.11/678.11-679.11. Cyprian claims that Fortunatus was consecrated by five bishops, not twenty-five as his opponents had claimed. But at 59.10 he falsely gives the impression that Privatus was the sole consecrator. His figures are not to be trusted.

Felicissimus had broken communion with Cyprian long before. The consecration of Fortunatus was a final and irrefutable token of separation and open warfare.[1] In an effort to gain support, Felicissimus and members of his party journeyed to Rome to win over Cornelius. Suffering under the cloud of potential persecutions and never a strong personality, Cornelius was moved enough by their persuasion to require a long and detailed missive from Cyprian mentioning the consecration of a Novatianist bishop at Carthage.[2] Perhaps Maximus' consecration caused Cornelius to reflect on the past support he had received from Cyprian.[3] Though the faction of Felicissimus could claim support among the ranks of Christians at Carthage, Cyprian was careful to point out the numerical superiority of his own party.[4] Most importantly, Cyprian claimed, if the position of one bishop could be challenged in this manner, all of the others would find themselves in a similar position.[5] Apparently Cyprian's pleas and persuasion fell on ready ears for we hear nothing of any break between him and Cornelius. But the weakness of the Roman bishop may have occasioned second thoughts

---

1. Fortunatus had been one of the original five to oppose Cyprian, Ep. 59.9/ 676.1-677.13. Also supra p. 139.
2. Ep. 59.9/676.1-677.13. Also 44.1/597.9.
3. A certain Felix is mentioned as another false bishop by Cyprian at 59.10/ 677.14-678.9. He is connected with Privatus but what the doctrine was that Privatus had formally professed is not known.
4. Ep. 59.15/684.7-685.19.
5. Ep. 59.18/687.16-689.10.

283

in Cyprian about his choice of ally.

The rumours of persecution that Cyprian had heard finally materialized, presenting more pressing problems than the actions of his Christian opponents. The internal policy of Decius towards the Christians and other dissident groups had been discontinued when more pressing problems posed by the Goths on the northern frontier had diverted his energy and resources. Gallus allowed the policy to lapse for the first two years of his reign, but the ravages of the plague and troubles on the imperial borders may have awakened his desire to supplicate the gods. The application of Decius' edict had ceased with the latter's death in June 251.[1] But Cyprian testifies to the report that Gallus was contemplating an edict which must have been designed to repeat the earlier provisions of Decius.[2] Not possessing Decius' resources, Gallus may have decided to proceed more gradually and aim first at the clergy rather than institute a full-scale sacrificial edict for all the inhabitants of the Empire on the Decian mode. Cyprian's references to edicts may refer only to the local actions of the governor of Proconsularis. Aside from Cornelius and Lucius at Rome, victims

---

1. Gilliam, "Trebonianus Gallus", pp. 305-11, has convincingly reconstructed the events and chronology surrounding the damnatio memoriae of Decius. Thus by July 15, 251, the damnatio memoriae had been voted, and the edict of persecution was a dead letter.

2. Damnatio, RE VIII A 1988; the edicts, Ep. 58.9/676.1-677.13; feralia edicta, Ep. 59.6/673.7-674.2.

284

are hard to find.[1] Eusebius is vaguer about the victims of Gallus and refers not to sacrifice but simply to the flight of holy men. No sacrifice or martyrs are named in the extract from Dionysius.[2]

The only direct evidence we have on the actions of Gallus is the banishment of Cornelius and his successor, Lucius.[3] Cornelius was banished to Centumcellae by order of the Emperor, probably in late May or early June of 253.[4] Cyprian sent a letter to him, stressing the great worth of

---

1. Alföldi, "Zu den Christenverfolgungen", p. 300, is right to dismiss the general consensus that Gallus renewed the edicts of Decius exactly, though he may finally have been contemplating such a step when revolt intervened. See CAH, p. 202, and Molthagen, Der römisches Staat, pp. 94 ff.

2. Eusebius, HE 7.1.

3. Ep. 60-61.1/695.11-21. Cyprian calls Lucius "confessor".

4. Lib. Pont., 152, places Lucius' succession on June 26, 253. Given the correspondence between Cyprian and Cornelius and the preparations to return Cornelius' body to the city after his death, a date in early June or late May would seem reasonable for the exile of Cornelius. See Jerome, Vir. Ill. 67, listing the date of Cornelius' death as the same as Cyprian's, that is, September 14 (AP 5). This tradition seems to appear in the Lib. Pont., 152, which lists the execution of Cornelius and his burial to September 14. The date of September 14 may have been the day on which the memory of Cornelius was celebrated, due to the lack of a bishop for 66 days.

285

his exile.[1] The letter points to Cornelius being accompanied by a large retinue of followers.[2] But no tradition supports the large number of confessors that Cyprian praises. Much of the content of the letter is directed towards Novatianus and his party. Cyprian was no doubt overjoyed to point to this glorious deed of Cornelius as a further blow for the Novatianist cause.[3] The only concrete mention of government policy confirms the conclusion that the action of Gallus was aimed at the clergy, not at the entire Christian congregation.[4]

Cornelius died a natural death.[5] The disorder in the Christian community of Rome must have been slight, for soon after Lucius received consecration as bishop until he himself was sent into exile (though soon to return).[6] In his own name and in the name of his colleague, Cyprian immediately felicitated him on his attainment of confessorship and his reinstatement as head of the congregation at Rome. Gallus had only been interested in half-measures; more serious problems were on his mind.

The Goths had proved a continued problem, and Aemilius Aemilianus, Gallus' successor as commander in Lower Moesia, was constantly occupied with them.[7] A

---

1. Ep. 60.
2. Ep. 60.1/691.8-692.7.
3. Ep. 60.3/693.20-694.12.
4. Ep. 60.2/692.8-693.19.
5. The variant tradition in the Lib. Pont., 152, is wrong. Eusebius, HE 7.1 mentions nothing about an execution. See Lawlor and Oulton, Eusebius, p. 237.
6. Ep. 61.1/695.10-21.
7. On the problems during Gallus'

286

successful though indecisive expedition against them by Aemilianus led to his proclamation by the troops.[1] Probably in August of 253, Aemilianus rushed upon Gallus before full preparations had been made for defense. Caught unaware at Interamna, the troops, rather than risk a hopeless battle, killed him and joined Aemilianus.[2] It must have been in the ensuing confusion that the new bishop of the Roman Church returned. Political upheaval reassured the Christians that they would be free from governmental interference at least for the time being.

Though Africa had been virtually untouched by the actions of Gallus, barbarian troubles added to the difficulties of the African provinces. From 253 to 262, Mauretania Caesariensis and Numidia were plagued by the revolts of mountain tribes.[3] It may have been at this time that Cyprian answered the appeals from the bishops of Numidia for money from the Carthaginian Church to redeem captives of the barbarian

---

7. (cont'd) reign on the Danube, see bibliography in Walser-Pekáry, Die Krise, p.26

1. Zosimus, 1.28; Zonaras, 12.21; PIR[2] A 330; CAH, p. 168. But Aurel. Vict., 34.8, preserves a variant version by which Aemilianus obtained the acclamation by corrupting the troops. This is suspect in light of the Greek sources and Victor's preoccupation with the corruption of the military. He also falsely records that Aemilianus died of the plague, 31.3.

2. Aurel. Vict., 31.2; also Epit. de Caes. 31.1.

3. See Rachet, Rome et les Berbères, pp. 238 ff.; Romanelli, Storia, pp. 460 ff.

raids.[1] Cyprian collected 100,000 sesterces in Carthage. Other sums, though smaller, were collected at different locations in the proconsular province.[2] But the effect of the barbarian invasions in Cyprian's province was small in comparison to the troubles that were seen in the 240's. Aside from this letter, no mention of barbarian disturbances appears in the correspondence.

Plague and threats of governmental action had thoroughly absorbed the mind and activities of the bishop of Carthage. But in the short period of peace before these troubles, Cyprian had had an opportunity to turn his mind towards less practical problems. Probably in late 251 or early 252, he had composed a treatise on the Lord's Prayer which took the form of a commentary. The obvious inspiration for the work was the similar composition by Tertullian.[3] Tertullian's consisted of two sections, the

1. Ep. 62. This epistle had been traditionally assigned to 253, in conjunction with the barbarian raids which took place then and are dated by the inscription to M. Aurelius Vitalis, EphEp 5.953. See Cagnat, L'armée romaine, p. 53; H. d'Escurac-Doisy, "M. Cornelius Octavianus et les révoltes indigènes du troisième siècle d'après une inscription de Caesarea", Libyca 1, Série Archéologie-Epigraphie (1953), pp. 181-7. But as Clarke, "Barbarian Disturbances" has pointed out, other disturbances could also have been the occasion of the letter. But the location in Numidia at least makes the identification possible.
2. Ep. 62.4/699.29-700.19.
3. The latest text with an extensive commentary is M. Réveillaud, Saint Cyprien: L'oraison dominicale, Etudes d'histoire et

288

first a commentary on the prayer itself, and the second a miscellany on different topics more or less related to the prayer. The disjointed state of Cyprian's treatise would indicate that it was in actuality a series of notes assembled as an aid in homiletic discourse.[1] He used Tertullian's commentary as the basis for his treatise. But Cyprian's work is more regularly planned and assembled than Tertullian's. In the De Dominica Oratione, chapters 7-27 are totally taken up in commentary; chapters 28-36 form a pendant to the commentary, discussing the times and attitudes necessary for the execution of the prayer in the proper manner. The whole is a more finished and organized product than Tertullian's.[2] It may be that as Cyprian came to know Tertullian he saw the dangers in his work.[3] Perhaps if Cyprian had had more time, other works of Tertullian would have been displaced by his own writings.[4] The base was Tertullian, but

---

3. (cont'd) de philosophie religieuses 58 (Paris, 1964). For date, Appendix III.

1. Barnes, Tert., p. 118.

2. E.v.d. Goltz, Das Gebet in der ältesten Christenheit (Leipzig, 1901), pp. 279-87, goes as far as postulating a common source rather than direct dependence. But the hypothesis is redundant. No other treatise in Latin of this type at this time is known, and we know that Cyprian was a close student of Tertullian. The work also requires no other source to account for structure or content.

3. For these, see Réveillaud, L'oraison dominicale, p. 5.

4. Unfortunately, this hypothesis lacks proof, but not verisimilitude.

Cyprian made use of him with an independence that characterizes all of his work.[1]

De Dominica Oratione opens with a theme common to all Cyprian's writings: the necessity to receive the divina praecepta which had played an instrumental part in his fight against his lapsist opponents.[2] Among these, the Lord's Prayer is the most important, for it was with its words that Christ himself instructed his people how to pray.[3] The form given by God must be observed with the requisite decorum and demeanor. Silence and modesty are essential.[4] Old and New Testament examples such as Hannah and the Pharisee in the temple are divine admonitions on the attitudes to be adopted in prayer.[5]

Having prescribed the necessary mental attitude, Cyprian begins a line by line commentary on the meaning of the prayer. He stresses its importance as an expression of the faith of the entire community.[6]

Following the commentary, he discusses the attendant circumstances that accompany prayer, giving the most detailed attention to the hours appropriate for prayer.[7] To the third, sixth and ninth hours sanctioned by the example of Daniel, the new dispensation of Christ has added other times appropriate for the expression of our sentiments towards God. Morning prayer

---

1. For the relation of the Ad Donatum and the Octavius, supra pp. 57 ff.
2. De Dom. Or. 1/267.1-13. Also supra pp. 209 f.
3. De Dom. Or. 2/267.14-268.7.
4. De Dom. Or. 4/268.18-269.10.
5. De Dom. Or. 5-7/269.11-271.3.
6. De Dom. Or. 8/271.4-272.6.
7. De Dom. Or. 34/292.4-21.

should be added so that the Lord's resurrection may be celebrated.[1] Other exegetic reasons are expounded for prayer at sunset and the decline of the day. But a true Christian should be in a state of prayer at all times. The night should be filled by petitions to the Lord.[2] Christians should constantly pray, that they not be forsaken by the Lord's divine light. Since the duties of prayer and thanksgiving to God are eternal, in this life as well let this act be a constant repetition of our thanks to God.[3]

Perhaps also dating from this interim period of quiet is a letter of Cyprian to Caecilius, bishop of Biltha in Proconsularis.[4] In essence the letter is a full-scale treatise in defense of the mixture of wine and water in the communion chalice.[5] Giving an exegesis of Biblical topoi, Cyprian demonstrates the Scriptural justification for the use of wine and water instead of water alone.[6]

The relaxation of pressure that marked the destruction of Gallus in July or August 253 provided an opportunity for the calling of another of the yearly councils that mark

---

1. De Dom. Or. 34/292.22-293.24.
2. Ibid.
3. De Dom. Or. 36/293.25-294.15.
4. Ep. 63. For the location, see Von Soden, "Prosop.", p.254; Mesnage, L'Afrique chrétienne, p. 193.
5. The treatise illustrates the fine line between letter and treatise which marks Cyprian's use of both genres. In fact, the Cheltenham List of 359-65 lists some of the treatises with the letters, 147, nos. 14 and 15.
6. Ep. 63.4-5/703.1-704.23.

Cyprian's episcopate.[1] The new council settled the defeat of those who favoured easy penance for the lapsed. Felicissimus' last effort to swing the Roman see over to his side was check-mated by Cyprian.[2] The threat that Cyprian felt from the lapsists disappears from his correspondence, and the council of 253 had time to be occupied with other matters.

One related question was considered by the sixty-six assembled bishops. Therapius, bishop of Bulla, either in Numidia or in Proconsularis, had given the priest Victor peace before the time stated by Cyprian. Faced with a fait accompli, however, Cyprian and his fellow bishops acquiesced, while reprimanding Therapius for his temerity. The recipient of the council's letter was Fidus, who was no doubt curious about the incident, and the letter served as a presentation of the official view.[3]

More relevant to Fidus' own concerns was the council's answer to his question on the principle of infant baptism. Fidus had maintained that infants ought not to be baptised during the second or third day after birth, in accordance with the Jewish law of circumcision which would not allow baptism until after the eighth day.

The early history of the Christian attitude to infant baptism remains confused. The practice was fairly widespread by the

---

1. The council of 253 took place later than usual, dated to perhaps early July by the letter to Lucius (Ep. 61). See Monceaux, HAC, p. 48, with reference to Ep. 64.
2. Supra p. 283.
3. Ep. 64.1/717.5 ad fin. The see of Fidus cannot be determined.

292

time of Tertullian.[1] Tertullian had argued against it as conferring a privilege before the recipient could understand the right and the responsibilities transmitted.[2] Cyprian took up a position opposite to that of Tertullian.

First, Cyprian proclaims that Christ's message was directed towards the saving of as many lives as possible. The child is a perfected creature and thus eligible for baptism.[3] The divine gift of peace is open to all, as the Scripture claims. Age is of no consequence.[4] The further arguments of Fidus on the uncleanliness of the new-born infant and the Judaic example are quickly settled: the Scripture proclaims all things clean, and Christians are freed from observance of the Mosaic rules by the coming of Christ who broke these bonds.[5]

The council marks a new period of peace for the African Church. The immediate threat of persecution had been removed, and time could be devoted to housekeeping details and theological argument. Aemilianus, however, was not in so fortunate a position. The victory at Interamna brought a reign of short duration. Though a plentiful coinage was issued attesting the confirmation of his position, with his wife Cornelia Supera declared Augusta, Aemilianus' plans were soon interrupted.[6]

---

1. De Bapt. 18.
2. Ibid. For the Eastern position, see Harnack, HD, II, pp. 142 ff. For bibliography, Quasten, Pat., pp. 278 ff.
3. Ep. 64.2/718.1-16.
4. Ep. 64.3/718.17-719.12.
5. Ep. 64.4/719.13-720.7.
6. CAH, p. 168; RIC IV.3, 150; Walser-Pekáry, Die Krise, pp. 27-8.

293

P. Licinius Valerianus, who was in charge of the troops on the Rhine, had been instructed to help Gallus quash the rebellion.[1] He arrived too late, however, for Gallus had been defeated and killed. But Valerianus' march ended the short reign of Aemilianus; the latter was put out of the way by his own troops who proclaimed Valerianus Emperor. At the news of his father's success, Gallienus was declared Caesar by the Senate.[2] By August or September 253, Valerianus was in sole control of the Empire.[3]

1.   PIR[2] L 258.
2.   Zosimus, 1.37.3.
3.   Barnes, "Some Persons in the Historia Augusta", Phoenix 26 (1972), p. 140, n. 1, has decisively shown that the proclamation of Valerianus is to be dated after 29 August 253. The terminus ante quem is given by ILS 531 from Gemellae, which is dated to October 253. Thus the accession of Valerianus falls between those two dates. The evidence does not allow a closer approximation. For the Alexandrian coinage, see J. Vogt, Die alexandrinischen Münzen: Grundlegung einer alexandrinischen Kaisergeschichte (2 vols. Stuttgart, 1924), Vol. II, p. 154.

Chapter VI: THE REBAPTISM CONTROVERSY

The temporary cessation of government activity against the Christians had allowed Cyprian to turn to problems of internal disunity. The victories he had achieved over the lapsists and the action he had taken against the Novatianists had not eliminated all opposition to his rule over the Christians at Carthage. There were others who found his administration irksome.

Cyprian's commanding personality and comparatively high social standing had been considered an obstacle by some from the beginning of his episcopate. The confessor Florentius did not hesitate to express his feelings against Cyprian, calling attention to his lack of humility.[1] More pressing was the charge of flight and cowardice that still clung to him from his exile during the Decian Persecution. Even after his death, Pontius would be forced to deal at length with this accusation.[2]

Cyprian replied to Florentius and attempted to discredit him, charging that Florentius was motivated by arrogance and pride.[3] He claimed that Florentius feared that his own martyrdom would be stained by further contact with the bishop. The persecution had left an enduring tension between the constituted authority of the

---

1. Ep. 66.3/728.7-729.10. In the heading, Florentius is addressed as cui et Puppiano fratri, the same type of agnomen formation as in Cyprian's name: Cyprianus qui et Thascius.
2. Vita 7.
3. Ep. 66.5/730.3-22.

295

bishops and the prestige and newly-won power of the martyrs and confessors.[1] Florentius had cut himself off from communion with the bishop and his supporters.[2] He had apparently joined the Novatianist faction or some other rigorist splinter group which severely disapproved of Cyprian's more lenient attitude.

Cyprian's rejoinder was to claim that Florentius had deserted God. He had with presumption assumed God's own prerogative as judge.[3] Bishops are constituted by God, and to question their judgment is to question the judgment of God.[4] He continues with irony, saying that Florentius has been the cause of division in the Church and that those who have fallen away were not worthy to have been members of the Church. The bishop invokes Peter's reply to Christ's question asking whether Peter too would leave him. Peter answered the Lord, "To whom shall we go?". So Cyprian implies that Florentius is a deserter of the true Church like chaff that should not be kept with the true grain.[5]

As to the more personal reproaches levelled against Cyprian, the bishop replied strongly pointing to the high status of a priest. Old Testament examples were brought forward to prove that he who disregards a priest courts death.[6] He quoted the words of the proconsul's edict against himself during the Decian Persecution as proof of

---

1. Ep. 66.1/726.10-727.9.
2. Ibid.
3. Ibid.
4. Ep. 66.2/727.10-728.6.
5. Ep. 66.8/732.11-733.11.
6. Ep. 66.3/728.7-729.10.

296

his own affliction.[1] He diplomatically neglects to mention his flight. He chided Florentius, saying that his conduct could only lead to schism, and therefore spelled disaster for the Church.[2] Florentius was displaying the very arrogance that lies at the root of heresy and schism. Even animals recognize their leaders. Florentius is worse than they for refusing to obey his.[3]

The charges of Florentius give a rare glimpse of those who still remained discontent with Cyprian's rule after the destruction of organized and strong opposition. Though such factions as the lapsists had ceased, and the party of Novatianus had lost its early momentum, individual cases of lapsed individuals, particularly the clergy, called for action. They could still provide foci for dissent, and a solution was therefore required.

The council which sat in the spring of 254 at Carthage, under the presidency of Cyprian, was presented with just such a problem, and the nature of the case involved far-reaching implications. Cyprian had, as an individual, dealt with at least one such case in Africa. Fortunatianus, bishop of Assuras, had, after sacrificing, begun to demand back his episcopal privileges.[4] Addressing Epictetus, probably the priest in charge of the congregation,

---

1. Ep. 66.4/729.11-732. This edict must refer to Decius, as we know of no such action taken during the short period of trouble under Gallus.
2. Ep. 66.5/730.3-22.
3. Ep. 66.6/730.23-731.5.
4. Ep. 65.1/721.15-722.24. The form is probably Assuras, though this is uncertain. See Benson, Cyprian, p. 302.

297

Cyprian fulminated against the lack of godliness displayed by Fortunatianus in such presumption.[1] But the situation at Assuras was merely a local matter. The case before the council of 254 was to affect Rome.

Two Spanish bishops had appealed to the council to act as judges in a dispute concerning the legitimacy of the bishops of Legio et Asturica and Emerita.[2] Felix and Sabinus, the two who had initiated the action, claimed that Martialis and Basilides had both succumbed in the persecution and possessed certificates for sacrifice.[3] Cyprian and his fellow bishops, in execution of the request, condemned them as idolaters, but allowed them to be received into communion though not to hold office.[4]

---

1. Von Soden, "Prosop.", p. 261, rightly observes that there is no indication that Epictetus was the bishop of Assuras. At the council of September 1, 256, the bishop mentioned from Assuras is Victor, SE 68.
2. Though the people of Emerita are also addressed, the close correspondence in the actions of Basilides and Martialis would indicate that their seats were close together. On their locations, see G.W. Clarke, "Prosopographical Notes on the Epistles of Cyprian", Latomus 30 (1971), pp. 1141-5.
3. Ep. 67.1/735-736.7. The sees of the two senders of the request are unknown. Whether Basilides was a libellaticus or a sacrificatus is unclear. In Martialis' case there is clear evidence that he had sacrificed (67.6). For Christianity in Spain, see Baus, HCH, p. 384. For the governors, Walser-Pekáry, Die Krise, p. 67.
4. Ep. 67.6/740.9-741.10, where the precedent of Cornelius is cleverly cited in

298

Sabinus, the successor of one of the two discredited bishops, had been elected in a council assembled from the nearest bishops of the same province in the presence of the laity.[1] Basilides journeyed to Rome to urge the bishop Stephen to re-instate him in the office from which he had been deposed.[2]

Lucius' episcopate at Rome had been of short duration. After eight months, the bishopric had fallen vacant and Stephen was elected.[3] Perhaps lingering plague caused the death of Lucius.[4] The newly-elected bishop still had to contend with the Novatianists, and may have been insecure in his position, being therefore more predisposed to leniency until he gained experience in office. In addition, as Cyprian states, the great distance between Rome and the troubled Spanish bishoprics would have made it difficult for Stephen to gather information on the case of Basilides.[5] So the

---

4. (cont'd) view of Stephen's actions.
1. Ep. 67.5/730.3-22.
2. Ibid.
3. The Liberian Catalogue blunders in assigning three years, eight months, and ten days to Lucius. Eusebius, HE 7.2 gives less than eight months, but his list generally includes numerous errors. See Lawlor and Oulton, Eusebius, p. 46, for a corrected table of Roman bishops.
4. In Ep. 68.5/748.11-749.2, Cyprian links Lucius and Cornelius as martyrs. The use of the term shows that they were both living witnesses to the faith: "in glorioso martyrio constituti, dandam esse lapsis pacem censuerunt". However, nothing can be inferred as to the actual manner of their deaths.
5. Ep. 67.5/730.3-22.

plea of Basilides found a favourable audience in Rome and further complicated the Spanish situation. The deception of Stephen must have been the origin of the Spanish plea to the African council.[1] The prestige of Carthage and the African Church was seen by the Spanish bishops as a necessary counterweight to the authority of the Roman see. Cyprian had the prestige of a long-established and successful episcopate. The outcome of the affair, however, remains unknown.[2]

At approximately the same time, a similar case occurred in Gaul.[3] Faustinus, bishop of Lyons, had written to Cyprian at least twice about Marcianus, bishop of Arles, who had joined the Novatianists.[4] In conjunction with the other bishops of Gaul,

---

1. For further discussion, infra p.333.
2. Mongelli, "La chiesa", p. 158, states that Cyprian prevailed, but there is no evidence to support this assertion, nor for his portrayal of Stephen as authoritarian. The prestige of Rome was the magnet that drew Basilides. No valid reason prevailed to stop Stephen from giving judgment and seeking to influence the Spanish episcopate.
3. Time deduced from Ep. 68.2/744.20-745.19, which probably refers to the council of spring 254.
4. Ep. 68.1/744.3-19. For the extent of Christianity in Gaul prior to 300, see Baus, HCH, p. 385. Arles is mentioned as possessing a bishop for the first time in Ep. 68. Interestingly, this is the first reference to the continuing dispute between these two sees for the control of Narbonensis. See A.H.M. Jones, The Later Roman Empire 284-602 (Oxford, 1964), Vol. II, p. 572.

300

Faustinus had also informed Stephen but the Roman bishop had taken no action.[1] Evidently Faustinus hoped that Cyprian would utilize his prestige to press Stephen to depose Marcianus. Cyprian complied with Faustinus' request and directed a letter to Stephen. He justified his letter by appealing to the harm that was being done to the peccatores who were being denied communion. He asked Stephen to direct a very full letter to Marcianus' Gallic colleagues which would persuade them not to continue to recognize the bishop of Arles.[2] Stephen was also asked to send a further letter to Arles itself, which should name another bishop to replace Marcianus.[3]

The African bishop thus recognized a special jurisdiction of the bishop of Rome over the election of a bishop for Arles.[4] The case is clearly different from that of the Spanish bishops with whom Cyprian did not hesitate to act directly. At Arles the Carthaginian bishop proceeded indirectly by first mobilizing Stephen.[5]

---

1. Ep. 68.2/744.20-745.19.
2. Ibid.
3. Ep. 68.3/745.20-746.22: "Dirigantur in provinciam et ad plebem Arelate consistentem a te litterae quibus abstento Marciano alius in loco eius substituatur".
4. The weakness of Gallic Christianity at this time may account for the special powers of the Roman bishop over the election of the bishop of Arles. Also the traditional closeness of Narbonensis to Italy ("Italia verius quam provincia") may help to explain the special relationship.
5. Baus, HCH, p. 359, equates the cases of Spain and Gaul. But clearly there is a distinction. Spain presents a case where

Cyprian's interference in the affairs of troubled sees was not confined to Gaul or Spain. Nearer home he had written to the people of Assuras about Fortunatianus who had fallen in the Decian Persecution.[1] Cyprian was energetic in his hunt for unfit or unsuitable bishops. Stephen heeded the African's admonitions to take action, at least in Gaul, but his motives are hidden. Most likely questions concerning such bishops came to the fore too early in his episcopate for him to be sure of himself. Cyprian reminded him of Lucius and Cornelius to galvanize him into action.[2] He also mentioned Biblical admonitions to the clergy to perform their duties as good shepherds.[3] Almost with prescience he reminds the Roman bishop that there should not be diverse opinions among those who possess a single spirit.[4] Cyprian closes by simply asking who has been substituted for Marcianus. His appeal to unity of spirit was sufficient incentive, so he thought, for Stephen to act.[5]

---

5. (cont'd) prestige is the central factor, and not special jurisdiction. At Arles, Cyprian implies that the Roman bishop was in a special position with regard to the election of a bishop for that see. The newness of the see may have been a factor, supra p. 301, n. 3.
1. Ep. 65.
2. Ep. 68.5/748.11-749.2.
3. Ep. 68.4/746.23-748.10.
4. Ep. 68.5/748.11-749.2.
5. The connections between Rome and Carthage were so close that Carthage might have been involved in the events leading to Stephen's election. This might explain the paternal tone of Ep. 68. But unfortu-

302

The frontal attack on Novatianus and other heretical clergy must have been taking its toll on the rigorists, for in 255 Cyprian received a letter from the bishop Magnus, of an unknown see, who was unsure of what to do about those who had come over from Novatianus and now asked for admission into the Catholic Church.[1] Cyprian's reply is strong and comprehensive. No exception was to be made for the Novatianists, even if they use the same symbol and formula as the Catholics in the rite of baptism.[2] Christ made no distinction when pointing out those who were his enemies among the various sects and divisions of the heretics, but he grouped them all together.[3]

The Church is one and single. Only the baptism of the Church can save, for only the Church has been granted the power to provide salvation.[4] To allow salvation to the Novatianist sacrament is to claim that Novatianus is within the Church. But Novatianus had made himself bishop, disregarding the legitimate successor of Fabianus as bishop of the Roman see. Thus he could not be counted among those within the Church.[5]

Anyone who violates the unity of the Church can only excite the anger of

---

5. (cont'd) nately, the record is blank. The Lib. Pont., 154, preserves only the information that Stephen was a resident of Rome, for what it is worth.

1. Ep. 69. For Magnus' see, see Von Soden, "Prosop.", p. 261.

2. Ep. 69.1/749.5-750.20; also 69.7/756.5-18.

3. Ep. 69.1/749.5-750.20.

4. Ep. 69.2-3/750.21-752.4.

5. Ep. 69.3/752.5-17.

303

God.[1] Thus the priest who was sent to chasten the sins of Jeroboam was forbidden to join him in food and drink. When the priest ignored this admonition, God struck him down. Further, when the disciples were sent by the Lord to preach the Gospels, they were forbidden to visit the Samaritans who were heretics. Evidently heretics and Gentiles were grouped in the same category.[2] Heretics can have no merit. As enemies of the bishops, how can they usurp what is not theirs to take? They have no right to baptism.[3] They have no right to the Holy Spirit and do not themselves possess it. Their baptism is not only unavailing but is positively harmful.[4]

Thus Cyprian established, in this letter to Magnus, the basic position he was to hold in the rebaptism controversy.[5] Baptism is only efficacious if the administrator of the sacrament possesses the Holy Spirit. No one outside the Church can possess the Holy Spirit, thus the baptism administered outside the Church, even if the same symbol is used, is of no worth. All heretics are equally without the possession of the Spirit. Novatianus, therefore, has neither the right nor the ability to administer a valid baptism.[6] Cyprian placed the efficacy of the sacrament not on the merit of the individual

---

1. Ep. 69.6/754.16-756.15.
2. Ibid.
3. Ep. 69.10/758.19 ff.
4. Ep. 69.9/758.1-18.
5. As Benson, Cyprian, p. 345 realized.
6. The obvious implications for the Donatist controversy of the next century are striking. On this subject, see Brisson, Autonomisme, pp. 78 ff., and Frend, DC, pp. 92 ff.

304

but on his relationship to a particular organization. The Holy Spirit is localized in the one true Church.[1]

But Cyprian found opposition and questioning not only in Africa but also at Rome. Stephen came out in favour of allowing the baptism of heretics its validity, if the name of Christ was part of the symbol.[2] What motivated Stephen's opposition to Cyprian is unknown. At least part of his staunch opposition may have found its origin in Cyprian's handling of the case of Marcianus of Arles.[3] By March of 255, when the opening forays of the controversy took place, Stephen had been in office for approximately one year and could afford to assert his authority, even against the prestige of Cyprian.[4]

Some idea of Stephen's arguments against Cyprian's position can be gained from an anonymous treatise on rebaptism preserved among Cyprian's works.[5] The author's

---

1. Thus Mongelli, "La chiesa", p. 160, is essentially wrong when he considers Cyprian to be concerned with the man rather than the sacrament. The institution is the central concern in Cyprian's theology of the sacraments.

2. Ep. 73.16/789.21-790.10.

3. H. Von Soden, "Der Ketzertaufstreit zwischen Stephanus von Rom und Cyprian von Karthago", QFIAB 12 (1909), pp. 7-8, sees this too strongly as the entr'acte of the rebaptism controversy. Rather, it added fuel to the fire. Neither position was of itself unassailable theologically.

4. Von Soden, "Der Ketzertaufstreit", p. 6, believes that it was Stephen's recognition of Novatianus' clerical grade.

5. The text can be found in Hartel,

305

personal virulence against his opponents

_____

5. (cont'd) part 3, pp. 69-92. The
date and provenance of the text have been
the centre of some controversy, see Altaner-
Stuiber, Pat., p. 177. The tone of the work
is anything but friendly and reasonable.
The author appears to be a bishop (chapters
1, 10, 19). The harsh tone adopted
towards Cyprian would imply an advanced stage
of the crisis. In chapter 1 the author
accuses Cyprian of acting from personal
motives. The controversy disappears from
the letters of Cyprian during the beginnings
of the Valerianic troubles. So a date in
256, perhaps after the council in the spring
of that year, remains the most reasonable
possibility. The Valerianic Persecution
seems to have left the question in limbo.
Later, good relations were established with
Rome and presumably with other dissenters
from Cyprian's position. The provenance is
the most difficult of all the questions. It
divided Africa internally as well as the
rest of the Christian world. A suggestion
has been made that the treatise is of Italian
origin and, in fact, corresponds to the
treatise mentioned in Ep. 73.4-5/781.1-15.
See J. Ernst, "Zeit und Heimat des Liber de
rebaptismate", ThQ 90 (1908), pp. 579-613;
91 (1909), pp. 20-64. But the absence of
remarks on Peter or Rome provides some
indication that it was not Italian. See
Monceaux, HAC, p. 92. The Biblical text
used seems to be closer in origin to African
versions than to Italian ones, Monceaux, p.
93. Therefore, the most likely place of
origin would seem to be Africa, perhaps
from a Numidian or Mauretanian opponent of
Cyprian.

matches Stephen's own approach.[1] The most potent argument is that Cyprian and his followers are violating tradition. The ancient tradition had allowed that the imposition of hands was sufficient for receiving heretics into the Church, if they had been baptised in the name of Jesus Christ. Any opinion which violates such authority is wrong and the work of a heretic.[2] As support for this tradition, the author cites the Scriptures. John the Baptist distinguished between two types of baptism, that of water and that of the Holy Spirit.[3] Even the Apostles did not immediately receive the Holy Spirit, but it descended upon them at length on the Day of Pentecost.[4]

The baptism of water is made efficacious by the name of Jesus Christ alone.[5] Once given, it should not be repeated but is valid forever.[6] More importantly for the present discussion, its efficacy is independent of the morals and person of the officiant who confers it.[7] Even a heretic or schismatic can confer grace by the use of

---

1. De Rebapt. 1/69-71.18, and Eusebius, HE 7.3.
2. Ibid. See also infra p. 312, for Cyprian's argument against such a position which had also been adopted by Stephen.
3. De Rebapt. 2-3/71.19-73.20.
4. De Rebapt. 6/75.32-76.1.
5. Ibid.
6. De Rebapt. 7/78.5-29; also 15/ 87.33-89.19.
7. De Rebapt. 4/73.21-74.27; 6-9/ 75.21-81.19; 15/87.33-89.19.

the Name in baptism.[1]

Thus the author brings both tradition and Scripture to support his point of view. Stephen had brought the weight of Roman tradition to bear on his side.[2] But the tradition on baptism was less consistent than the version of Rome and Cyprian's opponents would make it appear.

In Africa Cyprian could cite the precedent of the council of Agrippinus. Under his presidency, the bishops of Numidia and Africa Proconsularis established the precedent for Cyprian that rebaptism of heretics was in fact necessary.[3] On the whole, however, even in Africa tradition was against it, and Cyprian was forced to use reason to establish a counter-tradition.[4]

Even in the third century the differences between East and West were both striking and indicative of what would come in the future. Firmilian, bishop of Caesarea in Cappadocia, notes that the custom of rebaptising heretics had apostolic sanction.[5] Firmilian had himself taken part in a synod held at Iconium in Phrygia.[6] Probably at the same time, another synod met and decided in favour of rebaptism at Synnada, in the province of Asia.[7] Other

---

1. De Rebapt. 10/81.20-82.30.
2. Infra p. 312.
3. Ep. 71.4/774.13-20; 73.3/780.13-25. For the date of this council, supra p. 15.
4. Ep. 71.3/773.10-774.11.
5. Ep. 75.5/812.30-814.5; 75.19/822.18-823.5.
6. For the date of this council, probably circa 230, see Hefele, Histoire des conciles, I, part 1 (Paris, 1907), p. 307.
7. Eusebius, HE 7.7.5.

synods at unknown places in the East are also recorded as favouring this practice.[1] The great theologians of Alexandria, though not definite in their rejection of heretical baptism, expressed their doubts about its validity.[2] Firmilian had a great number of supporters in the East. The bishops of Cilicia, Cappadocia, Galatia and the neighboring provinces supported the position of Cyprian against Stephen.[3] Dionysius in Alexandria diplomatically hedged on the question, but he may at last have gone over to the Roman position.[4] Obviously the practice concerning the treatment of heretics presented a less uniform appearance than the Roman bishop would have liked.

Support for Cyprian's position was not solid throughout the African provinces. In the spring of 255 at the annual council, a letter arrived from a group of bishops in Numidia on the question of rebaptism.[5] The thirty-one bishops attending the council, with Cyprian as their leader, reaffirmed the position taken by Cyprian in his letter to Magnus. Heretics do not possess the Holy Spirit, nor are they a part of the Church.

---

1. Eusebius, HE 7.7.5.
2. Clement of Alex., Strom. 1.19; Origen, In Ioha. Comm. 6.25.
3. Eusebius, HE 7.5.1.
4. Eusebius, HE 7.7.4. See notes of Lawlor and Oulton, Eusebius, p. 241.
5. Ep. 70. See Von Soden, "Prosop.", for the sees and areas of these Numidian bishops. For the addition of Ianuarius, refer to Hartel's app. crit., p. 766. The addressee seems to be a corruption of the Januarius mentioned as the first recipient.

309

Therefore their baptism cannot be valid.[1] Cyprian's tone is one of gentle admonition rather than a proclamation of the truth. He knew that there was widespread dissatisfaction with his stand. Regardless of his support in the East and the previous decisions in Africa, the opposition of Rome presented a grave problem. He was unsure of his ground and ended his reply to the Numidian bishops with an invitation to a larger council to consider the matter further.

Cyprian's feeling that he lacked support is evidenced by his correspondence with bishops who were undecided on the truth of his position, even after the first council of 255. The opposition seems to have been particularly localized in Numidia and in Mauretania.[2] Quintus, one of Cyprian's correspondents, had been uncertain of the position to adopt and the distance of his see from Carthage had diminished the direct influence that Cyprian's personality could exert upon him.[3]

Cyprian presented his case with compelling logic, again using his definition of the Church as the central theme in his argument. Either the Catholic Church has baptism and the heretics do not, or the heretics possess the power to baptise and

---

1. Ep. 70.2-3/768.6-770.20.
2. Evidenced by Ep. 70, 72, and 73. By September 256, there is evidence that the area near Carthage in Proconsularis was also disaffected.
3. The see of Quintus lay in Mauretania, Ep. 72.1/775.1-776.13. Von Soden, "Prosop.", p. 269, identifies this Quintus as separate from the Quintus from Acbia in Numidia, and rightly so, SE 65.

the Catholic Church does not.[1] Cyprian argues that those coming from among heretics must be baptised. Obviously the Catholic Church is the one repository of grace, and therefore it alone is capable of giving baptism. This is not rebaptism, but simply baptism.[2] Cyprian distinguishes between those who had once been members of the Church and then joined a heresy and those who had never been members of the Church and were now entering it for the first time. The first group is accepted into the Church by the laying on of hands by the bishop.[3] But the second group enters as if they were pagans. Nothing can be common to sheep and to wolves. The second group must be baptised, as they come from a worthless baptism.

Cyprian could not ignore Stephen's opposition, and he attacked him by quoting from the New Testament in his letter to Quintus. He pointed to the example given in the dispute between Peter and Paul on the question of circumcision. Although Peter was the one upon whom the Lord established the Church, he did not claim anything for himself in an arrogant manner. He did not point to the fact that he was in the Church before Paul and ought, therefore, to be obeyed by those who, like Paul, had joined the Apostles later. Nor did Peter despise Paul because he had been a persecutor before his conversion, but he granted the force of Paul's argument. Cyprian emphasized that this was an example of concord and the legitimacy of reason. With pointed irony, he called attention to the lack of concord and reason in Peter's successor, the present

1. Ep. 71.1/771.1-772.15.
2. Ibid.
3. Ep. 71.2/772.16-773.9.

311

bishop of Rome, who claimed to be following ancient tradition.[1]

Stephen began to take the initiative in the East. The wide support that Cyprian enjoyed there called for action. Stephen broke off communion with the majority of bishops who supported Cyprian in the East, among whom were most of the bishops of Galatia, Cappadocia and Cilicia.[2]

This unyielding position had the effect not of breaking his adversary's will, but merely of destroying all hope of reconciliation or compromise. In the early winter of 256, Cyprian received a reply from Firmilian to a letter of his on heretical baptism.[3] The letter illustrates to what extent Stephen had destroyed any hope of bringing over the Eastern bishops to his point of view. It compares the conduct of Stephen to the perfidy of Judas. Firmilian states that just as one should not be grateful for the perfidy of Judas for making possible the passion of the Lord, so one should not thank the inhumanitas of Stephen for putting Cyprian's faith to the test and allowing us to witness it.[4]

---

1. Ep. 71.3/773.10-774.11.
2. Lawlor and Oulton, Eusebius, p. 238, take epestalkei to signify that Stephen communicated with the bishops in the East before he had done so with Cyprian. Since Stephen's letter in Eusebius is an extract, there is no certainty as to the time referred to in the tense of the verb.
3. Ep. 75. From time to time, doubts have been expressed as to the authenticity of this letter. For a reasoned defense, see Von Soden, "Der Ketzertaufstreit", p. 21.
4. Ep. 75.2/810.17-811.10.

Firmilian and the other supporters of rebaptism had been excommunicated by Stephen, and this further inflamed the Cappadocian's anger.[1]

Firmilian discounts the Roman tradition on the question of baptism, arguing that it has no apostolic foundation.[2] Not only is tradition thereby violated, but truth is enslaved to false custom. Even the Africans under the leadership of Cyprian have seen the falseness of past customs and now recognize the truth, rather than succumb with Rome to the false weight of antiquity.[3]

By allowing the efficacy of heretical baptism and all other acts when the name of Christ is used, Stephen is breaking the fundamental unity of the Church.[4] Firmilian strongly attacks this stance. If baptism given in the name of Christ is valid, regardless of the character of the baptiser, then the imposition of hands is valid in the same manner. Therefore, the stipulation that heretics can be received back into the Church once a bishop has imposed his hands falls to the ground.[5] Firmilian dilates on Stephen's blindness and error in allowing

---

1. Ep. 75.25/826.1 ff.
2. Ep. 75.5-6/812.30-814.4; 75.19/ 822.18-823.5.
3. Ep. 75.19/822.18-823.5. This further reinforces what has been made evident elsewhere in Cyprian, that the African custom on rebaptism was that of Rome, and the precedent of the council of Agrippinus must have been the only one that Cyprian could find to support his action. This also would explain the widespread opposition he encountered in his own province.
4. Ep. 75.18/822.6-17.
5. Ibid.

313

that remission of sins be given by heretics for they had not remained within the one Church which Christ had founded upon the rock.[1] He quotes from Matthew 16:19 and John 20:22:23 to show that it was only Peter and the Apostles and their legitimate successors, the bishops, who were given the power to remit sins.[2] Thus he is indignant that Stephen should glory in the rank of his episcopate as well as in his succession from Peter, at the same time as he destroys the unity of the very Church which Christ had committed to Peter.[3] In his stupidity Stephen had erected a new Church.

Cyprian's path was not smooth either.[4] The rational arguments which he brought forward could not, in emotional intensity, counter the argument that things had always been done in a certain way. Trouble flared up among the African bishops, and among the commonality of Carthage as well. The close

---

1. Ep. 75.17/821.14-822.6. This important passage is the first evidence we have for a Roman bishop explicitly claiming the successorship of Peter as a major prop to his authority, though it may not have been the first time this happened. G. Bardy, "L'autorité du Siège Romain et les contro-verses du IIIe siècle (230-270)", RSR 14 (1924), p. 396, assumes hastily that it was the first absolutely. He further states that the papacy had a tribunal in function at this early date, for which there is no evidence.
2. Ep. 75.16/820.24-821.13.
3. Ep. 75.17/821.14-822.6.
4. Eusebius, HE 7.5.4-5. Also Ep. 75.25/826.1 ff., which hints at the possibility that Cyprian or his legates were excommunicated.

connections with Rome evidenced in the Decian troubles had not lapsed.[1] Dissension was also introduced at Carthage.[2]

Cyprian tried to dampen the mutual hostility by praising the virtue of patience as a salutary remedy for disputes among Christian brethren.[3] Even while he was speaking, the congregation displayed a lack of patience and perhaps anger at the bishop.[4]

He appealed to his congregation's vanity. They were the true philosophers because they knew God. The patience displayed by the pagans was false, because they lacked this very knowledge.[5] Christians are true philosophers not in words but in deeds. They possess the true source of virtue and patience which is the Lord.[6] The Lord has long endured the sacrilegious rites and profane temples erected by man. He provides abundantly for both the pious and the impious, the godly and the ungodly.[7] Christ himself was a model of patience in word and in deed, imitating the divine patience of his Father. Even Judas was treated with endless

---

1. Supra p. 312.
2. Pontius' lack of discussion of this whole controversy is strong support for the rift the controversy must have caused.
3. This treatise is one of the few firmly dated; see Ep. 73.26/798.9-799.3, dating it to 256.
4. De Bono Pat. 1/397.1-12.
5. De Bono Pat. 2/397.13 ff. Perhaps this was also a covert attack on the Stoic proclivities of the presbyter Novatianus.
6. De Bono Pat. 2-3/397.13-399.2.
7. De Bono Pat. 4/399.3-400.9.

315

endurance by the Lord.[1] The Lord in His
patience will still receive the murderer
if he truly repents. Cyprian declares that
this is both the supreme example and the
model for Christians to emulate. He
exhorts his flock to adopt patience as they
adopt Christ. He overwhelms his congregation with Old and New Testament examples
of virtue.[2]

The Christian needs patience far more
than the pagan, for above the wearisome
toil of daily life he must face persecution,
behold the despoiling of his property, and
be forced perhaps to die.[3] Only by
enduring to the end can a Christian be
assured of hope and salvation. Thus
patience allows the Christian to be saved.[4]

In providing for the virtuous life,
patience allows the rejection of evil.
Charity, the foundation of Christian virtues,
cannot exist without it. None of the
virtues can survive its absence.[5] Job
provides an example of patience for all men.
The bodily ills that must be endured compel
us to be patient.[6]

Cyprian strengthens his case by arguing
the converse, pointing out the evils bred by
impatience, the mischief of the devil.
Behind Adam's fall, impatience is revealed.
The Bible is full of examples of the
disasters that overtook those who abandoned
this virtue.[7]

As a last inducement, Cyprian speaks of

---

1. De Bono Pat. 6/401.4-402.27.
2. De Bono Pat. 9-10/403.11-404.23.
3. De Bono Pat. 12/405.13-406.7.
4. De Bono Pat. 13/406.8-407.15.
5. De Bono Pat. 15-16/407.26-409.13.
6. De Bono Pat. 17-18/409.14-410.18.
7. De Bono Pat. 19-20/410.19-412.13.

316

the final glory and revenge that awaits the Christian as a reward for what he has endured. He paints a lurid picture of the fate of the persecutors. The Lord in His anger shall come like fire and render His vengeance.[1] The Christian should not take matters into his own hands. By adopting the example of divine patience, he will rest safely among the righteous and godly at the Final Judgment.[2]

But a sermon on the value of patience proved insufficient to check the internal squabblings of Cyprian's flock. The bishop was moved to expatiate further on the disadvantages of impatience and its concomitant evils - jealousy and envy. The short list of disadvantages was to lengthen to a full-scale catalogue of the disasters that such evils breed.

The world is an arena of combat. One must always be on guard to repel the advances and wiles of the adversary, and to resist such infiltrators as jealousy and envy. To beat back their attacks more easily, one must acquire knowledge of the origin and magnitude of these evils.[3]

The devil is the origin of envy and jealousy. He saw man made in the image of God and was overcome with both vices.[4] Envy and jealousy caused the fall of the angels. In imitating the devil, the Christian loses his way and also falls.[5]

Jealousy is the nursery of crime and the basis of transgression. By it, everything that is good is adulterated. To

1. De Bono Pat. 22-3/413.16-414.23.
2. De Bono Pat. 24/414.24-415.17.
3. De Zel. et Liv. 1-3/419.1-421.7.
4. De Zel. et Liv. 4/421.8-22.
5. De Zel. et Liv. 4/421.8-22.

the envious, no food or drink is sufficient. They are always tormented by the success of others. Their faces reveal the ravages of their disease. Pallor, trembling and ravings all betray the presence of the disease. Physical harm is far less dangerous. The cut of the sword or the thrust of a spear is less fatal.[1] Terrible as persecution is, to hate is a disaster beyond limit.

Cyprian exhorts his flock to stay themselves from such a deadly madness. Christ had called his followers sheep, that they be like lambs in innocence and simplicity. To be called Christian is not enough. One must actually imitate Christ in one's style of life.[2]

As the best defense against the perils described, Cyprian recommends a form of spiritual exercise. Use should be made of the Scriptures, and the Word of God should be imprinted on the mind. Living in accord with precept will ward off the devil. The things of this world must be despised. Love must replace hate. Believers must join their fellows in charity and brotherhood. If a man pleases God, heaven will be his reward.[3]

But with this exertion for his cause, Cyprian's position was still in danger. At the annual council of 256, more than twice as many bishops were present as had attended the council of the previous year. The topic was still rebaptism. The seventy-one bishops assembled were from both Africa Proconsularis and Numidia. The trouble with the Numidian bishops in the previous year had induced Cyprian to include them in council and to

1. De Zel. et Liv. 7-9/423.16-425.11.
2. De Zel. et Liv. 13/427.20-428.7.
3. De Zel. et Liv. 17-18/431.9-432.15.

318

present a unified front against Stephen.[1]

Hoping to impress Stephen with the size of the council, Cyprian directly approached him in the name of the council to sway him from his position. He stressed that the decision emanated from the council and not from himself personally.[2] He stated that he was reporting the decision of the council to Stephen in order to ask for his advice on a matter fraught with significance for the sacerdotal authority and unity of the Church.[3] His tone is one of reasoned argument throughout. Even Stephen's opposition to Cyprian is only obliquely hinted at in the closing words of the letter:

> "Ceterum scimus quosdam quod semel inbiberint nolle deponere nec propositum suum facile mutare, sed salvo inter collegas pacis et concordiae vinculo quaedam propria quae apud se semel sint usurpata retinere".[4]

In his letter Cyprian reports that the council's first decision was that those heretics and schismatics coming into the true Church ought to be baptised, and that it would not be sufficient for hands to be imposed to receive the Holy Spirit.[5] Cyprian

---

1. For number and composition, see Ep. 73.1/778.11-779.8, and 72.1/775.1-776.13. Monceaux, HAC, p. 49, thinks that the reference in 72.1 is to the conference held in 255. But the council of 255 was preoccupied with local unity.
2. Ep. 72.1/775.1-776.13.
3. Ibid.
4. Ep. 72.3/777.19-778.8.
5. Ep. 72.1/775.1-776.13.

supported this decision by pointing to the letter he had sent to Quintus which held that baptism by heretics is no baptism at all. He asked that the letter sent to Quintus and another sent by Cyprian's colleagues be appended to his letter to Stephen.[1]

The second decision of the council is again prefaced with an appeal to the consensus of those present. It had been decided that if priests or deacons had been originally ordained in the Church and then joined the heretics, they would be allowed to participate in communion, but only as laymen. They were not to retain the arms of ordination and honour by which they rebelled against the true Church.[2]

Perhaps Cyprian knew that his letter would have little effect, for he ended it on an essentially negative note, stressing that he was not trying to force Stephen to adopt his own position. In the administration of his office each bishop had the right to his own decision and was accountable for it only to God on the Day of Judgment.[3]

With his opponents in Africa, Cyprian was less gentle. The appeal of the Novatianists was direct and had created widespread trouble. Cyprian's main concern was to counter that appeal.[4] While his discussions with Rome centered solely on rational argument, those with the African bishops demanded a further appeal to the council under Agrippinus, quoting that council's decision as a legitimate

---

1. Ep. 72.1/775.1-776.13.
2. Ep. 72.2/776.14-777.23.
3. Ep. 72.3/777.24-778.7.
4. Ep. 73.2/779.9-780.11.

precedent.[1] At Rome, such a precedent would not have mattered.

Mauretania was one centre of dissension, and it was to Jubaianus, a Mauretanian bishop, that Cyprian directed his most complete theological statement on the legitimacy of his position.[2] Running through a list of heretics, he showed that none of their baptisms could be valid, even if the right formula had been used, because the faith they professed was not that of the Church.[3] As these individuals were engaged in nothing but blasphemy and perfidy, how could they presume to administer remission of sins through baptism? In giving the power to loose or bind to Peter, and after the Resurrection to all the Apostles, Christ made manifest that it was only those prelates, with their orderly succession, who are permitted to confer baptism.[4]

Some argued from Acts 8:14-17 that the already baptised Samaritans were received into the Church with the laying on of hands alone.[5] Cyprian's view was that this case was not relevant, for the Samaritans had believed in the true faith and, moreover, had been baptised by Philip the Apostle. Thus they had received a legitimate and ecclesiastical baptism.[6]

---

1. Ep. 71.4/774.12-20 and 73.3/780.12-24 for Agrippinus.
2. Jubaianus was probably from Mauretania. See Von Soden, "Prosop.", p. 261. Quintus was also probably a Mauretanian bishop.
3. Ep. 73.4/781.11-15.
4. Ep. 73.7/783.13-784.2.
5. Von Soden, "Der Ketzertaufstreit", p. 22.
6. Ep. 73.9/784.15-785.6.

Cyprian then struck out at Stephen. His opponents, when conquered by the logic of his position, fell back on custom. But the truth should prevail. Stephen had claimed in good faith that his practice had the sanction of the apostolic and Roman tradition, a strong argument which Rome had used as early as the difficulties caused by the Marcionites.[1] But Cyprian countered that the Apostles handed down a single Church and a single baptism in that same Church.[2] Cyprian's stress on reason sprang from an obvious cause. Carthage could point to no apostolic tradition; Rome could, and the prestige of that claim was of great importance. Both Tertullian and Irenaeus had argued that it formed the basis for distinguishing between true and heretical teachings.[3] Cyprian, however, interpreted the Scriptures and North African tradition to show that his view was more reasonable than that of his opponents. Basically his argument was that the tradition adhered to by Stephen was a falsification of the original

---

1. Stephen's appeal to a specifically Roman tradition has its roots in the late second century, see Irenaeus, Adv. Haereses 3.3.3. This statement of Irenaeus shows the strength of Stephen's argument, which rested not on the apostolic tradition alone but on the apostolic tradition at Rome. So the bishop of Rome, Victor, followed the same reasoning in his dispute with the Eastern bishops concerning the date of Easter at the end of the second century. See Baus, HCH, p. 271, and pp. 358 ff.
2. Ep. 73.13/787.8-788.2.
3. Tertullian, De Praescr. Haeret. 44.14; see also Irenaeus, Adv. Haereses 3.2.2.

apostolic practice.[1] Cyprian pursued his argument with ruthless logic. Even the martyrdom of the heretic availed him nothing.[2]

Finally he stressed his essential concern in his attack upon Stephen: if we allow the heretics baptism, we destroy the unity of the Church and the power of the bishops.[3] Cyprian's episcopate had been a constant striving for unity against a multitude of centrifugal forces. It had resulted in his relentless drive to preserve that unity. He believed that by allowing heretics the right of baptism, unity was not only endangered but it was sacrificed.

Cyprian's arguments, however, were of little avail. Driven to excommunicate Cyprian's allies in the East, Stephen was past the point of argument or persuasion. Stephen replied to the council's missive, according to Cyprian, with foolish pride, that "nihil innovetur nisi quod traditum est".[4] Thus the firm and basic answer of Rome stemmed from the concept that its own tradition was not only right but took precedence over any other factors.[5]

---

1. Ep. 73.14-15/788.3-792.19.
2. Ep. 73.21/794.17-795.14.
3. Ep. 73.25-26/797.17-799.3.
4. Ep. 74.1/799.6-18: "Si qui ergo a quacumque haeresi venient ad vos, nihil innovetur nisi quod traditum est, ut manus illis inponatur in paenitentiam cum ipsi haeretici proprie alterutrum ad se venientes non baptizent, sed communicent tantum". See Benson, Cyprian, pp. 402 ff., and D'Alès, S. Cyprien, p. 376.
5. I cannot understand how, in the face of this and other evidence, Bévenot can

Stephen generalized the problem which had essentially concerned the adherence of ex-Novatianists, into a proposition that anyone coming from whatever heresy could be received into the Church with the laying on of hands.[1]

Cyprian countered by developing a tradition based on the argument that the Bible urges us to baptise. The Scriptures paint heretics as lost and depraved. The Apostles themselves avoided them studiously, and we must do the same and not place human tradition above divine example.[2] Cyprian further chided Stephen for using the practice of the heretics as a precedent. Has the Church come to the point where it will follow the example of heretics?![3] He objected to Stephen's distinction over the use of Christ's Name in the baptismal formula. If heretics can provide grace efficaciously by the use of the Name, it follows that they will be allowed to use the Name for the laying on of hands.[4]

Then Cyprian turned to personal comments on the behaviour of the Roman bishop. He charges that Stephen has forgotten the commandment of Paul to Timothy. A bishop should be humble and teachable, not proud and insolent. Stephen had displayed the

---

5. (cont'd) characterize the conflict as an inter-African contest. The actions of Stephen in the East surely disprove this. See M. Bévenot, "A Bishop is Responsible to God Alone", RSR 39/40 (1951/2), Mélanges Jules Lebreton, p. 410.

1. Ep. 74.1/799.6-18. Also Ep. 74.5/ 802.22 ff. and 75.18.
2. Ep. 74.2/799.19-801.10.
3. Ep. 74.4/802.6-21.
4. Ep. 74.5/802.22-803.23.

324

opposite of these good qualities.[1] Cyprian closed by reaffirming his stand that all heretics who return to the Church should be baptised by the single and legitimate baptism, excepting those who had previously been baptised and had then gone over to the heretics. In an earlier letter, he had also affirmed that "salus extra ecclesiam non est".[2]

But the power and prestige of Rome were not so easily defeated. Opinion in Africa had to be marshalled to Cyprian's side. The growing size of the councils held in 255 and the spring of 256 betrays Cyprian's concern. Numidian and Mauretanian bishops were the most recalcitrant about falling into line. Cyprian must have spent much time in the summer of 256 preparing for a decisive conference which would show the unity of Africa. The council met on September 1, 256, under his presidency. The total of eighty-six bishops exceeded in size any of the previous councils of his epis- copate. An effort was made to draw in bishops from Numidia and Mauretania as well as from Africa.[3] Numidia was well-repre- sented by the attendance of at least twenty- five bishops. It is not certain that Mauretania was represented, but the provenance of five bishops is unknown and some of them may have been Mauretanian.[4] But even if a strong group of Mauretanian bishops opposed Cyprian, distance as well as theological convictions may have been a

---

1. Ep. 74.10/807.12-808.17.
2. Ep. 74.11/808.18-809.14. For a summary of argument, Benson, Cyprian, p. 401.
3. SE, praefatio, 435.
4. Von Soden, "Prosop.", pp. 251-4; also Mesnage, L'Afrique chrétienne, index.

factor in their low representation. So few Mauretanian bishoprics are located with certainty that no idea can be formed as to the percentage of them represented at the council.

The council opened with the plea to the Mauretanian bishops, in the form of a recitation of the letter of Jubaianus and Cyprian's reply to it. This had the advantage of calling attention to the opposition outside Proconsularis and at the same time giving Cyprian's fullest and most developed defense of his position on baptism.[1] His emphasis on the opposition of distant bishops may also have been designed to evade the opposition nearer to home.

Representations were apparently absent from several sees close to Carthage.[2] Indicative of Cyprian's hopelessness about his ability to convince Rome, and the divergent African opinion which must have cited Rome in its defense, is his admission that no action should be taken against those who opposed him. Perhaps this was an allusion to Stephen, who did not hesitate to impose his own views through excommunication.[3]

The record of the conference indicates that Cyprian's position was virtually rubber-stamped. The response of bishop after bishop repeats in various forms the necessity for the rebaptism of heretics. The absence of any record of correspondence from Stephen on the question indicates that the conference was primarily aimed at solidifying

1. SE, praefatio, 435.
2. Harnack, M&A, p. 324.
3. Supra p. 314, n. 4. It appears that at some time in the controversy, Cyprian was also excommunicated.

326

African opinion. Stephen's actions gave Cyprian ample warning that a simple increase in the number of his African opponents would not move him from his stance.

The council seems at least to have obtained its major objective. The correspondence of Cyprian contains no mention of any further controversy subsequent to the council of 256. Pontius neglects the entire episode, but he mentions the successor of Stephen, Xistus, as bonus et pacificus.[1] After the death of Stephen in early August 257, the conflict seems to have died out, though no solution acceptable to both sides appeared.[2]

The virulence of the controversy can be attributed in part to the authoritarian side of Stephen's personality. Xistus' relation to Stephen is unknown. The Liber Pontificalis describes his origin as Greek.[3] The greater strength of Cyprian's position in the East may have inclined Xistus to accept a compromise peace between Carthage and Rome more readily. Cyprian was a formidable figure for the new bishop to face. Further, the Novatianist Church had survived for a long period. It may have been between 255 and 257 that the majority of

---

1. Vita 14.1. Von Soden, "Der Ketzertaufstreit", p. 33, does not consider the reference in the Vita to be decisive. This would appear to be a mistake. Pontius' usual approach is not to mention, rather than to directly falsify Cyprian's conflicts.

2. See Eusebius, HE 7.5.3 and 7.9.1, for the attempted arbitration of Dionysius of Alexandria.

3. Lib. Pont., 155. Whether these statements in the Lib. Pont. refer to patria or origo is not clear.

327

Novatianist supporters crossed back to the Catholic faith and thus removed the immediate impediment to harmony between Cyprian and his Roman colleague. Though the conflict receded, however, the actual settlement of the dispute had to await Augustine in the West. In the East, the episcopate of Dionysius seems to have resulted in a settlement.[1]

The dispute on heretical baptism had served as a catalyst for Cyprian's conception of the role of the bishop in his community and for his view on the relationship of his see to Rome. There was no sudden break with Cyprian's previous convictions, but a crystalization of his opinions which had formerly been vague because there had been no need to clarify them. The two-year struggle with Stephen and its wide ramifications throughout the Christian world pressured Cyprian to develop further the concepts he first explicitly stated at the time of the controversy of the lapsed.

Cyprian had begun his episcopate with a conception that the powers of the bishop were final, at least within his own see.[2] He is guaranteed by the succession of the bishops from the Apostles in an orderly and uninterrupted chain.[3] Each bishop, though

---

1. See Baus, HCH, p. 363.
2. So Ep. 3.1/469.7-470.16. But note the characteristic response that asks that punishment be undertaken only as a last resort. At 3.3/471.16-472.17: "Magis enim optamus et cupimus contumelias et iniurias singulorum clementi patientia vincere quam sacerdotali licentia vincere".
3. Ep. 33. Also Ep. 64.1/621.4-622.3.

328

absolute with respect to the laity and clergy of his own see, is bound by certain limitations, even if his establishment is sanctioned and aided by the Lord.[1] Matthew 16:18 is employed as the basic example.[2] Samuel and Isaiah are also cited, and most notably the example of the disobedience of Core, Dathan and Abiron against Aaron.[3] Divine precept limits the scope of a bishop's activities. He cannot dissolve the former to create his own tradition.[4] Only dire circumstances can justify the abandonment of customary practice. Cyprian appointed new clergy on his own at the close of the Decian Persecution only after explaining that this was done in view of the extraordinary situation of the Church and the outstanding merits of the individuals concerned.[5]

Thus Cyprian's concept of the office of the bishop was absolutist, though tempered in some respects by popular opinion expressed by the lesser clergy and the laity.[6] He remained absolutist in viewing the Church as constituted solely upon the authority of the bishop. Withdrawal from communion with a legitimate bishop entailed withdrawal from the Church.[7] This was the absolutist claim

1. Ep. 33.1/566.4; 55.9/630.11-631.7.
2. De Unit. 4/212.8; Ep. 33.1/566.4; Ep. 75.6/820.28.
3. Ep. 55.4/625.19-626.17; 55.9/630.11-631.7; 68.8/663.13-664.15; 73.8/784.3-14.
4. Ep. 74.3/801.11-802.5.
5. Ep. 29, 38-40.
6. Harnack, HD, II, p. 85.
7. Ep. 33.1/566.1-517.8; 43.5/593.25-594 ad fin.; 45.3/602.4-603.3; 66.8/663.13-664.15; De Unit. 4/212.8.

329

which overrode all else. Unity was absolute and the bishops as vicars of the Apostles were the living pillars of the Church's foundation.[1] The strong reaction of Cyprian to the controversy over the lapsed and the Novatianist schism found much of its force in this concern. Any movement which defied the bishop raised the fundamental question of his legitimacy and, therefore, of the unity of the Church. It was more than fear for his own power that animated Cyprian; since the bishop is the key, any attack upon him invites heresy and anarchy. Roman governors were constantly concerned with the preservation of peace as part of their duty. A professor of rhetoric, thrust into a position of power, would take the Roman model to heart, particularly in view of the confirmation of his position in the Scriptures.[2] Cyprian had recognized further limits on the power of the bishop in respect to major theological decisions. During the Decian Persecution, when controversy over the lapsed was at its height, he refused to make any major decision on penance without first calling a council.[3]

The calling of a council leads us to Cyprian's conception of his own position vis-à-vis other bishops in the Church. The power of the bishops was founded upon

---

1. Ep. 55.9/630.11-631.7; 66.3/ 728.7-729.10.
2. Part of the reason for the growth of the monarchical episcopate may have been the gradual introduction of members of the upper classes as bishops. They carried over the imperial manner of administration into the life of the Church.
3. Ep. 17.3/522.20-523.10; 26, 32, etc.

330

the grant made by the Lord to Peter.[1] It is not merely a grant prior in time to that to the other Apostles, but it is a symbol of unity.[2] Peter stands as the symbol of the unity of the Catholic Church as opposed to those who, by leaving it, become heretics or schismatics.[3] As the see of St. Peter, Rome has the honour of being the ecclesia principalis.[4] But Rome's only claim is in being the original see of St. Peter; nothing is implied as to any special powers because of this honour. Cyprian's attitude towards Cornelius and Stephen was indicative of his theological conception of Rome. He did not hesitate to send his representatives to Rome to heal the break between Cornelius and Novatianus.[5] There is no indication that the Novatianist schism was more important because of the position of Rome in Cyprian's eyes. Rather, the importance was in the unity of the Church being attacked by the unlawful multiplication of bishops. Since each bishop participates in the unity of the Church, unlawful increases

---

1. Ep. 33; De Unit. 4/212.8 (both versions).

2. Koch, Cathedra Petri, p. 41, argues from De Bono Pat. 10 that the use of primatus is purely temporal. J. Chapman, Studies on the Early Papacy (London, 1928), p. 30, points out that this is a question of more than priority. Koch seems correct in supposing that Peter is a symbol of unity for all bishops.

3. Ep. 55.7/628.7 ad fin.

4. Ep. 59.14/683.1-684.7. See Ludwig, Heilige Märtyrerbischof, p. 73.

5. Ep. 45.1-2/599.11-602.3.

in their numbers destroy this unity.[1] The concept of the relationship of bishops to one another is not clear. Cyprian primarily relied upon two approaches, the conciliar one and the one involving direct intervention on his own initiative or on an appeal from the bishop himself.[2] In Africa the prestige of Carthage at least guaranteed his right to interfere, if not the success of his interference. But his relationship to Rome presented other difficulties.

His first major contacts had been with Cornelius who could only approach Cyprian in a position of weakness. Cyprian had not hesitated to interfere in the internal dispute on the question of election by using his own representative, and Cornelius had been desperate enough not to hinder his action. The constant presence of Novatianus must also have dampened any enthusiasm on the part of the Roman bishop to assert his own power.[3] The sees were too closely tied by a common Christian population which had too many contacts with each other for a course of independence.

But the election of Stephen presented a new type of problem. All the opponents whom Cyprian had so far encountered had no credentials to justify their legitimacy. The Carthaginian lapsists had no bishop leading them, and the later appointment of a bishop was, to Cyprian, illegal and schismatic. Novatianus also had presented a clear case,

---

1. De Unit. 5/213.14 ff.

2. The conciliar approach is well illustrated by the Spanish problem in Ep. 67. Intervention in Africa was a constant factor, see Ep. 64.

3. Ep. 48.

332

once Cyprian had recognized Cornelius. In so doing, Cyprian had automatically invalidated Novatianus' claim to wield the power of his bishopric in a legitimate manner.

But Stephen's election had been legitimate, and he was the head of a see that brooked no rivals in terms of prestige. At first Cyprian had adopted the tactics that had proved workable with Cornelius and Lucius. In receiving the appeal of the Spanish bishops at the council of 255, he had reasonably argued against Stephen's opinion on the legitimacy of Basilides.[1] Cyprian had intended not to contradict Stephen directly, but to ascribe the latter's reaction to a mistake in judgment, caused by the deception by Basilides. Thus a direct confrontation between Rome and Carthage was avoided. The Gallic troubles presented a more clear-cut confrontation and betrayed Cyprian's attitude towards the bishop and the Roman see. Cyprian did not hesitate to ask Stephen to correct his stand and depose Marcianus from his see at Arles.[2] More importantly, Cyprian claimed that both Cornelius and Lucius were his predecessors as well as Stephen's; since Stephen was their direct successor, he had all the more responsibility to follow their opinions.[3] The recognition of Peter was

---

1. Ep. 67.5/739.7-748.
2. Ep. 68.5/748.11-749.2.
3. Ep. 68.5/748.11-749.2: "antecessorum nostrorum...Quorum memoriam cum nos honoremus, multo magis tu, frater carissime, honorificare et servare gravitate et auctoritate tua debes, qui vicarius et successor eorum factus es". Thus Cyprian hardly expresses his recognition of Rome's preeminence in Spain and Gaul, as Baus, HCH,

333

symbolic for all bishops and not for Rome in particular. Cyprian refuted Stephen's claim to Roman tradition as a false tradition, which must give way before the rational coherence of his own view.[1] Of course the claim to Roman tradition would have been irrefutable had Cyprian recognized the supposed superiority of Rome. For the first time Cyprian was pitted against an opponent legitimately established. Against all of his earlier adversaries he could invoke the name of Peter and the power of the bishop. Against Stephen such a course was not open. The pressure of councils or of personal appeal was of no avail. Cyprian's prestige, all-embracing in Africa, failed to persuade Stephen to alter his views.

Stephen's intransigence led Cyprian to enunciate the principle that every bishop, because of his power and authority, can neither judge another bishop nor be judged by him.[2] Such a view precluded the possibility of a hierarchical principle.[3] Cyprian had originally been less flexible in his opinion of a bishop's independence.[4] But the stand-off between himself and Stephen had led him to deduce independence as the only principle that could assure a measure of unity within the Church. Its significance for Rome was the same as it was

---

3. (cont'd) p. 359. Recognition is only given for the see at Arles, which may have had a special relationship as a recently founded see.
1. Supra pp. 330 f.
2. SE, praefatio, 436.
3. Benson, Cyprian, p. 307. Bévenot, "A Bishop is Responsible", pp. 397-415, rightly sees this as a gradual evolution.
4. Ep. 71.1/771.3-772.15.

for Carthage, that is, a symbol of legitimacy.[1]

The development of Cyprian's conception of the episcopate was not the result of logical deduction or theological examination but the sequel to various practical considerations that arose from the continuing crises of his term as bishop. The schismatic tendencies of Novatianus and the lapsists led to the formulation and emphasis on the passage in Matthew. The persecutions led to a theological conception of God's means of chastisement and the approaching end of the world. The conflict with an equal adversary led to a formulation inherent but not explicitly stated in the De Unitate.[2] The conclusion that each bishop maintained his absolute independence, however, had required a legitimate opponent as its stimulus and could not have been provoked by bishops of the Novatianist persuasion. The oft-repeated description of Cyprian as a man of action rather than of theological speculation is well supported by the facts.[3]

Continuing confrontation between Rome and Carthage was avoided by the death of Stephen in March 257 and the accession of Xistus.[4] But one final crisis still loomed ahead for the bishop of Carthage.

---

1. Baus, HCH, p. 359, feels that Cyprian had failed to develop his thoughts logically on the implications of Matthew 16:18. Cyprian's use of this passage, however, is entirely different in character.
2. De Unit. 5/213.14-214.16.
3. See B. Altaner, "Cyprianus", in RAC III, p. 464.
4. For the date, Lawlor and Oulton, Eusebius, p. 46.

335

Chapter VII: SAINT CYPRIAN

The period during which Cyprian had been preoccupied by the rebaptism controversy was a time of turmoil for the Empire. Soon after his accession, Valerianus had raised his son Gallienus to the rank of Augustus.[1] The new Augustus soon saw action against German tribes along the Rhine, while his father was drawn to the East by a Persian attack.[2] The following three years were filled with disaster in the East and successes for Gallienus in the West.[3] By 257, Valerianus began his consulship at Rome. Gallienus may still have been on the western frontiers.[4] The troubles of the two Emperors were both continuous and disheartening.

Africa saw a continued resurgence of the Libyan tribes.[5] They seemed to have had little effect on the Christian community,

---

1. Zosimus, 1.30; Eutropius, 9.7; Aurel. Vict., 32.3; Epit. de Caes. 32.2.
2. T. Pekáry, "Bemerkungen zur Chronologie des Jahrzehnts 250-260 n. Chr.", Historia 11 (1962), p. 125. On the main problems, see Walser-Pekáry, Die Krise, pp. 28-50.
3. See E. Manni, L'impero di Gallieno (Rome, 1949), pp. 42 ff. on the date of the arrival of Valerianus in the East. See Pekáry, "Bemerkungen", p. 128, where he reports an inscription attesting the presence of Valerianus in Antioch on January 18, 255, AEpigr. 1957, n. 19.
4. Pekáry, "Bemerkungen", p. 125. See Manni, L'impero di Gallieno, p. 49.
5. See Rachet, Rome et les Berbères, pp.212 ff.

337

however, and Cyprian fails to mention their activities.1 As in the earlier 250's, the main area of operation was in Numidia and the Mauretanias. Africa Proconsularis and Tripolitania seem to have been relatively free of disturbance.2

But some of the consequences of the wider disturbances must have affected Africa. The joint reign of Valerianus and Gallienus saw the coinage of the Empire fall to its lowest worth.3 The constant warfare of the period must have sharply increased the general level of insecurity and the taxation requirements of the government. The temptation to find some reason for the terrible troubles which beset the Empire must, as usual, have been irresistible. Partial success in foreign affairs may have bred a desire to solve other problems more concretely. The uniformity desired by Decius to appease the gods had fallen short of success, and the hard-pressed government required an alternative outlet to relieve its frustrations.4

1. Supra p. 35 .
2. Romanelli, Storia, pp. 477 ff., and Rachet, Rome et les Berbères, pp. 240 ff.
3. CAH, p. 256, and references in Walser-Pekáry, Die Krise, p. 91.
4. Frend, M&P, p. 317, thinks that the canonical epistle of Gregory Thaumaturgus indicates social unrest among the Christians of Cappadocia led some to aid and join the invading barbarians in 255. But the reference to Canon VII is interpreted out of context. The epistle as a whole deals with crimes and their penalties with respect to ecclesiastical penance. The other canons display varieties of behaviour to be

The attitude of Valerianus towards the Christians in the first years of his reign remains an enigma. Dionysius of Alexandria paints a picture of favouritism on his part going so far as to call the court almost a church of God.[1] On the other hand, Zonaras reports that Valerianus had been a follower of Decius with respect to the Christians.[2] But the evidence indicates that neither version of his behaviour is correct. He may have held some office under Decius, but this of course does not guarantee anything about his own conduct as Emperor.[3] If Valerianus followed Decian policy, how does one explain the four-year lag between the succession of Valerianus and the initiation of persecution? In reporting the Emperor's rescript of 258, Cyprian describes various penalties for senatores, equites, and imperial freedmen who professed the Christian faith.[4] This might indicate that no strict policy had been followed until

---

4. (cont'd) expected in a period of turmoil. For instance, 6 deals with those detaining fleeing captives of the barbarians; 8, with those plundering deserted houses. Gregory is obviously horrified. It is not social unrest but simply the anarchy attendant on the disruption of daily life. It indicates nothing about particular social tensions on the part of the Christians. It certainly is no anticipation of the circumcelliones of the next century.

1. apud Eusebius, HE 7.10.3.
2. Zonaras, 12.20.
3. See PIR[2] L 258. The report of the HA is a fabrication, SHA Aurel. 5.4 ff. See Syme, Emperors, p. 21.
4. Ep. 80.1/839.8-840.12.

339

the actual beginning of persecution.[1]

Dionysius ascribes the origin of the persecution to the machination of Macrianus the _rationalis_.[2] Dionysius calls him "ho didaskalos kai ton ap Aiguptou magon archisunagogos".[3] The exact meaning of the term is obscure. The reference may simply be to an interest in magical practices of Egyptian origin.[4] Dionysius' account of the persecution makes it end with the fall of Macrianus and his sons, after their rebellion against Gallienus in 260/1.[5] Perhaps Gallienus had already stopped the persecution and Dionysius, in his gratitude, excused the conduct of Valerianus, foisting the responsibility for the persecution upon the unsuccessful pretender.[6] The quiet during the first years of the reign seemed to break the link of continuity with Decius.

---

1. Frend, _M&P_, pp. 315-6, is right in rejecting the theory of the Decian origin of this persecution. Benson, _Cyprian_, based his theory on the council held at Byzantium by Valerianus, _SHA Aurel._ 13 ff. Unfortunately, the entire section is fictional. See Syme, _Ammianus_, p. 133.
2. On Macrianus, _infra_ n. 4.
3. Eusebius, _HE_ 7.10.4.
4. See note of Lawlor and Oulton, _Eusebius_, p. 244. On Macrianus, see _PLRE_, p. 528, and PIR^2 F 549.
5. PIR^2 F 549.
6. So _CAH_, p. 252; Frend, _M&P_, pp. 315-316. P.J. Healy, _The Valerian Persecution. A Study of the Relations Between the Church and State in the Third Century A.D._ (London; Cambridge, Mass., 1905), p. 110, simply adopts Dionysius' account. Molthagen, _Der römisches Staat_, p. 85, thinks the account incredible, but this is unfounded.

340

Even if Valerianus had been constantly occupied with external foes during this period, the remainder of his reign saw no change in this situation.[1]

Some special impetus must have occasioned the sudden change in policy. Macrianus may have influenced the Emperor while in the East. There is no reason to dismiss this out of hand.[2] But the final decision was that of the Emperor. Perhaps the troubles that constantly assaulted the Empire drew him, in the brief respite of 257, to turn his attention towards eliminating internal plurality. Decius' example stood as a precedent. And perhaps the frustrations of his unsuccessful campaigns in the East were to be vented on a more pliant opponent. Even the financial needs of the beleagured Empire may have played a part.[3] Yet the mystery of Valerianus' own motives may also be due to a basic irrationalism rather than to a more recondite political factor.

Probably in August 257 a joint edict was issued in the name of both Emperors. Letters were sent to the provincial governors ordering that "qui Romanam religionem non colunt, debere Romanas caeremonias recognoscere".[4] Valerianus had learned from the mistakes of Decius. No general attack was made on disbelievers and Christians per se. The edict was directed solely against the clergy, and of these only the grades of

---

1. See chronology in Pekáry, "Bemerkungen" which is adopted here.
2. As Molthagen does, supra p.340,n.6.
3. See Frend, M&P, p. 316.
4. AP 1. Eusebius, HE 7.11.6-7 seems less exact, but it amounts to essentially the same procedure.

bishop and presbyter.[1] Church structure was the target. Valerianus rightly foresaw that the strength of the Christians lay in the organization they had constructed. Destroy this, and large numbers of the laity would probably succumb as they had under Decius. In this manner, the resources of the Empire would suffer less strain. The Decian method, even if thorough, was too costly.

The action of the government may have been sudden, and Cyprian probably received no warning. He was called before the proconsul at Carthage, Aspasius Paternus, on the 30th of August 257.[2] Paternus announced the terms of the edict to the bishop. Cyprian refused to fulfil the conditions specified by the Sacratissimi Imperatores. He replied that he was a Christian and recognized no other gods, though he added that a Christian supported the Emperor and his government by his prayers.[3] Paternus gave Cyprian an opportunity to retract his answer, but the bishop remained firm. Paternus inquired further about the presbyters of Carthage. Cyprian refused to give their names, strangely answering that "they will be found in the city".[4] Paternus read the provisions of the edict which forbade the meetings of Christians and their use of their cemeteries.[5] The desire to destroy

---

1. AP 1.5.
2. AP 1.1. This is the best information on the date of the persecution.
3. AP 1.2.
4. AP 1.5. Perhaps a half-ironical reply. On Paternus, PIR[2] A 1263; PLRE, p. 671, no. 3.
5. AP 1.7, conciliabula. For Chris-

342

Christian organization is manifest.

By order of the proconsul, Cyprian was exiled to Curubis.[1] It was not an unpleasant place, not far from Carthage and on the sea coast near Neapolis.[2] (Dionysius of Alexandria was exiled to a less pleasant location, Cephro, in the Libyan desert.[3]) Cyprian's old influence among the notables of Carthage could not save him as it had under Decius, but at least it may have lightened his suffering. Among his companions in exile was his future biographer, the deacon Pontius.[4] During his residence in the town, pagan friends, even senators and equites, came to persuade him to withdraw to a hidden and safer place of exile. Their offer was refused.[5] Perhaps the bishop did not expect the proceedings to end in his death. Further, the prestige of his position and his own conviction that his flight was ordained may have influenced his decision to wait out the order of banishment.

Other African bishops found the government less lenient in its application of the edict. Nine Numidian bishops were condemned to work in the mines, a harsh and

---

5. (cont'd) tian cemeteries, see Tertullian, Ad Scap. 4.

1. AP 1.4.

2. Vita 11.7.

3. Eusebius, HE 7.11.10. On his persecutor Aemilianus, see PLRE, p. 23, Mussius Aemilianus signo Aegippius. On Aemilianus, see Stein, Die Praefekten, pp. 143-5, with the additions and corrections of O.W. Reinmuth, "A Working List of the Prefects of Egypt 30 B.C. - 299 A.D.", BASP 4 (1967), pp. 119-20.

4. Vita 12.3.

5. Vita 14.3.

cruel sentence.[1] Unlike Cyprian, they received corporal punishment from the authorities to induce them to abjure.[2] The privations they endured were severe. Cyprian spent much of a letter to them bolstering their faith.[3] He also provided material support in the form of monies distributed by a sub-deacon and a few acolytes.[4] The letter may have had added significance in that Numidia had been one of the centres of opposition to Cyprian's position on rebaptism.

The appreciative bishops replied. Cyprian was praised for his stand before the proconsul. Evidently the Christians had already made copies of the imperial documents and were distributing them as a rallying point for opposition to the government.[5] Cyprian was lauded for his

---

1. Ep. 76. For the bishops, see Von Soden, "Prosop.", pp. 267 ff. On the use of the mines as a punishment for Christians, see the collection of evidence by J.G. Davies, "Condemnation to the Mines: a Neglected Chapter in the History of the Persecutions", Univ. of Birm. Historical Journal 6 (1957/8), pp. 99-107.

2. Ep. 76.2/829.3-830.12.

3. Ep. 76.6/832.11-23 implies that others as well as clergy were taken in the persecution. But the sense of the passage seems to be that by confessing, the laity share the spiritual rather than the actual sufferings of the martyrs.

4. Ep. 77.3/835.13-836.6.

5. Ep. 77.2/834.17-835.11. Perhaps best likened to an 18th century broadside or pamphlet. See B. Bailyn, The Ideological Origins of the American Revolution (Cambridge, Mass., 1971).

344

literary triumphs in giving support and impetus to the soldiers of Christ in resisting the onslaught of the enemy.[1] Other letters were also sent indicating the extensive and well-developed network of communications possessed by the Christians, and something about the hopelessness of the government's efforts to destroy their organizational structure.[2]

Cyprian's earlier career had seen his recourse to enthusiastic experiences during times of stress. In September 257, soon after the beginning of the exile, he experienced a vision recorded by Pontius.[3] Cyprian reported that on the day they had arrived in exile, the 14th of September 257, a vision of a youth of more than human stature was revealed to him while he slept. This youth led Cyprian to the proconsul. None of the ordinary questioning at such a trial took place. The judge simply began to note his verdict on the tablet. The youth, not speaking, read the tablet and with his hands signified to Cyprian that he would be put to death. Cyprian begged that a stay be granted so that he might put his affairs in order. The youth indicated with a nod that the stay would be granted, and and Cyprian awoke with joy.[4]

---

1. Ep. 77.2/834.17-835.11. Perhaps a reference to the Ad Fortunatum?
2. Ep. 78 and 79.
3. The date is given by Vita 13.3. There is no reason to doubt the vision if the authenticity of Pontius is accepted. See Appendix IV. Pontius' long exegesis of the meaning of dies would indicate that it was an abnormal pattern and therefore more likely to be genuine.
4. Vita 12.3-9.

345

It was perhaps the dream and the time of leisure provided by the exile that moved Cyprian to comply with the request of Fortunatus for a compendium of Scriptural citations to strengthen the resolve of the Christians to endure the persecution.[1] The persecution again raised the theory that had been most elaborately developed in the Ad Demetrianum. The end of the world is near, and the time of the Anti-Christ is at hand.[2] Cyprian complied with Fortunatus' request in order that courage should be accompanied by wisdom.[3] He states specifically that he is not providing a treatise so much as the material for one. The advantage of this was that with the help of Scriptural quotations, the reader could think his own thoughts through without being incumbered by Cyprian's style and ideas.[4]

The Scriptural quotations are arranged under thirteen headings. The first two show that neither the idols made by man nor the elements of the natural world are gods. Supported by quotations, Cyprian then shows the serious nature of idolatry with respect

---

1. Ad Fort., praefatio, 1/317.1-13. Fortunatus is often identified with the bishop Fortunatus of Thuccabor. Certainly praefatio 2 seems to point to a bishop, Quasten, Pat., p. 362. But there is no certainty as to whom is meant, since the name is common. The most recent text of the Ad Fortunatum is R. Weber (ed.), Opera Cypriani, Corpus Christianorum, Series Latina 3, Pars 1 (Turnholti, 1972).

2. Ad Fort., praefatio, 1/317.1-13.

3. Ibid.

4. Ad Fort. 3/352.19-353.19.

346

to the one true God.[1] He reaffirms a theme which had occupied him during the Decian Persecution, that these trials are sent by the Lord as a means of proving the faith of the Christians.[2] As a final consideration Cyprian treats, under four headings, the glorious rewards that await the success of the martyr. Whatever we experience, we will receive a just recompense.[3]

Since the government's measures were confined to priests alone, it may appear that this treatise was in fact designed for a larger audience. There is no doubt that the laity, in at least a few places, resisted the removal of their clergy.[4] Further, neither Cyprian nor the other clergy could be certain that the government would stop with measures directed against the officers and organization of the Church. A recurrence of the persecution under Decius always remained a possibility, and the moves against the priests must have excited widespread fear and unrest among the Christian population in general.[5]

Cyprian's exile lasted for approximately one year. The government must have been dissatisfied with its measures, for in early August 258, a new rescript on the question was submitted to the Senate.[6] It instituted new and harsher measures, providing that

---

1. Ad Fort. 3-8/323.20-331.7.
2. Ad Fort. 9/331.8-332.9.
3. Ad Fort. 10/332.6-334.9.
4. Ep. 76.2/829.3-830.13.
5. Just as the rumour in Africa of Gallus' actions in Rome, Ep. 64.
6. The date is sometime before the 6th of August, the date of the death of Xistus and his companions, see Ep. 80.1/839.8-840.13.

bishops, priests, and deacons should be punished immediately. Senators and _equites_ were to be deprived of their rank and goods. If they continued to persevere as Christians they were to be killed. High-born women were exiled and lost their property. _Caesariani_, or members of the imperial household, were to be sent as slaves to work the imperial estates if they confessed now or previously.[1] The test was still the sacrifice, as with the edict of Decius.[2] The rescript was less far-reaching than the Decian edict, however, still aiming its attack against Church leadership.[3] Perhaps the first victims were Xistus II, bishop of Rome, and four of his deacons.[4] The news of Xistus' death must have impressed upon Cyprian the imminent peril he was in.[5]

Sometime before September 13th, 258, Cyprian was recalled to Carthage to await a new trial under the revised terms of the rescript.[6] According to Pontius, he was visited by various members of senatorial and equestrian rank during his stay in his _horti_, men who urged him to withdraw and who offered him sanctuary. Pontius praises Cyprian's refusal of their offers, explaining

---

1. Ep. 80.1/839.8-840.13.
2. _AP_ 3.5. See Molthagen, _Der römische Staat_, p. 93.
3. Molthagen, Ibid., comes to the conclusion that all that was wanted was loyalty. But the specific nature of the edict points rather to a more demanding result expected by Valerianus.
4. Ep. 80.1/839.8-840.13. See the report of the _Lib. Pont._, 156, which differs and is wrong.
5. _Vita_ 14.1; Ep. 80.1/839.8-840.13.
6. _Vita_ 15.1 and _AP_ 2.2.

that the bishop was no longer prey to mundane cares but thought only of the glory of his approaching martyrdom.[1] However, Cyprian's own letter to his clergy (Ep. 81) shows that when he had been ordered to appear before the proconsul at Utica, he retired for a while from his gardens ("ut de hortis nostris interim secederem"). The force of interim must be taken to indicate that Cyprian withdrew only for a short period of time. He had decided that a bishop should die in his own see. Presumably the withdrawal was only until the proconsul, on his judicial circuit, reached Carthage; then the bishop would return there to die.

That Pontius did not mention the circumstances conveyed by Epistle 81 is curious; he had certainly read the letter, and echoes of it appear in the Vita.[2] Had Pontius mentioned Cyprian's temporary "flight", however, perhaps the increasing tension that characterizes his portrayal of his hero's approaching execution would have suffered diminution. It may be that Pontius saw it only as a brief disruption of a divinely inspired plan, and for that reason not worthy of mention.

The rumour of Cyprian's impending trial sped through Carthage. At the news, Christian and pagan both rushed to see the spectacle of his trial and death.[3] While the laity kept vigil all night outside the house of the princeps, Cyprian and his companions spent a pleasant night together inside.[4]

---

1. Vita 14.3-4.
2. Vita 19.2 reminiscent of Ep. 81.1.
3. Vita 15.4.
4. Vita 15.4 and 16.4.

On the 14th, Cyprian was led from the house of the _princeps_ to his place of trial. The bishop was surrounded on all sides by the crowd that his fame attracted as he was led before the proconsul. On the way he passed by the stadium, recalling one of the Christian metaphors for martyr.[1] He finally arrived at the _praetorium_ to which Galerius Maximus had come after his convalescence in the Ager Sexti.[2]

Cyprian was brought before Galerius Maximus, and the trial commenced.

Maximus: You are Thascius Cyprianus?

Cyprian: I am.

Maximus: You put yourself forward as leader for these men of sacrilegious mind?

Cyprian: Yes.

Maximus: The most sacred Emperors order you to perform the requisite ceremonies.

Cyprian: I will not do it.

Maximus: Consult your best interests.

Cyprian: Do what you are ordered to do.[3]

---

1. _Vita_ 16.4. On the topographical features here, see _RE_ X[2] 2160 ff., and for a reconciliation, see notes of Pellegrino, _Vita, ad loc._.
2. _AP_ 2.4 and 3.2.
3. _AP_ 3.3-6. See Reitzenstein, "Die Nachrichten", pp. 10 ff., for the sentences:

350

After this, the proconsul discussed the sentence with his _concilium_.[1] He then turned to Cyprian and, describing his complicity in the criminality of the Christians, sentenced him to death by beheading.[2] The behaviour of the bishop so moved his followers that they asked to be executed with him.

Cyprian was led away to execution, surrounded by a military escort including tribunes and centurions.[3] He was taken to the Ager Sexti, a large valley surrounded by trees.[4] The immensity of the crowd obscured the scene for many, and some of the spectators climbed the surrounding trees to obtain a better view of the bishop's execution.[5] Cyprian covered his eyes with his hands and urged the executioner to perform his task.[6] According to Pontius,

---

3. (cont'd) "Fac, quod tibi praeceptum est. In re tam iusta nulla est consultatio".
1. For the obvious lack of interest of Pontius in the proceedings and his report of them, see _Vita_ 15.8. See also _Vita_ 11.1 for earlier process and Pontius' remarks about _Acta_.
2. _AP_ 4 and _Vita_ 17.1-3.
3. _Vita_ 18.1 and _AP_ 5.1-2.
4. _Vita_ 18.2 and _AP_ 5.2.
5. _Vita_ 18.3.
6. _Vita_ 18.4; _AP_ 5.5. The _AP_ mentions that Cyprian divested himself of his _dalmatica_, the long woolen undergarment worn by priests during mass. It also states that he prostrated himself in prayer. The account in the _AP_ may be expanding its information according to the author's expectation of how a typical martyr would behave. Pontius' account seems straightforward here, except for the Biblical parallel.

351

the executioner could hardly hold his
sword with his trembling right hand.
Finally the hour ordained for the bishop's
death arrived, and the executioner was
granted the heavenly power to deal the fatal
blow.[1] Thus died the first martyred bishop
of Carthage.

To save the body from the curiosity of
the pagans, it was buried at once. At
night, however, the body was uncovered and
conveyed in procession by torchlight to the
area of Macrobius Candidianus, on the
street of Mappaliensis near the fish ponds,
and there it was reburied.[2]

A few days later the proconsul died.
Cyprian was not the only African bishop
to perish. On January 26th of the following
year, Theogenes, bishop of Hippo, died in
the persecution. Agapius and Secundinus
also perished.[3] But of the clerical martyrs

---

1. Vita 18.4. The same topos of the
inability of the forces of evil to kill the
martyr occurs in the Pass. Perpet. 21, where
it is the will of Perpetua which allows her
death to occur: "fortasse tanta femina
aliter non potuisset occidi, quae ab inmundo
spiritu timebatur, nisi ipsa voluisset".
Pontius may well have been influenced by
this passage. AP 5 mentions no difficulty
which hindered Cyprian's death.

2. AP 5.6-7. For an attempt at
precise geographical placement of these
sites, see Audollent, Carthage romaine,
p. 353.

3. For the death of Theogenes and the
others, see Augustine, Sermo 273.7.
Secundinus may have been identical with one
of the two mentioned in the Cyprianic
corpus, either the bishop of Carpos or
Cedias. See Von Soden, "Prosop.", pp. 267-9.

352

it was the death of Cyprian which made the greatest impression. In the _Passio Mariani et Jacobi_ Cyprian appears leading the martyrs into paradise.[1] In the _Passio SS. Montani et Lucii_ he again appears as a teacher of the blessed, and he plays a conspicuous part in the revelation.[2]

But the opposition to his memory still persisted.[3] His episcopate had been filled by one crisis after another. The middle-aged professor of rhetoric had found himself in a position demanding persistence and the will to conquer. He had met his trials with success. It was with almost an ironic appropriateness that a century and a half later Augustine would spend the night with his mother in an oratory dedicated to St. Cyprian, before setting out on the journey to Rome which was to alter his career.[4]

---

1. _Passio Mariani et Jacobi_ 6.10.
2. _Passio SS. Montani et Lucii_ 11.2; 13.1; 21.3a.
3. As evidenced by the _Vita_.
4. Augustine, _Conf._ 5.8.15.

EPILOGUE

The force of the character and personality of the martyred bishop was manifested soon after his death. In the spring of 259, the martyrdom of Marianus, Jacobus, and other Christians resulted from the continuation of the same persecution which had taken Cyprian's life. While in prison, the <u>lector</u> Marianus had a vision in which he found himself before a tribunal of magnificent aspect and proportion. Groups of confessors were brought before the judge who ordered them off to die. As Marianus' turn came to face the judge, a great voice shouted: "This way, Marianus". It was Cyprian, sitting at the right hand of the judge, stretching out his hand to raise Marianus to a higher place on the tribunal.[1] Another African martyr from the same persecution also saw Cyprian in a divinely inspired vision.[2]

Cyprian's commanding ability and character had been most important for the future of the Church in Africa. Faced with initial opposition to his election, he consolidated his position with rigorous and direct action, shoring up the discipline of

---

1. Chapter 6 of <u>Passio Mariani et Jacobi</u>, Knopf-Kruger, <u>Ausgewählte Märtyrerakten</u>, p. 70. For the authenticity of this martyrdom and that of Lucius and Montanus, see Delehaye, <u>Les passions</u>, pp. 59 ff. On the date, see Monceaux, <u>HAC</u>, pp. 153 ff.
2. This may be found in chapter 11 of <u>Passio SS. Montani et Lucii</u>, Knopf-Kruger, <u>Ausgewählte Märtyrerakten</u>, pp. 77 ff., good evidence of Cyprian's prestige.

the Carthaginian Church. That infusion of stamina produced unanticipated results.

The persecution which opened in 250 provided a major challenge to his personal resources. The action of the authorities had resulted in wholesale apostasy. When the persecution ended, Cyprian was confronted with the election of Novatianus as a rival bishop in Rome, and he had to deal with the latter's rigorist attitude towards the lapsed. While Cyprian's own early thoughts on penance had leaned towards firmness, the actions of Novatianus threatened to rend the Church. It was at this point that his talents as an administrator and his personal strength were required.

The great persecution at the beginning of the fourth century was to leave the African Church divided until Islam swept over the whole of North Africa and Christianity receded into Europe. Again the question was between rigour and leniency with regard to those, particularly the clergy, who had given way in the persecution.[1] Though the Donatists claimed Cyprian as a direct precursor and maintained they were pursuing his concept of the Church, they were wrong in one-sidedly stressing one aspect of the bishop's work.[2] Cyprian's central

---

1. For the Donatist controversy, see Frend, DC, pp. 1-24.
2. Augustine, C. Crescon. Donat. ii.31.39 and iii.3. Also Frend, DC, pp. 318-20. R.F. Evans, One and Holy. The Church in Latin Patristic Thought (London, 1972), p. 67, has pointed out that there are two separate attitudes manifested by Cyprian concerning discipline and Church unity. In questions dealing with the

service to the Church was his preservation of unity in the face of the opposing rigorist and non-rigorist factions. The weakness that ensued from the schism of the fourth century would have been greatly magnified had the split occurred in the much weaker Church of the mid-third century.

By throwing his weight to Cornelius and, in union with him, firmly opposing all adversaries, Cyprian was able to use the combined prestige of Rome and Carthage to hold in check any threat to Church unity. The treatises on the lapsed and the De Unitate are in this way the most important writings of his career.

The fading threat of Novatianism in Africa was soon followed by the controversy over rebaptism, and here Cyprian again found himself on perilous ground. Taking his stand in opposition to Rome and other African bishops, Cyprian risked a split in the Church. In the earlier Novatianist controversy, he had been able to call upon the support of established bishops like Cornelius. Here, the split was among the bishops themselves. The weight of office and alliance with the Roman see could no longer be brought to bear. Cyprian tried an approach based on reason, constantly calling councils to reinforce and publicize his point of view. From the year 255 on, each of the councils on the question of rebaptism

---

2. (cont'd) discipline of laymen and the readmission of schismatics, Cyprian could allow diversity; but where the issue was a dereliction of duty on the part of the bishops who sacrificed to pagan gods and then retained their sees, he would allow no compromise.

357

had a larger number of bishops in attendance than had the preceding ones. The death of Stephen and the Valerianic Persecution intervened, however, so the test was postponed. With Stephen's death, the entire matter was dropped.

The potential for disunity stirred up by the rebaptism controversy was thus averted, and Church unity and discipline was maintained. In this case too, Cyprian's major concern had been with Church unity. His recognition of the independence of the decisions of each bishop was an affirmation of that unity.[1]

Cyprian raised his own and his bishopric's prestige to a level of major influence, as his letters to the bishops of Gaul and Spain would indicate. But no known innovations mark his conduct in this field. His attitude towards the concept of Roman primacy is one fraught with difficulties. The concept is absent from his writings, except insofar as the prominence and vitality of the Roman Church are admitted, Cyprian's stress on the powers of the bishop, however, and the further development of the monarchical episcopate, reinforced his position vis-à-vis his flock and increased the likelihood of the development of a hierarchy among bishops.[2] Thus the active work of the bishop was crucial for the development of African Christianity. It provided the stable background for a struggling and persecuted Church to develop in an area in which distance and diversity of peoples might have destroyed it, as Donatism was later to do.

Complementary to his effect as an

1. Ep. 72.3/780.13-24.
2. See Harnack, HD, II, pp. 84 ff.

358

administrator and, to a great extent, as its direct result, Cyprian composed a number of treatises and letters which were of wide-spread influence.[1] The first great writer of the African Church was outside the ecclesiastical hierarchy; Tertullian had turned from the Catholic Church and joined a rival. It was Cyprian who provided the Christians of Africa with a literary heritage which was a direct product of a specifically clerical bias.

Some found his writings not quite to their taste however. Lactantius complained that the Christian faith had lacked suitable apologists and publicists, though he noted Cyprian's eloquence and output as an exception. He insisted that as Cyprian's writings were steeped in Christian content and meaning, they had no effect outside the faithful. Non-Christians had even derided him by renaming him Coprianus.[2] Lactantius' judgment on the Ad Demetrianum is not far from the truth; but that work was dedicated to the healing of internal disputes and was not intended to be a full and reasoned apology for Christianity.

Among Christian writers, Cyprian's works were held in high regard. In the second half of the fourth century, Pacianus of Barcelona frequently called upon his authority in his own fight against the Novatianists.[3] Jerome's letters are full of references to Cyprian's works, and he notes that the bishop's writings will be an antidote to the poison of the epistles of Novatianus.[4] Jerome had the highest praise

---

1. See Vita 7 on contemporary influence.
2. Lactantius, Div. Inst. 5.1.
3. Ep. 1 ad Sempronianum.
4. Ep. 10.3/492.5-13.

359

for Cyprian's style and thought.[1] He was especially familiar with the works of the African bishop.[2] Augustine's opinion of Cyprian's style was high but tempered.[3] He recognized the latter's widespread influence and dedicated several sermons to his memory.[4] He saw in Cyprian's earlier writings, however, a certain profusion of terms which hampered the effect of his eloquence.[5] Cyprian's utilization of classical rhetoric became a precedent for Augustine.[6] He paid tribute to the martyr by quoting from almost all of his treatises and from a fair sampling of the letters.[7]

In contrast to most Christian Latin authors, Cyprian was also known in the East. Eusebius records that he found a letter of Cyprian and his African colleagues which supported an anti-Novatianist position and which was written

---

1. Ep. 58.10/665.5-24, where Cyprian is compared to Tertullian, to the latter's disadvantage.
2. Harnack, GAL I, 2nd half-volume, pp. 704-6, where the testimonia of Jerome on Cyprian are cited extensively.
3. Augustine, De Doctr. Christ. 4.14.
4. For influence, C. Duas Epp. Pelag. 4.8 (21). The sermons are 309-13.
5. Ibid.
6. Augustine, De Doctr. Christ. 2.40. See H. Hagendahl, Latin Fathers and the Classics. A Study on the Apologists, Jerome and Other Christian Writers, Studia graeca et latina gothoburgensia, 6 (Göteborg, 1958), pp. 385-7.
7. Harnack, GAL, I, 2nd half-volume, p. 713. Also Monceaux, HAC, p. 365.

360

in Latin.[1] In the late fourth century, a speech on Cyprian's life is preserved from the pen of Gregory Nazianzus.[2] But the confusion in Gregory's writing would indicate that, at least to a Greek writer of that period, Cyprian had become simply a name for veneration. None of Cyprian's letters were used in Gregory's Oratio.

It was as one would expect in Africa that Cyprian made his greatest impact. The Donatist bishops relied on his writings as if they were equivalent to Scripture.[3] The separatist bishops often quoted the judgment of the council of September 256 as a justification for rebaptism.[4] Soon after the outbreak of the schism, they apparently assembled a collection of his letters to justify their views on asceticism, martyrdom, and the removal of an unworthy bishop from his see.[5]

Augustine, the major Catholic controversialist, had to cope extensively with the Donatists' interpretation of Cyprian. He had to maintain the bishop's authority and at the same time preserve his own position against the Donatists' citations

---

1. Eusebius, HE 6.43.3-7.3. It is unclear if this is to be identified with one of the letters in the corpus or not. The letter was presumably also addressed to the Church of Antioch, in the same manner as the lost letter to which Firmilian of Cappadocia wrote Epistle 75 as a reply.

2. The oration of Gregory Nazianzus on Cyprian is number twenty-four, to be found in PG 11.

3. Augustine, De Bapt. c. Donat. 2 (3) 41.

4. Ibid, 11.1.2. PL 11,iii,126.

5. See Frend, DC, p. 131.

from his writings. He dealt with this problem in two steps. To dispel any notion of absolute authority in Cyprian's writings he made a clear separation between the Scriptures and the Cyprianic corpus.[1] Those points cited by the Donatists could be disputed on the grounds that the author was in fact fallible.[2] The second and more important step was to interpret Cyprian's writings according to the Catholic point of view, and thereby fault the reasoning of the Donatists.[3] Both as a model and as a potential adversary, Cyprian was of prime importance to the bishop of Hippo.

Cyprian's fame extended beyond the narrower sphere of theology and Church discipline. The Spanish Christian poet, Prudentius, writing in the second half of the fourth century, composed one of his hymns to martyrs in Cyprian's honour.[4] In Africa itself, Cyprian was always popular. Three basilicas were consecrated to his memory.[5] The populace of Carthage celebrated at night about his tomb.[6] Even at the time of the Vandal invasion in the fifth century his cult was strong at Carthage. He was among the most honoured

---

1. Augustine, C. Crescon. Donat. 2.41 (39).
2. Ep. 93 ad Vincentium 10 (35).
3. Ep. 23 ad Hieron..
4. Prudentius, Peri Steph. 13, though here as in Gregory there appears to be confusion with Cyprian of Antioch. On Prudentius, see Altaner-Stuiber, Pat., pp. 407-9.
5. On these, see Monceaux, HAC, pp. 372 ff., and Cabrol-Leclercq, Dictionnaire III, pt. 2, pp. 3214-5.
6. Augustine, Sermo 311.5.

of saints.[1]

Memory of Cyprian remained fresh both in Africa and in other parts of the Christian West.[2] His position as bishop and his martyrdom were major factors in the popular veneration, but his true worth was to be found, as Augustine and others perceived, in the works which his pen had produced and which had become an important heritage for the Western Church.

---

1. Procop., Vandal. 1.21.
2. On Rome, see Monceaux, HAC, p. 359.

Appendix I: THE CHRONOLOGY OF THE LETTERS

The chronological order of the letters is as follows:

5-43	The Decian Persecution
44-66	The episcopates of Lucius and Cornelius
67-75	The rebaptism controversy
76-81	The Valerianic Persecution

Though these large groups are well defined, the chronological relationships between the individual letters are a matter of controversy. After the first major attempt at an accurate chronology by Bishop Pearson in the Oxford edition of 1681, several major rival schemata have been put forward.[1] The manuscripts provide no help as the letters seem to have been put together from separate private collections. The order of the letters in the manuscripts is almost random.[2] The only method of proceeding is to examine the cross-references in the letters themselves. Cyprian displayed extensive care with his correspondence.[3]

Epistles 1-4, 62 and 63 provide no precise indication of date. The absence of any reference to a trial or persecution would date 1-4 to the first years of Cyprian's

---

1. For the Oxford edition, see Hartel, part 3, praefatio, and for the major schemata, reference should be made to Harnack, GAL, pp. 339 ff.

2. For discussion, see Von Soden, "Die Cyprianische Briefsammlung", pp. 19 ff.

3. Ep. 20.1/527.4-15.

episcopate; they are probably a result of the annual council. Epistle 62 was commonly dated to 253 because of the barbarian eruptions into Numidia in that year.[1] Epistle 63 falls into no discernible time period.

The Decian Persecution (5-43)

The opening of the collection is dated by the execution of Fabianus on January 20/21 250 - which seems almost simultaneous with Cyprian's flight from Carthage. The other firm point we have is epistle 20 to the Roman clergy from Cyprian, which refers to a packet of 13 previously written letters which will be forwarded to them.[2] The letters specified in epistle 20 appear to include 5-7 and 10-19.[3] The order followed by the latest chronological treatment of the letters appears to be accurate. This order is 7, 5/6, 14, 13, 11, 10, 12, 15-20.[4] Epistle 18.1 says iam aestatem coepisse, indicating that it was written in the summer of 250. Therefore we have a broad interval for the relative dating of the letters

---

1. Monceaux, HAC, p. 258. But as Harnack, GAL, p. 348, and Clarke, "Barbarian Disturbances" recognized, there is no exact dating possible.
2. For detailed discussion, reference will be made to the relevant section of L. Duquenne, Chronologie des lettres de S. Cyprien. Le dossier de la persécution de Dèce, Subsidia hagiographica, 54 (Brussels, 1972).
3. Duquenne, Chronologie des lettres, p. 100 and references there.
4. Duquenne, Chronologie des lettres, pp. 58 ff., and p. 159.

between the death of Fabianus in January 250 and the summer of the same year. Epistle 19 appears to have been written soon after 18.[1] Epistle 20 itself was most likely sent directly after the last letter mentioned in the catalogue which it contains. Thus a date for the letter in mid-summer 250, perhaps July, cannot be far wrong.[2]

The attack on Cyprian by the Roman clergy in epistle 8 and his response contained in epistle 9 appear to have followed one another immediately. They can only be dated sometime in the period between the outbreak of the persecution and letter 20. A closer approximation is impossible.[3]

The exchange of letters between Celerinus and Lucianus, epistles 21 and 22, also falls during the same period.[4] But the multitude of events mentioned seems to indicate that a fair amount of time had elapsed since the beginning of the persecution. Thus a date in July appears probable.[5]

Epistle 23 was written after the set

---

1. Duquenne, _Chronologie des lettres_, pp. 95-6.
2. Duquenne, _Chronologie des lettres_, p. 96.
3. Duquenne, _Chronologie des lettres_, p. 120, opts for a date sometime in March or April for epistle 8, and in April or May for epistle 9, but all one can do is speculate.
4. Duquenne, _Chronologie des lettres_, p. 120.
5. Harnack's dating, _GAL_, p. 343, is vitiated by his assumption of different phases of persecution.

367

comprising 24 and 25.[1] Neither of them betrays the anger and anxiety Cyprian felt on the receipt of epistle 23 and which finds expression in epistle 26.[2] Epistles 27 and 28 are Cyprian's response to the declaration of Lucianus in epistle 23 and an attempt to gain the support of both the Roman clergy and the confessors grouped about Moyses.[3] Though epistle 33 contains neither the name of its author nor that of an addressee, it is most probably the response of Cyprian to the lapsed after the furor raised by epistle 23. Epistle 29 is to be dated in conjunction with 33, which probably mentions both 23 and 33.[4] Following his defense of his position to the Christians of Carthage, Cyprian made his case further known at Rome, sending epistles 33 and 29 with the covering letter 35.[5] The presbyter now in charge at Rome, Novatianus, warmly supported Cyprian's measures.[6] Further support was also provided by the prestigious band of confessors at Rome in epistle 31. Cyprian soon communicated the confessors' letter to his clergy.[7] Soon after, Novatianus further

---

1. Duquenne, _Chronologie des lettres_, pp. 136-7.
2. Ep. 26.1/539.1 ff.. Duquenne, _Chronologie des lettres_, points to the lack of knowledge on the part of Caledonius of Cyprian's whereabouts as evidence for the date, p. 136. But this may be only the result of Caledonius' personal ignorance.
3. Duquenne, _Chronologie des lettres_, pp. 137 ff.
4. Ep. 29.1/547.12 ff.
5. Ep. 35.1/571.9 ff. Reference to Duquenne, _Chronologie des lettres_, p. 139.
6. Ep. 30.
7. Ep. 32.

clarified his position in another letter to the Carthaginian bishop.[1]

These letters all soon follow July, and can possibly be dated to the period August/ September 250.[2] But the volume of correspondence and the time necessary for the letters to travel to their destination might allow them to be dated sometime in the early autumn of the same year.

Thus the letters of the corpus discussed above would seem to have been composed according to the following order: 8/9?, 21/22?, 24, 25, 23, 26, 27/28, 33, 29, 35, 30/31, 32, 36.

Epistle 37 is to be dated to February 251, a year after the death of Fabianus.[3] Epistle 34 was most probably at the same time, but one cannot positively discern the relative order of 37 and 34.[4] The same question arises in connection with the appointments of new clergy mentioned in epistles 38, 39 and 40. Thus the order of this section of the correspondence is likely: 34, 37, 38, 39, 40.

The last three letters, 41-43, are the product of a new situation, the schism

1. Ep. 36. Duquenne, Chronologie des lettres, p. 140.

2. Duquenne, Chronologie des lettres, p. 140, chooses August as the date for this letter and posits a lucuna in the correspondence for the autumn of 250. But the amount of correspondence perhaps indicates that at least some of the letters ran into the autumn of 250.

3. Ep. 37.2/577.6, which was written a year after the death of Fabianus in January 250.

4. Duquenne, Chronologie des lettres, p. 144.

of Felicissimus. Epistle 41 seems to mark the first appearance of this new problem. Epistle 42 is the answer to 41. Epistle 43 marks the end of the Decian series. It was written in the spring of 251.[1]

The episcopates of Lucius and Cornelius (44-66)

Letter 44 is dated approximately by Cornelius' consecration which falls in March 251.[2] Letters 45 and 46 date from the same short period; 47 mentions 46 and therefore follows. Letter 48, judging by Cyprian's attitude to Cornelius, appears early, though later than 44, as the return of Stephen and Pompeius had already taken place.[3] Letters 49 and 50 are answered by 51; 50 and 52 answer each other. Letter 53 is obviously close in time to 49 and may have come as a covering letter included with Cornelius' announcement of his winning over the confessors. Letter 54 answers 53. All of these must follow around late March or early April 251, from the council mentioned in 44. Letter 55 is after Cyprian had gone over to Cornelius but has no precise date. Letter 56 has no exact date, except that it falls prior to Easter 252. Letter 57 is the letter of the council of 252, the date for which is given as the Ides of May in 59.10. Letter 58 is probably in anticipation

---

1. For the date of Easter in 251, see Duquenne, Chronologie des lettres, Appendix I, p. 166, who rightly sees that it is impossible to assign an exact date for the African celebration in 251, as the method of calculation used is unknown.
2. Lib. Pont., 151.
3. Ep. 48.4/607.20-608.14.

370

of Gallus' persecution, but no closer date
can be surmised - perhaps the early summer
of 253 is appropriate. So probably with 59,
only after May 252.[1] Letter 60 follows 59,
as now Cornelius has been banished by the
government, i.e., prior to June 23, 253.[2]
Letter 61 refers to Lucius and the death of
Cornelius.[3] For 62 and 63, see above page
365. Letter 64 is dated to the council of
the spring of 253; 65 is undatable
precisely, but it follows the persecution,
as does 66.[4]

The rebaptism controversy (67-75)

Letter 67 dates to the council of 254,
held probably in the spring, and after the
consecration of Stephen in March 254. The
letter may actually fall in May, since
enough time would have elapsed for a
journey by Basilides to Stephen.[5] Letter 68
may date from the same period, but the order
of 67 and 68 is uncertain; each contains no
mention of the rebaptism controversy.
Letter 69 is the first statement of the
controversy.[6] Letter 70 dates to the
council in the spring of 255; 71 follows 70.
Letter 72 follows the council but has no
exact position.[7] Letter 73 follows 70 and
71.[8] Letter 74 is prior to the council of
September 1, 256.[9] Letter 75 dates to the

---

1. Ep. 59.10/677.14-678.10.
2. Dated by Lib. Pont., 151.
3. Ep. 61.1/695.12-21.
4. Ep. 66.4/729.11-732.
5. Ep. 67.5/739.7-740.8.
6. i.e., Ep. 69.10/758.19-759.10.
7. Ep. 72.1/775.3-776.13.
8. Ep. 73.1/778.11-779.8.
9. Bayard, Correspondance, I, p. 279,

winter of 256, but before Firmilian knew of the council of September 256.[1]

The Valerianic Persecution (76-81)

Letter 76 dates to the beginning of August 257; 77 is in response to 76, and 78 to 76; 79 is also in response to 76, followed by 80 and 81. The order is: 76, 77/78/79, 80, 81.

---

9. (cont'd) is not correct.
1. Ep. 75.25/826.1-30, ad fin..

372

Appendix II: THE AUTHORSHIP OF THE QUOD IDOLA DII NON SINT

The Quod Idola Dii Non Sint is now accepted as Cyprianic in the standard reference works.[1] Though it was also ascribed to Cyprian by ancient authors, its authenticity has been the subject of much dispute.[2] Its inclusion in the standard reference works has been the result of an extensive comparison between its style and usage and other accepted writings of Cyprian.[3] The nature of the Quod Idola militates against its ascription to Cyprian.

The treatise is a condensation of the Octavius and the Apologeticum.[4] It bears few traces of adaptation and is basically an epitome of the two sources. This is so untypical of any other extant work of Cyprian that it must become suspect.[5] The one source utilized by Cyprian which we can

---

1. Quasten, Pat., pp. 363-4, and Altaner-Stuiber, Pat., p. 174.
2. Jerome, Ep. 70.5; Augustine, De Baptismo 6.44.77; and De Unic. Bapt. c. Petilian. 4.
3. The basic demonstration is by Koch, CU, pp. 1-78.
4. Chapters 1-9 are based closely on Oct. 18-23.2; chapters 10-15, on Apol. 21-23.
5. Benson, Cyprian, p. 7, tried to meet the objection by claiming it as a juvenile work of Cyprian. But as far as we know, Cyprian did not accept Christianity until a period of his life too late for such an hypothesis.

reliably check is Tertullian. In works in which Cyprian utilizes material from Tertullian, direct adaptation and condensation are never the methods he employs. Cyprian may use elements from Tertullian, such as those in the De Dominica Oratione, but they are changed and arranged in an entirely new manner.[1] The conceptual framework is against his authorship of the Quod Idola.[2]

Furthermore, the work seems to contain resemblances to Lactantius' Divinae Institutiones.[3] The following is a table of some of the more striking ones:[4]

Quod Idola		Div. Inst.
1	resembles	7.15
2	resembles	1.13.16
3	resembles	1.15.1-10
6	resembles	2.15.1
6	resembles	2.15.6-8
13	resembles	4.15.23

Though an attempt has been made to explain away these similarities, they seem too convincing to have been arrived at independently.[5] Similarity may be accounted for by postulating a third and unknown source, but

1. Supra pp. 288-90.
2. Becker (1967), pp. 94-5, recognized this objection.
3. See Diller, "Tertullian-Minucius", pp. 98-114 and 216-39.
4. The table is based on Diller, "Tertullian-Minucius", and B. Axelson, "Echtheits-und textkritische Kleinigkeiten", Eranos 39 (1941), pp. 67-74.
5. Simonetti, "Sulla paternità", pp. 265 ff.

374

there is no evidence of its existence. The possibility remains that Lactantius utilized the Quod Idola, but the immaturity of the work and the availability of both the Octavius and the Apologeticum would militate against this.

A demonstration based on language which has found widespread support is unsatisfactory. The paucity of comparative styles from the period and location invalidates any basis for comparison. A similar and equally fallacious approach was used to prove that almost all of the works of the appendix were by Pontius.[1] Since the range of vocabulary and style for a valid comparison is not available, similarity of expression proves nothing about authorship. Such an approach, particularly in assessing the works of a highly standardized and rhetorical tradition, is insufficient.

---

1. A. D'Alès, "Le diacre Pontius", RSR (1918), pp. 319-78.

375

Appendix III:
THE CHRONOLOGY OF THE TREATISES

The extant and accepted treatises of Cyprian are twelve in number, including two collections of Biblical passages, the Testimonia and the Ad Fortunatum. They contain few chronological indications.

Chapter 7 of Pontius' Vita, however, has long been recognized to contain a listing of the treatises in what appears to be their relative chronological sequence.[1] Attempts have been made to prove the listing inaccurate, but they carry little conviction.[2] The listing would seem to be as follows:

1. Ad Donatum

   Vita 7.3: "quis emolumentum gratiae per fidem proficientis ostenderet?"

2. De Habitu Virginum

   Vita 7.4: "Quis virgines ad congruentem pudicitiae disciplinam...coerceret?"

3. De Lapsis

   Vita 7.5: "Quis doceret paenitentiam lapsos"

4. De Unitate

   Vita 7.5: "veritatem haereticos, schismaticos unitatem"

---

1. See Harnack, GAL, p. 362, and Schanz-Hosius, p. 343.
2. For example, Koch, CU, pp. 148-83, on the Ad Fortunatum.

377

5. De Dominica Oratione

Vita 7.5: "filios Dei pacem et evangelicae precis legem?"

6. Ad Demetrianum

Vita 7.6: "Per quem gentiles blasphemi repercussis in se Quae nobis ingerunt vincerentur?"

7. De Mortalitate

Vita 7.7: "A quo Christiani mollioris affectus circa amissionem suorum aut, quod...spe futurorum?"

8. De Opere et Eleemosynis

Vita 7.8: "Unde sic misericordiam... disceremus?"

9. De Bono Patientiae

Vita 7.8: "Unde...patientiam disceremus?"

10. De Zelo et Livore

Vita 7.9: "Quis livorem...inhiberet?"

11. Ad Fortunatum

Vita 7.10: "Quis martyres tantos... erigeret?"

The accuracy of this listing is verified by other extant chronological indications.[1]

---

1. The inclusion of the Ad Donatum does not destroy the reliability of the list though generally taken to be composed before Cyprian's election to the bishopric. Its inclusion here merely demonstrates Pontius' desire to heighten the effect of Cyprian's escape.

Missing from the list is the _Testimonia_, which Cyprian recognized as a compendium and not as a treatise.[1] It would therefore not strictly fall within the scope of this list. The same objection could be brought against the _Ad Fortunatum_, in which Cyprian makes the same disclaimer.[2] But the fact that the treatise centres on martyrdom would justify its inclusion for Pontius, who was anxious to prove that Cyprian's own martyrdom was justly delayed.[3]

In addition to listing the treatises, chapter 7 of the _Vita_ closes with a statement that seems to refer to a further treatise by Cyprian:[4]

"Quis denique tot confessores
frontium notatarum secunda
inscriptione signatos et ad
exemplum martyrii superstites
reservatos incentivo tubae
caelestis animaret?"

Some attempts have been made to identify this passage with letter 76.[5] But the length of 76 seems too disproportionate to the other treatises. It would appear that

---

1. _Test._ I, _praefatio_, 36 in Hartel.
2. _Ad Fort._, _praefatio_, 316 in Hartel.
3. This is obviously the central point of _Vita_ 7.
4. _Vita_ 7.11.
5. Monceaux, _HAC_, p. 247; so Corssen, "Das Martyrium", p. 137, who considers the work as a treatise and not part of the corpus of letters. Such a decision is very difficult to make, as letter 63 demonstrates.

379

Pontius refers to a lost work here, perhaps written soon before Cyprian's execution and lost at the time of his death.[1]

The Ad Donatum appears to have been composed soon after Cyprian's conversion, around 246.[2]

The De Lapsis and De Unitate were read at the council in the spring of 251 and probably composed in March 251.[3]

The Ad Demetrianum appears to refer to a great political catastrophe in chapter 17, which the death of Decius alone would justify. The mention of illness in chapter 6, probably the plague, would make it fall any time after 250/1.[4]

The De Bono Patientiae is dated by a reference in epistle 73.26 to the spring of 256.

Thus the external indications reinforce Pontius' list. Any attempt at more exact indications would involve extensive hypothesis and guesswork. The schema adopted in the text has been based on what has appeared to be a likely choice rather than an absolutely justifiable one.

Chapter 21 of the De Habitu Virginum ("audite virgines ut parentem")

---

1. Pontius would have known of it, because he was in the company of the bishop.
2. Supra p. 118.
3. Ep. 54.4/623.16-624.3.
4. Chapter V, p. 269, n. 1. The possibility that chapter 17 refers to the events of 253 seems excluded by Cyprian's emphasis upon the unexpectedness of the retribution: "nec hoc casu accidisse aliquis existimet aut fuisse fortuitum putet".

points to the composition of the work during Cyprian's episcopate. The absence of any mention of persecution or of Cyprian's later preoccupation with the dissolution of the world would indicate an early date, seconded by the evidence of Pontius who places it second in his series. The spring council of 249 was probably the occasion of the treatise and of epistle 4.

The De Dominica Oratione contains no indications as to date. Pontius places it after the De Unitate, so it would fall after March 251. The most likely period is late 251 or early 252, between the two persecutions.

Chapter 17 of the Ad Demetrianum points to its having been composed after the death of Decius. The appearance and the development of the theme of the nearing dissolution of the world is also found here in chapter 23, a strand of Cyprianic thought first developed after the Decian Persecution. The position in Pontius' series would make the year 252 a reasonable setting.

The plague started in the West as early as 250.[1] However, its virulence was marked from 252. The other terminus is 256, attested by the De Bono Patientiae from Pontius' list. The connection with the so-called persecution of Gallus and the widespread effects of the plague circa 252 however would point to that year as the period for the composition of the De Mortalitate. Pontius lists the De Opere et Eleemosynis directly after the De Mortalitate and it would best seem to fit here in light of Pontius' description of Cyprian's

_____

1. Supra pp. 269 ff.

381

behaviour during the plague.[1]

De Bono Patientiae is dated by the reference in 73.26 to early 256. Cyprian informs Jubaianus that "libellum nunc de bono patientiae quantum valuit nostra mediocritas permittente Domino et inspirante conscripsimus".

De Zelo et Livore follows, according to Pontius, and so it is after early 256, perhaps connected with the opposition that Cyprian experienced to his stand on rebaptism. So a date some time in 256 would seem reasonable.[2]

The _Ad Fortunatum_, a collection of Biblical passages relating to martyrdom, corresponds to the last composition listed by Pontius.[3] A connection with the Valerianic Persecution is most likely (i.e., it is to be dated to 257, perhaps after August, during Cyprian's exile at Curubis).[4]

All three books of the _Testimonia_ appear to have been written by Cyprian.[5] The stand taken in III.28 on sins against God points to a date early in the episcopate. An added confirmation is the absence of any reference to persecution. A date prior to Cyprian's investiture as bishop has been proposed.[6]

---

1. _Vita_ 9.1 ff.
2. _Supra_ p. 303.
3. _Vita_ 7.9.
4. Koch, _CU_, pp. 149-83, tries to connect the treatise with the persecution of Gallus, basing himself on an analysis of style and word usage, but the ineffectiveness of this method has been treated above. Furthermore, the theory contradicts the evidence presented by Pontius, which should hold unless there is a strong indication to the contrary.
5. Quasten, _Pat._, p. 362.
6. Benson, _Cyprian_, p. 19.

But the preface seems to be that of a bishop rather than a presbyter.[1]

Thus the treatises would appear to have been composed in the following sequence:

1.	Ad Donatum	circa 246
2.	Testimonia	before 250
3.	De Habitu Virginum	249
4.	De Lapsis	March 251
5.	De Unitate	March 251
6.	De Dominica Oratione	late 251/early 252
7.	Ad Demetrianum	252
8.	De Mortalitate	252
9.	De Opere et Eleemosynis	252/3
10.	De Bono Patientiae	early 256
11.	De Zelo et Livore	summer 256
12.	Ad Fortunatum	after August 257

---

1. Hartel, p. 35.

383

Appendix IV: THE _VITA CYPRIANI_

Though included in the Cheltenham List composed between 359 and 365, the _Vita Cypriani_ listed there is anonymous, as it is in all manuscripts of the _Vita_ before the 12th century.[1] In his catalogue of Christian writers, Jerome mentions Pontius, a deacon of Cyprian, who accompanied the bishop into exile and composed a distinguished account of his passion and life.[2] For obvious reasons, this Pontius has been identified with the author of the anonymous _Vita_ which we now possess. Jerome's acquaintance with Paul of Concordia is the likely source for this information. The _Vita_ may have been anonymous by the second half of the fourth century.[3] In spite of the explicit statement of Jerome, however, the authenticity of both author and content has been challenged.[4]

1. For the Cheltenham List of 359-65, see T. Mommsen, "Zur lateinischen Stichometrie", _Hermes_ 21 (1886), pp. 142-56 = _Gesammelte Schriften_, VII (Berlin, 1909), pp. 283-98.
2. Jerome, _Vir. Ill._ 68.
3. For Paul of Concordia, see Jerome, _Vir. Ill._ 53. The Cheltenham List makes anonymity a possibility. Hartel had doubts, heading his Vienna text of the _Vita_ "Pontio diacono vulgo adscripta", in his introduction, xc.
4. Against authenticity, Reitzenstein, "Die Nachrichten", pp. 46-69. Also, J. Martin, "Die Vita et Passio Cypriani", _HJ_ 39 (1918/19), pp. 674-712, thought it an unhistorical compilation from the end of the third century.

The attempt to overthrow the traditional authorship of Pontius and the Acta Proconsularia which he utilizes is not convincing.[1] Besides an erroneous consideration of the manuscript tradition of the Acta, the main thrust in the attempt to discredit Pontius arose from the relationship of the Vita to other works of Christian literature, with special emphasis upon the correspondence between the Passio Perpetuae and the narrative of the Vita.[2] But the confusion resulted from a lack of appreciation of ancient rhetorical education. Imitation was an essential part of any literary work.[3] Thus the presence of similar expressions and the description of similar incidents, such as the acts of martyrs, will invoke similar language. While there may be a certain loss of detail which must be guarded against, the general authenticity of a work cannot be challenged on this ground. The description of battles according to traditional formulae does not guarantee that they are fictitious.

Jerome's testimony is also of importance. No other ancient account of Cyprian's life is known. Jerome had direct access to a source who had intimate knowledge of Cyprian's circle. There can be no doubt that his reference to Pontius is to the work which we now possess. The

---

1. For a detailed refutation, see P. Franchi de' Cavalieri, "Di un nuovo studio sugli Acta Proconsularia di s. Cipriano", Studi Romani, Riv. di archeol. e storia, 2 (1914), pp. 189-215.
2. Reitzenstein, "Die Nachrichten", p. 61.
3. See the discussion on Minucius Felix in text, infra pp. 51 ff.

importance of Cyprian as bishop and writer would almost ensure the survival of a work as favourable to him as the _Vita_. There is no trace of any other such work in antiquity.[1] Most importantly, the _Vita_ is listed as early perhaps as 359 on the Cheltenham List, which would preclude Reitzenstein's argument that the author depended on a late Medieval or Humanist document.[2] That the _Vita_ listed on the Cheltenham List is the same _Vita_ that we now possess cannot, of course, be ascertained.[3]

Contradictions between the _Vita_ and Cyprian's own statements are no guarantee of lack of authenticity.[4] In discussing the election of Cyprian to the episcopate, for example, the author of the _Vita_ mentions the resistance of his opponents.[5] He affirms that Cyprian treated the men so benevolently that afterwards he counted them among his closest friends. Cyprian's own correspondence, however, shows that the men who had opposed his election remained hostile and later challenged him on the issue of the

---

1. Reitzenstein, "Die Nachrichten", pp. 9-10, utilized a small selection of manuscripts in his analysis of the tradition of the _Acta_, none earlier than the 11th century. The differences he found cannot be interpreted as evidence for falsification but simply of a continuing manuscript tradition.
2. Reitzenstein, "Die Nachrichten", p. 12.
3. Reitzenstein, "Die Nachrichten", pp. 9-10.
4. This was one of the points of attack of Martin, "Die Vita et Passio", p. 697.
5. _Vita_ 5.6.

lapsed.[1] By making so contrary a statement, would not Pontius cast doubts on his own truthfulness? The discrepancy makes sense if we view the general apologetic tendency of the Vita in the light of the circumstances after Cyprian's death, and in relation to Cyprian's controversy with Stephen over the question of rebaptism.

The same point is strengthened by comparing the Ad Donatum version of Cyprian's conversion with that in the Vita. The latter implies that Cyprian underwent an easy and painless conversion.[2] The Ad Donatum, however, points to considerable confusion, doubt, and disillusion with the world prior to his conversion.[3]

Indicative of Pontius' approach is the point that the conversion of Cyprian was an effortless process in which the seeds of the new religion, once sown, bore immediate fruit.[4] Even the Biblical example of the conversion of the eunuch, quoted by Pontius as a parallel, pales in comparison with Cyprian's achievement. For the eunuch was a Jew and therefore predisposed to the Christian message; whereas Cyprian, whose antecedents were pagan, was able to equal the pace and depth of the Jew's conversion.[5]

Thus the turmoil expressed by the Ad Donatum is totally neglected. The method of the Vita is obvious. Unlike much hagiography, there is no assembling of false and impossible details, but a close adherence to the facts which can be verified from the

---

1. Ep. 43.1/591.5 ff; 43.3/592.6 ff.
2. Vita 2 ff.
3. Ad Don. 3 and 5.
4. Vita 2.9.
5. Vita 3.1.

388

works of Cyprian himself. But in the _Vita_ the facts are toned down and certain aspects are exaggerated. The speed of Cyprian's advancement in the ecclesiastical hierarchy is now made to match his unparalleled progress in the faith. The speed is not false, but the underlying tensions are dissipated in the interests of praise and uniformity. The same type of procedure appears in the _Vita_ again and again. The treatment of the five presbyters and the elimination of any indication of the rebaptism controversy are of a piece with the recounting of Cyprian's conversion. The account of the Christian hero is emphasized, but the picture of the human struggle is lost.[1]

Other than Pontius' own statements in the _Vita_, nothing further is known of him beyond his bare mention by Jerome. It seems likely that he was present with Cyprian from the time of the latter's conversion.[2] He was also present at his execution and with him the night before in the house of the _princeps_.[3] Pontius indicates that he was not with Cyprian during any part of his pre-Christian career. Some of his information for the period immediately after Cyprian's conversion came from the oral reports of older men,

---

1. For a reasoned statement on the historical value of the work, see Pellegrino, _Vita_, pp. 62-3. Monceaux, _HAC_, p. 31, is too sceptical. Benson, _Cyprian_, p. 9, is not critical enough.
2. The absence of Pontius' name in the letters would seem to indicate that he was with the bishop.
3. _Vita_ 19.5.

389

presumably Cyprian's contemporaries.[1] According to Jerome, Pontius was a deacon, but his evidence for this is not clear. Opening the Vita, the author alludes to the abundance of documents which preserve the memory of the martyrdoms of catechumens and lay members of the Church while Cyprian, a man of eloquence and a priest, might have his memory effaced.[2] Pontius' bias towards the clergy appears to support Jerome's statement that he held some position in the ecclesiastical hierarchy.[3]

An attempt has been made to associate the author of the Vita with a dedication from Curubis to a C. Helvius Honoratus, who bore the nickname of Pontius.[4] The inscription was set up to commemorate the beneficence of Honoratus in aiding in the distribution of the alimenta. He had held the highest municipal offices. But the existence of a relationship between this man and the author of the Vita cannot be proved. It has been claimed that the author was

---

1. Vita 2.3: "si qua de antiquioribus comperi".
2. Vita 1.2.
3. Vita 4.1 was used by Harnack, "Das Leben", p. 15, as proof, but the de nobis has since been satisfactorily changed to de novis and can no longer be used to indicate the ecclesiastical state of the author. See Bayard, "Notes sur la Vita", pp. 206-10.
4. Thus H. Dessau, "Pontius, der Biograph Cyprians", Hermes 51 (1916), pp. 65-72. Obviously Dessau was prone to this approach to ancient authors, i.e., Minucius Felix and Caecilius Natalis. The inscription is CIL VIII, 977 and 979 = ILS 5319 and 5320. Pontius is presumably an agnomen, as Dessau thinks.

390

particularly favourable to Curubis as a place of exile for Cyprian.[1] Pontius praises the physical surroundings of Curubis and the good behaviour of the citizens in providing all the necessities of life for the exiled bishop.[2] The step from praise of a locality to residence in it, however, is not a necessary one. The number of Honoratus' municipal offices would also indicate a man of greater age than Pontius, though some relationship to the family of Honoratus is possible. There is no certain way to evaluate the relationship due to the paucity of information available.

No other work has been preserved from the pen of Pontius. Some of the other works which have come down in the Cyprianic corpus may in fact be his, but there is not enough evidence to assign any other tract to him.[3]

The actual facts are few in number, but the tendency of the Vita may shed some light upon the period during which it was written. Pontius does not pretend to give a full biography of Cyprian, but rather desires to provide a record which would preserve his memory.[4] Though the writings

---

1. Vita 11.7-12.2.
2. Ibid.
3. D'Alès, "Le diacre Pontius", pp. 319-78, argues that other works in the corpus should be assigned to Pontius, i.e., the De Laude Martyrii, the Quod Idola Dii Non Sint, Passio Mariani et Jacobi and Passio SS. Montani et Lucii. But the similarities of thought and style to which he points as evidence are too widespread to indicate Pontius alone authored the works.
4. Vita 1.1: "summatim pauca conscribere".

of Cyprian were assured of survival, Pontius feared that the memory of his glorious death and his great accomplishments as bishop could not survive without an account of his martyrdom.[1]

No space is given in the Vita to Cyprian's pagan background. It starts at once with its hero's conversion.[2] The conversion is taken as a model for what the conversion of all Christians should be like.[3] The steps from a neophyte to bishop are covered in the same manner.[4] The false stress on amity with the presbyters who opposed his election has already been noted.[5] A great deal of treatment is devoted to the necessity and God-given design of his flight during the Decian Persecution.[6] Cyprian's steadfastness and care for both Christian and pagan during the plague receive unlimited praise.[7] Pontius describes the intervening peace between the plague and the Valerianic Persecution without alluding to the vitally important rebaptism controversy. The only allusion to Rome is the news of the death of Xistus II.[8] The panegyrical content of the Vita has led some to deny it the status of biography.[9]

---

1. Vita 1.1.
2. Vita 2.1.
3. Pontius puts him above a famous Biblical example, Vita 2.4, the eunuch baptised by Philip (I Tim. 3:6).
4. Vita 2.
5. Supra p. 139.
6. Vita 7.1 ff.
7. Vita 9.1 ff.
8. Xistus II, Vita 14.1.
9. Bardenhewer, Geschichte, II, p. 446; Monceaux, HAC, p. 192; Altaner-Stuiber, Pat., p. 172, ein Panegyrikus.

392

The _Vita_ appears to have been written soon after Cyprian's death in September 258. The exact time of composition cannot be determined. But Pontius' selection of material is due less to the dictates of panegyric than to the necessity of defense, although no explicit statement about opposition to Cyprian occurs beyond that at his election.[1] Pontius' stress on the justification of the flight in 250, however, would indicate at least one of the charges against him. More important is the total absence of any information on the rebaptism crisis which dominated the last years of his episcopate. There was certain opposition to Cyprian's stand within the African Church.[2] The lack of discussion of the lapsed and the emphasis on reconciliation implies that Pontius is basically concerned with writing Cyprian's defense. The African Church seems not to have been unified in its estimation of the great Carthaginian bishop. Pontius' emphasis on Cyprian's having been the first martyred bishop of Carthage sounds like the reply to a charge of cowardice, perhaps arising out of the first persecution.[3] His opening statement on the recording of the martyrdoms of catechumens and laymen makes little sense unless at least part of the opposition was among the laity. This would also explain the stress on the support that the _plebs_ of Carthage had given Cyprian in his election as bishop. Cyprian's dominating personality and strong control over the North African Church made him many enemies, as his correspondence

---

1. Even the rebaptism crisis is not mentioned.
2. _Supra_ p. 320.
3. _Vita_ 19.1 ff.

indicates. With his removal by death, the party about him, which would have included Pontius, was deprived of its strongest support. The _Vita_ may have functioned as a defense of Pontius as well as of his hero. So too the stress on the _plebs_ may have indicated opposition between the less fortunate members of the Church and men like Cyprian who possessed wealth and education.[1] With the need for defense, there is little wonder that Pontius skims over Cyprian's earlier life as a pagan. Panegyric is a misnomer. The _Vita_ is a biography designed for defense against the various charges that threatened to condemn the memory of the first of the Carthaginian bishops to be martyred.[2]

---

1. Harnack, "Das Leben", p. 40, sees in the portrait presented by Pontius the ancient type of the aristocratic man, presumably adapted to a Christian ethic. But the Christian colour is too strong for this. What he has actually portrayed is the ideal Christian bishop - which is a different animal altogether.

2. Evaluation of Pontius' statements demands care, not disbelief. Exaggeration was his métier, not falsification.

Appendix V:
DID CYPRIAN COMPILE HIS OWN <u>FLORILEGIUM</u>?

The usefulness of the <u>Ad Quirinum</u> to
Christians for refutation or for the
acquisition of Biblical learning is
apparent. Cyprian was later to repeat the
experiment with the <u>Ad Fortunatum</u>.[1] This
raises the question as to whether all of the
extensive Biblical quotation found in
Cyprian is based on an anthology prior to
his own.[2] It has been suggested that
Cyprian's whole network of Biblical
quotation is based on <u>florilegia</u> which had
existed prior to his collection of
passages in the <u>Ad Quirinum</u>.[3] These
<u>Testimonia Inedita</u> would have formed the
basis of the Biblical quotations scattered
throughout his work. But such an hypothesis
needlessly complicates an understanding of
Cyprian's use of <u>florilegia</u>. In the preface
to the first two books of the <u>Testimonia</u>,

---

1. See Goetz, <u>Geschichte</u>, p. 439.
2. For a reconstruction of the African
Bible in use in the third century, see Von
Soden, "Neue Testament", pp. 1-20. See also
G.J.D. Aalders, <u>Tertullianus' Citaten uit de
Evangeliën en de oudlatijnsche Bijbelverta-
lingen</u> (Amsterdam, 1932); and T.P. O'Malley,
<u>Tertullian and the Bible. Language-Imagery-
Exegesis</u>, <u>Latinitas Christianorum Primaeva</u>,
21 (Utrecht, 1967); also Chadwick,
"Florilegium", pp. 1131-52.
3. For this hypothesis, see Réveillaud,
<u>L'oraison dominicale</u>, introduction, pp. 7-
24. He calls this collection the
"Testimonia Inedita", which will be
adopted here for convenience.

Cyprian explicitly states that he composed the work on the request of Quirinus, presumably because no other such collection was then available.[1] He goes on to state that the collection was compiled directly from memory, eschewing the mention of any other source.[2] Unless one is willing to accuse Cyprian of a definite, fairly obvious, and perhaps easily refutable lie, one must discard the notion of a collection of Testimonia Inedita available for consultation. The resemblances and linkages of the other sets of Biblical quotations can easily be explained by making Cyprian himself the collector of a florilegium on which he could constantly draw. There is no need to postulate an intermediate source between the bishop and the Bible.[3]

---

1. This seems a strong presumption against Réveillaud's hypothesis in itself.
2. Test., praefatio, 1/36 ff.: "sed quantum mediocris memoria suggerebat".
3. Réveillaud, L'oraison dominicale, pp. 20-1, further argues from the similarity between the Biblical quotations in Cyprian and Firmilian's letter (Ep. 75) that there is a common source for them. He asserts the origin of the T.I. is Caesarea from the correspondence (p. 22). Although the citations permeate the work of the Carthaginian bishop, why is there no other evidence that the T.I. existed? If it had been known among the bishop's intimates, why was there no effort to circulate it? The common citations in Firmilian and Cyprian can be explained. The translator of Firmilian's epistle simply changed the quotations into the form known in Africa; or,

396

---

3. (cont'd) in the later copying of the letter, the copyists switched to a more familiar and (perhaps in their eyes) more correct Biblical text. As for non-publication, other Cyprianic works have been lost. See A. von Harnack, "Über verlorene Briefe und Aktenstücke, die sich aus der Cyprianischen Briefsammlung ermitteln lassen", TU N.F. 23, hft. 2a (Leipzig, 1902). There is certainly no reason to complicate matters further by adopting the hypothesis which has been presented by Réveillaud.

Appendix VI:
CYPRIAN'S DE UNITATE, CHAPTER 4

The status of chapter 4 in the De Unitate is the most controversial of all Cyprianic conundrums. Many have taken it as the central text on Cyprian's relationship to the bishop of Rome. Both Catholic and Protestant scholars have often been divided on the basis of religious rather than scholarly loyalties.

Chapter 4 has been transmitted in three forms. One is the Textus Receptus which Hartel printed as the legitimate text; the second is a so-called Primacy Text which Catholic scholars have taken to support the position of Roman supremacy; and the third is a conflated version of both.[1] The origin of the controversy lay in the 16th century. The edition brought out by Manutius in 1563 at Rome contained certain additions which form the basis of the Primacy Text. The printing of the text was made against the advice of Latino Latini, who then withdrew his name from Manutius' edition.[2] The edition of Pamelius in 1568 repeated the text found in the Manutius edition. Latini was consulted by him, but no changes or actual consultation of Latini's collations were made by Pamelius. The Oxford text of Pearson and Fell, which was one of the milestones of Cyprianic scholarship, left out the additions. They were replaced in the edition under the editorship of Dom Morin.[3]

---

1. Bévenot, St. Cyprian's 'De Unitate', pp. 1 ff., for the manuscript families.
2. Hartel, p. x.
3. For these editions, see Hartel, praefatio, lxx ff.

399

In the Vienna corpus, which came to be the standard text, Hartel rejected the suggestions. His stance was followed by the last full-scale biographer of Cyprian in English, Archbishop Benson.[1] The problem remained in this state until the appearance of the articles of Dom Chapman.[2] Chapman's essential contribution was to discern that there was not one text plus an interpolated version, but that there were in reality two texts, the Primacy Text and the Textus Receptus (P.T. and T.R.). It is around these two versions that the controversy has raged since Chapman's discovery.

The problem generated by the two versions has resolved itself into a number of questions of which two are of prime importance. Is one version genuine and the other not, and do the different versions of the text affect materially the view of Cyprian's relation to Rome. Koch tried to argue that the P.T. was an interpolated version, and that the T.R. was genuine and unchanged from the hands of Cyprian.[3] Chapman claimed that both versions were Cyprian's, and that Cyprian had himself later reworked the chapter during the controversy with Stephen on the rebaptism of heretics.[4] Chapman made the telling point against Koch that epistle 43.5 establishes that the power given to Peter is not merely a matter of temporal priority but also of rank.

---

1. Benson, Cyprian, p. 324.
2. Chapman, "Les interpolations", passim.
3. H. Koch, Cyprian und der römische Primat, eine Kirchen-und dogmengeschichtlich Studie, TU 35, hft. 1 (Leipzig, 1910) for this argument.
4. Chapman, Studies, pp. 18-50.

400

Chapman saw part of the problem when he remarked that Cyprian's theory of the foundation of the Church was incomplete. Koch's reply to the question was the Cathedra Petri. He restated his position that the P.T. was an interpolated version, and that there was no effective or theoretical primacy of the bishop of Rome in the third century.[1] A new direction was introduced into the discussion by the appearance of Bévenot's St. Cyprian's 'De Unitate' (London, 1939), which was based on a more thorough study of the manuscripts and had received its impetus from an article by Van Den Eynde.[2] Van Den Eynde attacked the problem by assuming Cyprianic authorship of both (which Chapman had fairly established) and by comparing both the style and the Scriptural quotations of the two versions to other extant works of definite Cyprianic authorship particularly the letters. From his analysis he deduced that the P.T. was composed before 255 and the T.R. afterwards. Unfortunately he based much of his analysis on the temporal occurrence of Scriptural quotations neglecting to consider the loss of numerous letters - which is obvious from references in the extant correspondence as well as in the Testimonia and which imply a wide knowledge of the Biblical text. He also placed too much reliance on Hartel's index of Scriptural quotations, which is recognizably incomplete. Attempts at refutation were made

---

1. Koch, Cathedra Petri, pp. 107 ff., and pp. 154 ff.
2. D. Van Den Eynde, "La double édition du De Unitate de S. Cyprien", RHE 29 (1933), pp. 5-24.

by Lebreton and Frances.[1]

Bévenot approached the problem by thoroughly re-studying the manuscript tradition. His conclusions supported those of Van Den Eynde. His arguments centered around the composition of both chapters, arguing that the additions to the P.T. were more coherent and sensible than those to the T.R. for the conflated version. But the rationalization does not quite hold. The additions to the T.R. are not confusing and are less economical than the other set. They all centre around the addition of statements referring to the name of Peter, which is what one might expect. Bévenot's explanation, as he himself admits, is in the last instance the same as Van Den Eynde's, but he has provided important material for the study of the manuscript tradition. He grants that certain proof is not obtainable.[2] His is the view which most economically fits the facts, and it is the view adopted here, that the P.T. was the first version of the text and the T.R. the second, and that both were from the hands of Cyprian.[3]

---

1. J. Lebreton, "La double édition du De Unitate de S. Cyprien", RSR 24 (1934), pp. 456-67.

2. See Bévenot, Tradition of Manuscripts, p. 172.

3. Bévenot, St. Cyprian's 'De Unitate', p. 65. For a restatement of Bévenot's position against the criticism of J. Le Moyne, RevBén 63 (1953), pp. 70-115, see his "Primatus Petro datur", pp. 19-35.

Appendix VII: THE ADVERSUS JUDAEOS

There is more dispute concerning the Adversus Judaeos. It is already included among Cyprian's works in the Cheltenham List of 359-65, so its inclusion in the corpus was early. Von Soden argues that the piece entered the Cyprianic corpus at Rome in the first half of the fourth century.[1] Because of this and because of resemblances in style and expression, Harnack concluded that it was authored by Novatianus himself.[2] But such resemblances are insufficient in themselves to prove authorship. Bardenhewer more cautiously concludes that the work cannot be positively assigned to any one author.[3] More recently, Peterson has convincingly shown that the work is heavily dependent upon the homily of Melito on the Passion.[4] The question of authorship cannot be solved.[5]

1. Von Soden, "Die Cyprianische Briefsammlung", p. 221.
2. Harnack, GAL, p. 404.
3. Bardenhewer, Geschichte, II, p. 442.
4. E. Peterson, "Ps.-Cyprian, Adversus Judaeos und Mileto von Sardes", Vigiliae Christianae 6 (1952), pp. 33-43.
5. A new text of the Adversus Judaeos has recently been published: D. Van Damme, Pseudo-Cyprian Adversus Judaeos, gegen die Judenchristen: die älteste lateinische Predigt, Paradosis 22 (Freiburg, Switz., 1969). The text is a great improvement over Hartel. For a balanced review, one should take special note of S.G. Hall, JThS N.S. 21 (1970), pp. 183-9.

403

Appendix VIII: THE AUTHORSHIP AND DATE OF THE AD NOVATIANUM

The dating and place of the Ad Novatianum have caused difficulty. Harnack[1] attempted to assign it to Xistus II, but his attempt has met with little favour.[2] There has also been extensive dispute over the place of origin of the Biblical text, but the general consensus favours Africa. Koch[3] feels that it is a composition exercise and not by a bishop, but this conclusion is not justified merely by extensive use of imitation, a factor common to all ancient works. So little other comparable work than Cyprian's is extant that to speak of imitation is not legitimate. Given that the work was composed in Africa approximately contemporaneously with the events described in it, there remains the question of ascertaining a more exact date of composition.

The first indication of dating is provided by chapter 1: "et ab ecclesia separatus". This would establish a terminus after the councils at Rome and Carthage in the summer of 251. The central reference is in chapter 6 where the author refers to two persecutions, the first of which is the Decian. (This may, however, be a gloss, though the manuscripts are uninformative on this point.) If composed in Africa, the second persecution must be that of Valerianus, dating the work to 257 or after. The persecution of Gallus seems to have left

---

1. Harnack, GAL, p. 387.
2. See Koch, CU, pp. 359 ff.
3. Koch, CU, pp. 359 ff.

Africa unscathed.[1] Socrates states that Novatianus perished during the Valerianic Persecution, but no other evidence is available.[2] The martyr listed in the Martyrium Romanum under June 27 and 28 probably has no connection with Novatianus, who would hardly have been entered in the roles of Catholic martyrs. An inscription from a richly engraved gravestone found at San Lorenzo reads:

NOVATIANO BEATISSIMO/MARTYRI GAUDENTIUS DIAC./FEC.

This probably has nothing to do with our Novatianus, as the failure to include his title of episcopus is fatal.[3] So a date during or soon after the Valerianic Persecution would appear most likely. The generally held opinion is that the work is the product of a bishop. This has been challenged by Koch.[4] But the opening of chapter 1, particularly the phrase "cogitanti mihi quidnam agere de miserandis fratribus" creates a strong presumption that Koch is wrong.

1. Ep. 58.5/660.6-661.13 and Ep. 61.
2. Socrates, HE 4.28.
3. See D. Van Den Eynde, "L'inscription sépulcrale de Novatien", RHE 33 (1937), part 2, pp. 792-4.
4. Koch, CU, p. 418.

406

EDITIONS, COMMENTARIES AND TRANSLATIONS

ACTA ET PASSIONES

Beek, C. van, Passio Sanctarum Perpetuae et Felicitatis, I (Neumagen, 1936).

Knopf, R., Krüger, G., Ruhbach, G., Ausgewählte Märtyrerakten[4], Sammlung ausgewählter kirchen-und dogmengeschichtlicher Quellenschriften, N.F. 3 (Tübingen, 1965).

Robinson, J.A., "The Passion of S. Perpetua", Texts and Studies, Contributions to Biblical and Patristic Literature, Vol. I, no. 2 (Cambridge, 1891).

CYPRIAN

Bévenot, M., "A New Cyprianic Fragment", Bulletin of the John Rylands Library 28, 1 (1944), pp. 76-82.

Bévenot, M., St. Cyprian: The Lapsed. The Unity of the Catholic Church, ACW, 25 (Westminster, Md., 1957).

Bévenot, M., De Lapsis and De Unitate, in Opera Cypriani, Corpus Christianorum, Series Latina 3, Pars 1 (Turnholti, 1972).

Damme, D. Van, Pseudo-Cyprian Adversus Judaeos, gegen die Judenchristen: die älteste lateinische Predigt, Paradosis, 22 (Freiburg, Switz., 1969).

Hartel, W., Corpus Scriptorum Ecclesiasticorum Latinorum 3, S. Thasci Caecili Cypriani Opera Omnia (Vienna, 1868-71), parts 1-3.

Keenan, A.E., De Habitu Virginum, Patristic Studies, 34 (Washington, D.C., 1932).

407

Réveillaud, M., _Saint Cyprien: L'oraison dominicale_, Etudes d'histoire et de philosophie religieuses, 58 (Paris, 1964).

Weber, R., _Ad Fortunatum_ and _Ad Quirinum_, in _Opera Cypriani_, _Corpus Christianorum_, _Series Latina_ 3, Pars 1 (Turnholti, 1972).

HERODIAN

Whittaker, C.R., _Herodian_, Books 1-8 (2 vols. Cambridge, Mass., I: 1969; II: 1970), _Loeb Classical Library_.

LIBER PONTIFICALIS

Duchesne, L., _Le liber pontificalis_, _Bibliothèque des écoles françaises d'Athènes et de Rome_, 2 (Paris, 1886).

MARTYROLOGIUM HIERONYMIANUM

Delehaye, H., and Quentin, H., _Martyrologium Hieronymianum_, _Acta Sanctorum, collecta...a Sociis Bollandianis_, Nou., ii, 2 (Brussels, 1931).

MINUCIUS FELIX

Beaujeu, J., _Minucius Félix: Octavius_ (Paris, 1964).

NOVATIANUS

Diercks, G.F., _Opera Novatiani_, _Corpus Christianorum_, _Series Latina_ 4 (Turnholti, 1972).

Fausset, W.Y., _Novatian: De Trinitate_, _Cambridge Patristic Texts_ (Cambridge, 1909).

Weyer, H., _Novatianus: De Trinitate: Über den dreifaltigen Gott_, _Testimonia_, 2 (Dusseldorf, 1962).

408

PONTIUS

Harnack, A. von, "Das Leben Cyprians von Pontius: die erste christliche Biographie", TU 39 hft. 3 (Leipzig, 1913).

Pellegrino, M., Ponzio: Vita e martirio de San Cipriano, Verba Seniorum, 3 (Alba, 1955).

BIBLIOGRAPHY

The following bibliography includes those works cited in the notes which deal with Roman History and Christianity. Peripheral works mentioned in the notes or text will not be found below.

Aalders, G.J.D., _Tertullianus' Citaten uit de Evangeliën en de oudlatijnsche Bijbelvertalingen_ (1932).

Achelis, H., _Virgines subintroductae_ (Leipzig, 1902).

Adam, K., _Das sogenannte Bussedikt des Papstes Kallistus_, Veröffentl. aus dem kirchenhistor. Seminar München, 4, 5 (Munich, 1917).

Albertini, E., _L'Afrique romaine_, revised by M.L. Leschi (Algiers, 1950).

Alès, A.D', _La théologie de Tertullien_ (Paris, 1905).

"Le diacre Pontius", _RSR_ (1918), pp. 319-78.

La théologie de S. Cyprien (Paris, 1922).

Novatien: Etude sur la théologie romaine au milieu du troisième siècle (Paris, 1924).

Alföldi, A., "Zu den Christenverfolgungen in der Mitte des 3. Jahrhunderts", _Klio_ 31 (1938), pp. 323-48 = _Studien zur Geschichte der Weltkrise des 3. Jahrhunderts nach Christus_ (Darmstadt, 1967), pp. 285-311.

Altaner, B., and Stuiber, A., _Patrologie_.

Leben, Schriften und Lehre der Kirchenväter7 (Freiburg, 1966).

Audollent, A., Carthage romaine, 146 avant Jésus-Christ - 698 après Jésus-Christ, Bibliothèque des écoles françaises d'Athènes et de Rome, fasc. 84 (Paris, 1901).

Axelson, B., Das Prioritätsproblem Tertullian - Minucius Felix, Skrifter utgivna av Vetenskaps-Societeten i Lund, 27 (Lund, 1941).

"Echtheits-und testkritische Kleinigkeiten", Eranos 39 (1941), pp. 67-74.

Baradez, J., Fossatum Africae, Arts et métiers graphiques (Paris, 1949).

Barbero, G., "Seneca e la Conversione di San Cipriano", Rivista di Studi Classici 10 (1962), pp. 16-23.

Barbieri, G., L'Albo senatorio da Settimio Severo a Carino 193-285, Studi pubblicati dall' Istituto Italiano per la Storia antica, fasc. 6 (Rome, 1952).

Bardenhewer, O., Geschichte der altkirchlichen Literatur (5 vols. Freiburg i.Br., 1913-32).

Bardy, G., "L'autorité du Siège Romain et les controverses du IIIe siècle (230-270)", RSR 14 (1924), pp. 255-72; 385-99.

La théologie de l'église de Saint Irénée au concile de Nicée, Unam Sanctam, 14 (Paris, 1947).

La question des langues dans l'église ancienne, I, Etude de théologie historique (Paris, 1948).

Barnes, T.D., "The Family and Career of

Septimius Severus", Historia 16 (1967), pp. 87-107.

"Pre-Decian Acta Martyrum", JThS N.S. 19 (1968), pp. 509-31.

"Legislation Against the Christians", JRS 58 (1968), pp. 32-50.

"The Lost Kaisergeschichte and the Latin Historical Tradition", Bonner Historia-Augusta-Colloquium 1968/69 (1970), pp. 13-43.

"Three Neglected Martyrs", JThS N.S. 22 (1971), pp. 159-61.

Tertullian: A Historical and Literary Study (Oxford, 1971).

"Some Persons in the Historia Augusta", Phoenix 26 (1972), pp. 140-82.

Batiffol, P., L'église naissante et le catholicisme^6 (Paris, 1913).

Baudrillart, A., Meyer, A. de, and Gauwenbergh, E. van, Dictionnaire d'histoire et de géographie ecclésiastiques (Paris, 1912 ff.).

Baus, K., Handbook of Church History, I: From the Apostolic Community to Constantine (Montreal, 1965), Eng. trans. of third German edition, ed. J. Dolan and H. Jedin.

Bayard, L., "Notes sur la Vita Cypriani et sur Lucianus", RP N.S. 38 (1914), pp. 206-10.

St. Cyprien: Correspondance^2 (2 vols. Paris, 1945).

Beck, A., Römisches Recht bei Tertullian und Cyprian, Schriften der Königsberger gelehrten Gesellschaft, Geisteswiss. Kl., 7, hft.2 (1930).

Becker, C., "Der Octavius des Minucius Felix", SBBayer, hft. 2(Munich, 1967).

Benson, E.W., Cyprian: His Life, His Times, His Work (London, 1897).

Bévenot, M., St. Cyprian's 'De Unitate'. Chapter 4 in the Light of the Manuscripts, Bellarmine Series, 4 (London, 1939).

"A Bishop is Responsible to God Alone", RSR 39/40, Mélanges Jules Lebreton (1951/52), pp. 397-415.

"Primatus Petro datur: St. Cyprian on the Papacy", JThS N.S. 5 (1954), pp. 19-35.

"Hi, qui sacrificaverunt. A Significant Variant in St. Cyprian's De Unitate", JThS N.S. 5 (1954), pp. 68-72.

"In solidum and St. Cyprian: A Correction", JThS N.S. 6 (1955), pp. 244-8.

"The Sacrament of Penance and St. Cyprian's De Lapsis", ThSt 16 (1955), pp. 175-213.

The Tradition of Manuscripts: A Study in the Transmission of St. Cyprian's Treatises (Oxford, 1961).

Birley, A., Septimius Severus. The African Emperor (London, 1971).

Bowersock, G.W., Greek Sophists in the Roman Empire (Oxford, 1969).

Brisson, J.P., Autonomisme et christianisme dans l'Afrique romaine de Septime Sévère à l'invasion vandale (Paris, 1958).

Brown, P., _Augustine of Hippo_ (London, 1967).

"Christianity and Local Culture in Late Roman Africa", _JRS_ 58 (1968), pp. 85-95= _Religion and Society in the Age of Saint Augustine_ (London, 1972), pp. 279-300.

The World of Late Antiquity from Marcus Aurelius to Muhammad (London, 1971).

Bureth, P., _Les titulatures impériales dans les papyrus, les ostraca et les inscriptions d'Egypte (30 a.c. - 284 p.c.), Papyrologica Bruxellensia_, 2 (Brussels, 1964).

Cabrol, F., and Leclercq, H., _Dictionnaire d'archéologie chrétienne et de liturgie_ (15 vols. Paris, 1903-53).

Cagnat, R., _L'armée romaine d'Afrique et l'occupation militaire de l'Afrique sous les Empereurs²_ (Paris, 1913).

Cambridge Ancient History, XII: _The Imperial Crisis and Recovery A.D. 193-324_, ed. S.A. Cook, F.E. Adcock, M.P. Charlesworth, N.H. Baynes (Cambridge, 1939).

Carcopino, J., "L'insurrection de 253 d'après une inscription de Miliana récemment découverte", _Revue Africaine_ 60 (1919), pp. 369-83.

Chadwick, H., "St. Peter and St. Paul in Rome: The Problem of the _Memoria Apostolorum ad Catacumbas_", _JThS_ N.S. 8 (1957), pp. 31-52.

Early Christian Thought and the Classical Tradition. Studies in Justin, Clement, and Origen (Oxford, 1966).

Chapman, J., "The Order of the Treatises and Letters in the Manuscripts of St.

Cyprian", JThS 4 (1902), pp. 103-23.

"Les interpolations dans le traité de S. Cyprien sur l'unité de l'église", RevBén 19 (1902), pp. 246-54; 357-73; 20 (1903), pp. 26-51.

Studies on the Early Papacy (London, 1928).

Chartier, M.-C., "La discipline pénitentielle d'après les écrits de saint Cyprien", Antonianum 14 (1939), pp. 17-42; 135-56.

Clarke, G.W., "The Literary Setting of the Octavius of Minucius Felix", JRH 3 (1964/5), pp. 195-211.

"The Secular Profession of St. Cyprian of Carthage", Latomus 24 (1965), pp. 633-8.

"Minucius Felix: Octavius 4.6", CPh 61 (1966), pp. 252-3.

"The Historical Setting of the Octavius of Minucius Felix", JRH 4 (1966-7), pp. 267-86.

"Some Observations on the Persecution of Decius", Antichthon 3 (1969), pp. 63-76.

"The Barbarian Disturbances in North Africa of the Mid-Third Century", Antichthon 4 (1970), pp. 76-84.

"The Epistles of Cyprian", Auckland Classical Essays Presented to E.M. Blaiklock (Auckland, 1970), pp. 203-21.

"Prosopographical Notes on the Epistles of Cyprian", Latomus 30 (1971), pp. 1141-5.

Colombo, S., "S. Cipriano di Cartagine:

L'uomo e lo scrittore", Didaskaleion N.S. 6 (1928), pp. 1-80.

Corssen, P., "Das Martyrium des Bischofs Cyprian", ZNW 18 (1917/18), pp. 118-39; 202-16.

Croix, G.E.M. de Ste., "Aspects of the 'Great' Persecution", HThR 47 (1954), pp. 75-109.

Crook, J.A., Law and Life of Rome (London, 1967).

Davies, J.G., "Condemnation to the Mines: A Neglected Chapter in the History of the Persecutions", University of Birmingham Historical Journal 6 (1957/8), pp. 99-107.

Dekkers, E., Clavis Patrum Latinorum^2, Sacris Erudiri, 3 (Steenbrugge, 1961).

Delehaye, H., Les passions des martyrs et les genres littéraires^2, Subsidia hagiographica 13B (Brussels, 1966).

Dessau, H., Über einige Inschriften aus Cirta", Hermes 15 (1880), pp. 471-4.

"Minucius Felix und Caecilius Natalis", Hermes 40 (1905), pp. 373-86.

"Pontius, der Biograph Cyprians", Hermes 51 (1916), pp. 65-72.

Diehl, E., Inscriptiones latinae christianae veteres (3 vols. Berlin, 1925-31), with supplement by J. Moreau and H.I. Marrou.

Dill, S., Roman Society in the Last Century of the Western Empire. From the Fall of Paganism to the Advent of the Barbarians^2 (London, 1899).

Diller, H., "In Sachen Tertullian-Minucius Felix", Philologus 90 (1935), pp. 98-114; 216-39.

Dodds, E.R., Pagan and Christian in an Age of Anxiety. Some Aspects of Religious Experience from Marcus Aurelius to Constantine (Cambridge, 1965).

Donna, R., "Note on St. Cyprian's De Habitu Virginum: Its Source and Influence", Traditio 4 (1946), pp. 399-407.

Duquenne, L., Chronologie des lettres de S. Cyprien. Le dossier de la persécution de Dèce, Subsidia hagiographica, 54 (Brussels, 1972).

Eck, W., "Das Eindringen des Christentums in den Senatorenstand", Chiron 1 (1971).

Ernst, J., "Zeit und Heimat des Liber de rebaptismate", ThQ 90 (1908), pp. 579-613; 91 (1909), pp. 20-64.

Escurac-Doisy, H. d', "M. Cornelius Octavianus et les révoltes indigènes du troisième siècle d'après une inscription de Caesarea", Libyca 1, Série Archéologie-Epigraphie (1953), pp. 181-7.

Evans, R.F., One and Holy. The Church in Latin Patristic Thought (London, 1972).

Eynde, D. Van Den, "La double édition du De Unitate de S. Cyprien", RHE 29 (1933), pp. 5-24.

"L'inscription sépulcrale de Novatien", RHE 33 (1937), part 2, pp. 792-4.

Favez, C., "La fuite de S. Cyprien lors de la persécution de Décius", REL 19 (1941), pp. 191-201.

Ferguson, J., "Aspects of Early Christianity in North Africa", in Africa in Classical Antiquity (Ibadan, 1969), ed. Ferguson and L.A. Thompson.

Festugière, A.M.J., Personal Religion Among

the Greeks, Sather Classical Lectures, 26 (Los Angeles and Berkeley, 1954).

Franchi de'Cavalieri, P., "Di un nuovo studio sugli Acta Proconsularia di s. Cipriano", Studi Romani, Riv. di archeol. e storia 2 (1914), pp. 189-215= Scritti Agiografici, II: 1900-1946, Studi e Testi 222 (Vatican City, 1962), pp. 229-54.

Frend, W.H.C., The Donatist Church. A Movement of Protest in Roman North Africa (Oxford, 1952).

Martyrdom and Persecution in the Early Church. A Study of a Conflict from the Maccabees to Donatus (London, 1965).

Freppel, C.E., Saint Cyprien et l'église d'Afrique au IIIe siècle (Paris, 1865).

Fuchs, H., Der geistige Widerstand gegen Rom in der antiken Welt (Berlin, 1938).

Gagé, J., "Nouveaux aspects de l'Afrique chrétienne", Annales de l'Ecole des Hautes-Etudes de Gand 1 (1937), pp. 181-224.

Garnsey, P., Social Status and Legal Privilege in the Roman Empire (Oxford, 1970).

Gilliam, J.F., "Trebonianus Gallus and the Decii: III et I cos", Studi in Onore di Aristide Calderini e Roberto Paribeni 1 (Milan, 1956), pp. 305-11.

Goetz, C.G., Geschichte der Cyprianischen Literatur (Basel, 1891).

"Der alte Anfang und die ursprüngliche Form von Cyprians Schrift Ad Donatum", TU N.F. 19, hft. 1c (1899), pp. 1-16.

Goltz, E.v.d., Das Gebet in der ältesten

Christenheit (Leipzig, 1901).

Graham, A., _Roman Africa_ (London, 1902).

Gsell, S., _Histoire ancienne de l'Afrique du nord_ (8 vols. Paris, 1913-28).

Inscriptions latines de l'Algérie. Inscriptions de la Proconsulaire (Paris, 1922).

Hagendahl, H., _Latin Fathers and the Classics. A Study on the Apologists, Jerome and Other Christian Writers, Studia graeca et latina gothoburgensia_, 6 (Göteborg, 1958).

Hall, S.G., _JThS_ N.S. 21 (1970), pp. 183-9, for his review of D. Van Damme, _Pseudo-Cyprian Adversus Judaeos, gegen die Judenchristen: die älteste lateinische Predigt, Paradosis_, 22 (Freiburg, Switz., 1969).

Harnack, A. von, _Geschichte der altchristlichen Literatur bis Eusebius: Die Überlieferung und der Bestand_ (2 half-volumes Leipzig, 1893-8); _Die Chronologie_ (2 vols. Leipzig, 1904).

History of Dogma^3 (7 vols. New York, 1894-9), trans. N. Buchanan.

"Cyprian als Enthusiast", _ZNW_ 3 (1902), pp. 177-91.

"Über verlorene Briefe und Aktenstücke, die sich aus der Cyprianischen Briefsammlung ermitteln lassen", _TU_ N.F. 23, hft. 2a (Leipzig, 1902).

Die Mission und Ausbreitung des Christentums in den ersten drei Jahrhunderten^3 (2 vols. Leipzig, 1915).

Haywood, R.M., _Roman Africa_, in T. Frank (ed.), _An Economic Survey of Ancient_

Rome (6 vols. Baltimore, 1933-40), Vol. IV.

Healy, P.J., The Valerian Persecution. A Study of the Relations Between the Church and State in the Third Century A.D. (London; Cambridge, Mass., 1905).

Hefele, C.J. von, Histoire des conciles d'après les documents originaux^2 (Paris, 1907 ff.), ed. and trans. H. Leclercq.

Hirzel, R., Der Dialog, ein literarhistorischer Versuch (2 vols. Leipzig, 1895).

Hoppenbrouwers, H.A.M., Recherches sur la terminologie du martyre de Tertullien à Lactance, Latinitas Christianorum Primaeva, 15 (Nijmegen, 1961).

Horbury, W., "Tertullian on Jews in the Light of De Spectaculis 30.5-6", JThS 23 (1972), pp. 455-8.

Hummel, E.L., The Concept of Martyrdom According to St. Cyprian of Carthage, Studies in Christian Antiquity, 9 (Washington, 1946).

Jones, A.H.M., The Later Roman Empire 284-602 (3 vols. Oxford, 1964).

Jones, A.H.M., Martindale, J.R., and Morris, J., The Prosopography of the Later Roman Empire, I: A.D. 260-395 (Cambridge, 1971).

Jourjon, M., Cyprien de Carthage, Eglise d'hier et d'aujourd'hui (Paris, 1957).

Joyce, G.H., "Private Penance in the Early Church", JThS 42 (1941), pp. 18-42.

Kajanto, I., Onomastic Studies in the Early Christian Inscriptions of Rome and Carthage, Acta Instituti Romani

Finlandiae, vol. 2, no. 1 (Helsinki, 1963).

Knipfing, J.H., "The Libelli of the Decian Persecution", HThR 16 (1923), pp. 345-90.

Koch, H., "Virgines Christi", TU 31, hft. 2 (1907).

Cyprian und der römische Primat, eine kirchen- und dogmengeschichtlich Studie, TU 35, hft. 1 (Leipzig, 1910).

Cyprianische Untersuchungen, Arbeiten zur Kirchengeschichte, 4 (Bonn, 1926).

Cathedra Petri, Beihefte zur Zeitschrift für die neutestamentliche Wissenschaft, 11 (Giessen, 1930).

Labriolle, P. de, "Le 'mariage spirituel' dans l'antiquité chrétienne", RH 137 (1921), pp. 204-25.

Histoire de la littérature latine chrétienne³, Collection d'études anciennes (2 vols. Paris, 1947).

Lapeyre, G.G., and Pellegrin, A., Carthage latine et chrétienne, Bibliothèque historique (Paris, 1950).

Lauffer, S. (ed.), Diokletians Preisedikt, Texte und Kommentare, 5 (Berlin, 1971).

Lawlor, H.J., and Oulton, J.E.L., Eusebius: The Ecclesiastical History and the Martyrs of Palestine, II (London, 1928).

Lebreton, J., "La double édition du De Unitate de S. Cyprien", RSR 24 (1934), pp. 456-67.

Le Saint, W.P., Tertullian: Treatises on Marriage and Remarriage, ACW 13 (Westminster, Md., 1951).

Ludwig, J., Der heilige Märtyrerbischof Cyprian von Karthago (Munich, 1951).

Macmullen, R., Enemies of the Roman Order. Treason, Unrest, and Alienation in the Empire (Cambridge, Mass., 1966).

Manni, E., L'impero di Gallieno (Rome, 1949).

Marrou, H.-I., Histoire de l'éducation dans l'antiquité⁶ (Paris, 1965).

Martin, J., "Die Vita et Passio Cypriani", HJ 39 (1918/19), pp. 674-712.

Mattingly, H., "The Reign of Aemilian", JRS 25 (1935), pp. 55-8.

Melin, B., Studia in corpus Cyprianeum, Commentatio academica (Uppsala, 1946).

Mengis, H.K., "Ein altes Verzeichnis cyprianischer Schriften", BPW 38 (1918), pp. 326-36.

Mesnage, J., L'Afrique chrétienne: Evêchés et ruines antiques (Paris, 1912).

Millar, F., A Study of Cassius Dio (Oxford, 1964).

"Local Cultures in the Roman Empire: Libyan, Punic and Latin in Roman Africa", JRS 58 (1968), pp. 126-34.

"Paul of Samosata, Zenobia and Aurelian: the Church, Local Culture and Political Allegiance in Third-Century Syria", JRS 61 (1971), pp. 1-17.

Molthagen, J., Der römische Staat und die Christen im zweiten und dritten Jahrhundert, Hypomnemata 28 (Göttingen, 1970).

Mommsen, T., "Zur lateinischen Stichometrie", Hermes 21 (1886), pp. 142-56 = Gesammelte Schriften, VII (Berlin, 1909) pp. 283-98.

Monceaux, P., Histoire littéraire de

l'Afrique chrétienne depuis les origines jusqu'à l'invasion arabe (7 vols. Paris, 1901-23).

Mongelli, G., "La chiesa di Cartagine contro Roma durante l'episcopato di S. Cipriano (249-258)", Miscellanea Francescana 59 (1959), pp. 104-201.

Moreau, J., Die Christenverfolgung im römischen Reich^2, Aus der Welt der Religion. Forschungen und Berichte, N.F. 2 (Berlin, 1961).

Nautin, P., Lettres et écrivains chrétiens des IIe et IIIe siècles, Patristica, 2 (Paris, 1961).

Nock, A.D., Conversion. The Old and the New in Religion from Alexander the Great to Augustine of Hippo (Oxford, 1933).

O'Malley, T.P., Tertullian and the Bible. Language-Imagery-Exegesis, Latinitas Christianorum Primaeva, 21 (Utrecht, 1967).

Parker, H.M.D., A History of the Roman World 138-337^2, Methuen's History of the Greek and Roman World, 7 (London, 1958).

Pekáry, T., "Bemerkungen zur Chronologie des Jahrzehnts 250-260 n. Chr.", Historia 11 (1962), pp. 123-8.

Pellegrino, M., Studi su l'antica apologetica, Ed. di storia e letteratura (Rome, 1947).

Peterson, E., "Ps.-Cyprian, Adversus Judaeos und Mileto von Sardes", Vigiliae Christianae 6 (1952), pp. 33-43.

Pflaum, H.G., Les carrière procuratoriennes équestres sous le Haut-Empire romain, Inst. franç. d'Archéol. de Beyrouth. Bib., archéol. et hist., 57 (Paris,

1960/61).

Picard, G.C., *La civilisation de l'Afrique romaine* (Paris, 1959).

Pick, B., *Die antiken Münzen Nord-Griechenlands, I: Die antiken Münzen von Dacien und Moesian* (Berlin, 1898).

Plumpe, J.C., "Ecclesia mater", *TAPA* 70 (1939), pp. 535-55.

Poschmann, B., "Zur Bussfrage in der cyprianischen Zeit", *ZKT* 37 (1913), pp. 25-54; 244-65.

"Die altchristliche Busse", *Hdb. der DG* 4, 3 (Freiburg i.Br., 1951), pp. 18-41.

Penance and the Anointing of the Sick (Montreal, 1964), trans. and revised by F. Courtney.

Quasten, J., *Patrology* (3 vols. Utrecht-Antwerp, 1950-60).

Rachet, M., *Rome et les Berbères. Un problème militaire d'Auguste à Dioclétien*, Collection Latomus, 110 (Brussels, 1970).

Ramsey, H.L., "On Early Insertions in the Third Book of St. Cyprian's *Testimonia*", *JThS* 2 (1901), pp. 276-88.

Reinmuth, O.W., "A Working List of the Prefects of Egypt 30 B.C. to 299 A.D.. Their names, terms of office, and references to them which have appeared since A. Stein, *Die Praefekten von Aegypten* (1950)", *BASP* 4 (1967), pp. 75-128.

Reitzenstein, R., "Die Nachrichten über den Tod Cyprians", *SBHeidel*, Phil.-hist. Kl. (1913), Abhand. 14, pp. 1-76.

Rémondon, R., _La crise de l'Empire romain²_, _Nouvelle Clio_ (Paris, 1970).

Romanelli, P., _Storia delle Provincie Romane dell' Africa, Studi Pubblicati dall'Istituto Italiano per la Storia antica_, fasc. 14 (Rome, 1959).

Rostovtzeff, M., _The Social and Economic History of the Roman Empire²_ (2 vols. Oxford, 1957).

Routh, M.J., _Reliquiae Sacrae²_ (5 vols. Oxford, 1846).

Ruysschaert, J., "La commémoration de Cyprien et de Corneille in Callisti", _RHE_ 61 (1966), pp. 455-84.

Sanday, W.A., "The Cheltenham List of the Canonical Books of the Old and New Testament and of the Writings of Cyprian", _Studia biblica et ecclesiastica_ 3 (Oxford, 1891), pp. 117-304.

Saumagne, C., "La persécution de Dèce en Afrique", _Byzantion_ 32 (1962), pp. 1-29.

Schanz, M., Hosius, C., and Krüger, G., _Geschichte der römischen Litteratur_, III³ (Munich, 1922).

Simonetti, M., "Sulla paternità del _Quod Idola Dii Non Sint_", _Maia_ 3 (1950), pp. 265-88.

Soden, H. von, "Die Cyprianische Briefsammlung: Geschichte ihrer Entstehung und Überlieferung", _TU_ N.F. 25, hft. 3 (Leipzig, 1904).

"Die Prosopographie des afrikanischen Episkopats zur Zeit Cyprians", _QFIAB_ 12 (1909), pp. 247-70.

"Das lateinische Neue Testament zur Zeit Cyprians", _TU_ 33 (Leipzig, 1909).

"Der Ketzertaufstreit swischen Stephanus von Rom und Cyprian von Karthago", QFIAB 12 (1909), pp. 1-42.

Sordi, M., "L'apologia del martire romano Apollonio come fonte dell'Apologeticum di Tertulliano e i rapporti fra Tertulliano e Minucio", Rivista di Storia della chiesa in Italia 18 (1964), pp. 169-88.

Spanneut, M., Le stoicisme des pères de l'église de Clément de Rome à Clément d'Alexandrie, Patristica Sorbonensia, 1 (Paris, 1957).

Tertullien et les premiers moralistes africains (Paris, 1969).

Stein, A., "Zur Chronologie der römischen Kaiser von Decius bis Diocletianus", Archiv für Papyrusforschung 7 (1924), pp. 30-51.

Die Praefekten von Aegypten in der römischen Kaiserzeit, Diss. Bernenses, series 1, fasc. 1 (Bern, 1950).

Sullivan, D.D., The Life of the North Africans as Revealed in the Works of St. Cyprian, Patristic Studies, 37 (Washington, 1933).

Sumner, G.V., "Germanicus and Drusus Caesar", Latomus 26 (1967), pp. 413-35.

Syme, R., Ammianus and the Historia Augusta (Oxford, 1968).

Emperors and Biography. Studies in the Historia Augusta (Oxford, 1971).

Taylor, J.H., "St. Cyprian and the Reconciliation of Apostates", ThSt 3 (1942), pp. 27-46.

Thomasson, B.E., Die Statthalter der

römischen Provinzen Nordafrikas von Augustus bis Diocletianus, Acta Instituti Romani Regni Sueciae, 8° IX:2 (2 vols. Lund, 1960).

Turner, C.H., "Two Early Lists of St. Cyprian's Works", CR 6 (1892), pp. 205-9= Studies in Early Church History (Oxford, 1912), pp. 263-5.

"Prolegomena to the Testimonia and Ad Fortunatum of St. Cyprian", JThS 29 (1928), pp. 113-36; 31 (1930), pp. 225-46.

Vanbeck, A., "La pénitence dans S. Cyprien", Revue d'histoire et de littérature religeuses N.S. 4 (1913), pp. 422-42.

Vogt, H.J., Coetus Sanctorum. Der Kirchenbegriff des Novatian und die Geschichte seiner Sonderkirche, Theophaneia, Beiträge zur Religions- und Kirchengeschichte des Altertums (Bonn, 1968).

Vogt, J., Die alexandrinischen Münzen: Grundlegung einer alexandrinischen Kaisergeschichte (2 vols. Stuttgart, 1924).

Voss, B.R., Der Dialog in der frühchristlichen Literatur, Studia et testimonia antiqua, 9 (Munich, 1970).

Walser, G., and Pekáry, T., Die Krise des römischen Reiches. Bericht über die Forschungen zur Geschichte des 3. Jahrhunderts (193-284 n. Chr.) von 1939 bis 1959 (Berlin, 1962).

Watson, E.W., "The Style and Language of St. Cyprian", Studia biblica et ecclesiastica 4 (1896), pp. 189-324.

"The De Opere et Eleemosynis of St. Cyprian", JThS 2 (1901), pp. 433-8.

"The De Habitu Virginum of St. Cyprian", JThS 22 (1921), pp. 361-7.

Weiss, J., "Ein neugefundenes Kanon-Verzeichnis in Hilgenfeld", Zeit. für wiss. Theol. 30 (1887), pp. 157-71.

Wiles, M.F., "The Theological Legacy of St. Cyprian", JEH 14 (1963), pp. 139-49.

INDEX

435